SPIX'S MACAW

SPIX'S MACAW

The Race to Save the
WORLD'S RAREST BIRD

Tony Juniper

ATRIA BOOKS

New York   London   Toronto   Sydney   Singapore

ATRIA BOOKS
1230 Avenue of the Americas
New York, NY 10020

ISBN: 0-7434-7550-X

First Atria Books trade paperback edition November 2003

10 9 8 7 6 5 4 3 2 1

ATRIA BOOKS is a trademark of Simon & Schuster, Inc.

Manufactured in the United States of America

For information regarding special discounts for bulk purchases, please contact
Simon & Schuster Special Sales at 1-800-456-6798 or business@simonandschuster.com.

For my Mother and Father

Contents

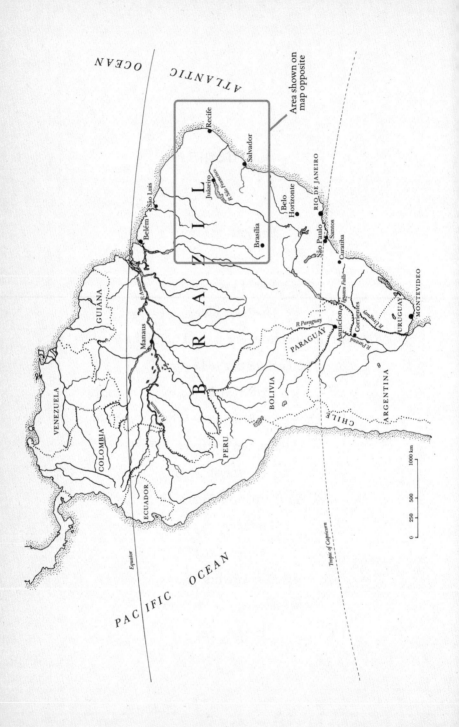

Area shown on
map opposite

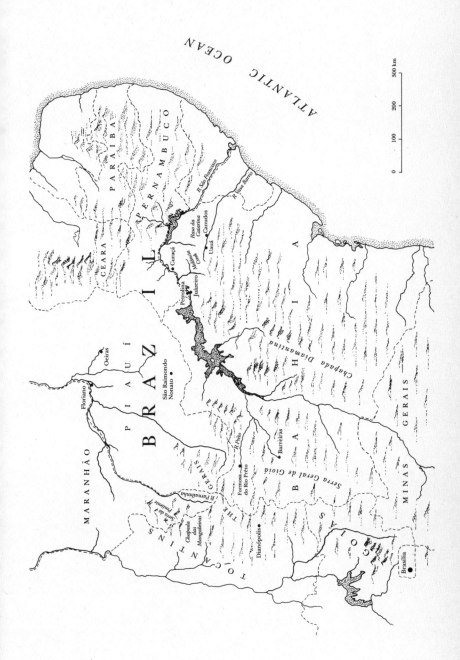

SPIX'S MACAW

The Real Macaw

The blue parrot came to rest on a bare sun-bleached branch that stuck out from the bushy crown of a craggy old caraiba tree. The magnificent old plant, some 25 meters tall, was one in a long ribbon of trees that fringed a winding creek. The parrot had chosen a high branch, a natural vantage point. From his lofty position, the bird scanned the flat thorny cactus scrub that lay around in all directions. He climbed to a branch slightly lower down, using his feet and beak, checking behind and above for airborne predators. When hawks were hunting, a second of relaxation could cost him his life. Once the parrot was satisfied he was safe, he cried out—quite a harsh call, but thin, with a trilling quality. He received a distant reply, and then another.

Moments later, from around a bend in the creek, two parrots appeared, flying fast and strong above the treetops. They followed the line of the green-fringed channel, their long tails flexed and strained against the air, their flowing blue plumes acting as a rudder to steer a course toward the huge tree. They spread their tails, rotated their wings backwards, and fluttered to rest next to the bird already perched there. The thin branches swayed as they took the parrots' weight. The birds' scaly gray feet gripped tightly as the branches rocked gently back and forth. The parrots fluffed out their bodies and flight feathers and waggled their tails to ensure that their plumage lay correctly. This ritual ensured they would be ready for instant flight should they need to leave in a hurry. Finally, every feather in place, they settled down on the caraiba tree.

The trio were the adult male parrot who had first made the call and a pair of young adults. More chatter followed, then the birds indulged in friendly fencing with their hooked black bills. Their sharp yellowish eyes regarded one another carefully, their dark pupils dilating. Then, once more scanning the surrounding land, the first bird began to climb down the caraiba tree. Beneath it was a pool of muddy water.

As the first bird went lower, his companions nervously followed, very quiet now, anxious not to attract unwelcome attention. Going to the ground to drink was dangerous. It was a necessary daily chore, but they didn't like it. Not only were hawks still a threat, but snakes and other predators could catch them down there. There had recently been a population explosion among the local wild cats, and the parrots needed extra caution. They tilted their heads to get a better view of the ground, paying particular attention to the bushy cover at the edge of the creek.

They stopped once more and again checked for danger, then fluttered, one by one, the last five meters to the moist sandy ground of the creek bed. As they landed and cast shadows over the margins of the pool, tadpoles scattered into the murky brown water at the center. Whether the larvae of the frogs would progress to a terrestrial existence depended on more rain. This pool would evaporate soon under the hot tropical sun.

The parrots drank deep and fast. Taking their fill in seconds, they immediately flew back up to the bare top of the tree. They called once more, and then took off again down the creek calling loudly. Two kilometers upstream they stopped to perch in another of the tall trees. They knew that they would find food there. It was late in the day and dusk would soon fall, but a meal of the caraiba's seeds would see them through the night.

When the baking sunshine of the day was extinguished, a suffocating cloak of warmth rose from the parched earth. It was time to roost. Two of the birds, the pair, would spend the night in a hollow in one of the tall trees. They regularly slept there and felt safe. Their companion, the single male bird, perched atop a tall spiny cactus.

The tall trees that bordered the seasonally flooded creeks formed a rare green oasis. The rest of the woodland—if you could call it woodland—was mostly low and composed of tangled thickets of spindly thornbushes and cacti. There were baked open areas where little at all grew. It was a melancholy landscape, especially in the heat of the dry season, when the stillness and quiet gave a paradoxically wintry feeling. In all directions its vastness rolled in endless undulations toward an ever-receding horizon. Located in the interior of northeastern Brazil, these dry thorny woodlands—the caatinga—occupied an immense area, some 800,000 square kilometers in all—considerably larger than the state of Texas, or about three times the size of the island of Great Britain. Amid sharp rocks, viciously spined cacti, the lancelike thorns of the bushes, and brutal, unrelenting heat, this peculiar place felt lonely, an isolated and forgotten corner of the world.

Drought turned the forest into a desolate and brittle chaos. Animals could hide in the shade, but the plants could not. Adapted to the desiccating climate, the plants eked out the precious water in whatever way they could. Some had thick waxy leaves, others potatolike tuber roots or fine hairs to scavenge moisture from the air. Most trees and shrubs were deciduous, and even those said to be evergreen lost their leaves in the worst droughts. And when the droughts dragged on, as they frequently did, there was death. Creatures that succumbed didn't rot; the dry heat drained their body fluids and mummified them. Sheep and goats killed by lack of food and water lay like specimens preserved for museum display.

The energy in the winds was small and the airstreams that came brought little rain. It was a harsh place and had become known as the backlands—a forgotten country scorned by the outside world as a desolate wasteland fit only for goats and sheep.

In the good years dark clouds spawned violent thunderstorms that brought relief from the unforgiving drought. As the lifeless desert was for a short time banished, the caatinga became a brief paradise of green dotted with white, yellow, and red flowers. When the first rains fell, it was as if the drops of moisture were hitting the face of a red-hot iron. Flashed back into vapor, the first specks of water could not penetrate the earth. If the rain continued to fall, the baked red soil would first become darkly stained, damp, and then moistened. Tiny rivulets formed, then streams, and finally substantial bodies of water accumulated in the creeks.

What little rain there was fell in a four- or five-month period, generally from about November to April. Most of the year, even in "wet" years, it did not rain at all. But because the creeks that drained the land during the brief annual deluges retained some of the moisture in their deep fine soils, ribbons of tall green trees grew there— little streaks of green in the great dry wilderness.

In this uncompromising environment, the blue parrots had made their home. Tested and honed by the punishing climate, their bodies and instincts had been molded into the alert exotic blue creatures that flew there now. Perhaps, like many other animals found in these tough lands, they had first evolved in kinder and wetter conditions, but now found themselves driven by thousands of years of climatic change to the precious few areas of moister habitat within the caatinga. The tree-lined creek was one such place.

Exquisite blue creatures some 60 centimeters long, darker above, slightly more turquoise below, their heads were paler and grayer, and at a distance sometimes appeared almost white. Depending on the angle and intensity of light, the birds sometimes showed a greenish cast. When they fluffed out their head feathers, they took on a different appearance and looked almost reptilian, an impression enhanced by their intense bare faces. Their outward resemblance to small dinosaurs reinforced the impression that these curious birds were descended from a remote past.

A t first light the next day, the trio of blue parrots collected together once more at the top of the huge bare-branched tree and resumed their daily routine. Their first port of call was a fruiting faveleira tree down the creek toward the main river. As the parrots approached their destination and breakfast, they were greeted by a screeching flock of Blue-winged Macaws, a type of small macaw known locally as a *maracana*. These birds were already feeding in the dense green foliage of the fruit tree's crown. Despite their bright green plumage, their striking white faces, and red and blue patches, to an observer on the ground or even an aerial predator they were almost invisible.

These smaller and mainly green macaws shared the creekside woods with their larger blue cousins. Relations between the species were generally quite amicable, unless one of the smaller macaws sat on one of the favorite perches of the bigger ones. If they trespassed in this way, they would be angrily driven off. Although there were several other species of parrot living in the creek, the little *maracanas* were the only other kind of macaw. They were also the only other birds the bigger blue species deigned to have any social contact with.

Amid the chattering and bickering of the busy *maracanas*, a distant growl registered in the blue birds' finely tuned senses. The sound grew closer. It was a rare sound in this remote place—the sound of a vehicle. The blue parrots knew that the approaching sound often meant trouble. Besides the hawks, wild cats, and snakes, the three blue macaws had come to know a still more deadly predator. And that lethal hunter was on the prowl again now. This predator stalked his prey by both night and day. This predator never gave up: If one method of capture failed, he tried a new one. He took babies from their nests and even stole eggs.

The birds fled upstream once more until they arrived at a tall caraiba tree with dense foliage covering the branches in its crown. They had already eaten well and felt able to rest. As the dazzling sun grew hotter, the parrots melted into the shadows to doze, preen, and chatter. They disappeared into the dappled light and shade cast by the long waxy leaves of the caraiba tree. Just as they relaxed, the birds were shocked to full alertness by a startling shrill screeching sound. It was the scream of a distressed parrot, a panic-laden cry made by a wounded bird facing a predator. The macaws' curiosity was aroused. They were compelled to respond to the call.

They fluttered to an opening in the caraiba's dense canopy to gain a better view of the creek. Finding no line of sight to the source of the sound, they cautiously flew toward it. The noise was coming from a bend in the creek some distance away. The three birds approached. As they drew nearer they could see on the ground a struggling parrot. It appeared unable to move from its place on the creek bed even though it was violently writhing. The single blue macaw approached while the pair remained at a distance. His natural caution overtaken, the parrot descended to a low perch closer to the bird struggling on the ground.

As he settled, two men burst forth and ran toward him. They crashed over dry sticks and leaves that lay on the sandy bed of the creek. Terrified, the macaw took to his wings, but he couldn't fly. The spot where he had perched was covered in bird lime, a glue substance used to trap birds. It had trapped him.

Seconds later he was inside a nylon net. The men snapped the branch he was involuntarily gripping and wound the mesh around it, trapping him. The bird's sharp hooked beak tore at the net, but it wouldn't give. Then the blue macaw, still inside the net and glued to the perch, was caged in a wire mesh-fronted crate. He lay panting on the floor covered in glue, tangled in the net where he had no choice but to grip the branch to which he was stuck. He called out, but there was no answer; his companions were already far away. It was the end of April 1987.

The trapper and his assistant sat on the huge fallen trunk of a dead caraiba tree and smiled. Dressed in modern city clothes, they had arrived in a four-wheel-drive vehicle—a rare sight in this poor area where local transport was more often by horse or mule. They smoked cigarettes and talked for a while. Then they rose to their feet and approached the crate. One of the men put on thick leather gloves while his assistant opened the door. The gloved man picked up the bird, still inside the net, while his companion cut away the nylon with a penknife. The parrot's feet were prized from the broken branch and a scrap of cloth was used to clean some of the glue from its feet. The blue bird, paralyzed with fear, was put back into the crate and the door was once more wired fast.

The gloved man stood back and regarded his prize with obvious pleasure. The sight of the caged blue parrot took his thoughts back to when he was a boy of eleven. A neighbor had asked him to look after some young parrots he was raising. Soon after, the neighbor had had to leave the area and told the boy he could keep the birds. When they were ready for sale, he put them in a cart and took them around the streets in his town and found that they sold very well. The boy got some more parrots and, as time went by, became more knowledgeable and serious about his surprisingly lucrative vocation. By the time he was seventeen he had bought himself a second-hand car—quite an achievement in this part of the world. He marveled at his good fortune—the birds had helped him escape the grinding poverty suffered by the poor rural people in the caatinga. He was lucky enough to have a small house in town that he shared with his wife and three young children. He only came to the country for more parrots.

As the years went by, his reputation as a parrot dealer grew, first in Brazil and then internationally. If you wanted to buy a Brazilian macaw, he was your man. He had first caught some of the special blue caatinga macaws in the early 1980s, when he took a couple of babies from their nest. He traded the azure bundles of fluff for a car; this time it was brand new. Since then he had not looked back. It was easy money—better still, it was big money. Capturing another of these special blue parrots was a real achievement.

All kinds of blue macaw were in big demand, but the trapper had caught this parrot to fulfill an order placed by a foreign collector. It would now travel via a series of dealers working as part of the criminal underworld of the international bird trade.

Unlike some common parrots, this one was not destined for a run-of-the-mill pet keeper but for an elite collector who would fully appreciate the rarity and value of such a trophy. Blue macaws fetched excellent prices, but the caatinga macaw was different. This bird was like a Rembrandt or a Picasso. Yet unlike a painting by a great master, this bird was a temporary treasure only. One day he would die, his value would be gone, and another would be demanded to replace him. No matter how many were caught, there was relentless demand for more.

As the long, hot dry season passed, the traumatic memory of the last trapping faded, but the surviving pair of blue parrots remained very nervous. Any people near the creek sent them into fast flight. The normal activities of the sparse local population—the odd ranch hand passing by on horseback or people from one of the isolated houses nearby collecting leafy branches for their goats and sheep to eat—created panic. The birds took no chances even with these casual visitors. They would take flight up the creek until they had traveled what they regarded as a safe distance.

The pair of blue parrots nested in a particular hole that had been used by their kind for generations. High up in one of the big trees, it had been formed by the fall of a huge branch some five decades before. Almost every year since then a pair of the blue parrots had laid their eggs in that same favorite refuge. The hollow was dry and the nesting area was some distance down into the tree from the exit to the outside world. It was just right—the ideal place to raise babies. But such a location was valuable and the blue macaws didn't have an exclusive claim.

Most of the best tree holes in the creek were accounted for in some way. The woodpeckers, black vultures, the other parrots, like the *maracanas*, and even snakes liked to use tree cavities as well. Lately bees introduced from Africa had also moved into the creek. Swarms of these insects were especially dangerous when they wanted to take possession of a tree hole. They had stung parrots to death in order to take over a prime site.

With the arrival of the wet season, the birds spent more time around the nest hollow, both to defend it from unwanted squatters and to prepare themselves for breeding. A couple of weeks later, in mid-December, the female bird stayed inside during the day. She had laid three white eggs. They rested in the bottom of the hollow where she would now devote most of her time to maintaining the correct temperature and humidity for the tiny embryos to grow and then hatch.

One night, when the two parrots were asleep with their eggs in the nest hole, the drone of a vehicle was heard once more in the creek. The birds would not venture out; owls were a real danger after dark. They sat tight even when they heard scraping sounds on the outside of the tree. They heard whispering human voices by the hole and huddled silently. But when they felt a presence come inside, they fled. The female made her move for the entrance first. In the darkness all she could see was the gloomy disc of the predawn sky. She made for it, climbing the inside of the tree trunk, a familiar enough task in the day but in the near total darkness unnatural and frightening. As she spread her wings for flight, she became constrained. She was in a net. Something powerful and unyielding grasped her body. As she struggled to free herself from her captor, her mate struggled past and fluttered free of the hollow. He found his wings and took off down the creek into the darkness as fast as he could.

In the nest the three eggs lay smashed. The two trappers had reached inside for young birds in the hope that they could take baby macaws too—they would fetch an even better price than the sleek adult bird. They were too early for that, however, and their clumsy groping in the dark broke the fragile white shells and spilled the contents into the base of the hollow. The blood-streaked yolks slowly congealed in the wood shavings at the bottom of the nest chamber. Disappointed not to find chicks, the trappers were pleased that they at least had caught one of the adult macaws before someone else did. It was Christmas Eve 1987. The capture of the blue parrot would certainly brighten the trappers' festivities.

The macaw soon found herself in a crate ready for loading into the back of the four-wheel-drive vehicle. It was now daylight and the men prepared for departure along the long dusty track that led back the main tarmac road. Just before leaving, they saw a man approaching on foot. He stopped and asked what they were doing.

The stranger seemed harmless enough, certainly not a policeman, so the trappers boasted about the valuable creature they had taken that morning. The man asked to see it. The chief trapper opened the rear door of the jeep and pulled an old blanket to one side revealing the blue bird in its crate. It recoiled at the sudden bright light and shrank back into the shadows. The man was impressed. He asked if he might take a photo of the gorgeous blue creature. After the trapper had shrugged his consent, the man took a Polaroid camera from his green bag, carefully composed his picture, and pressed the shutter. He waited a few moments, then peeled the paper backing from the print to reveal the image of the caged parrot.

He did not know it, but the image that was gradually appearing on the Polaroid as it dried in the warm morning air was of the last wild female of the blue caatinga parrots. After her capture, only her partner remained. He was the last Spix.

CHAPTER 2

The First Spix

On June 3, 1817, Johann Baptist Ritter von Spix and his traveling companion and fellow scientist, Carl Friedrich Philipp von Martius, set sail for the Atlantic Ocean from Gibraltar. They had arrived in the bustling port some weeks previously from Trieste on the Adriatic. Along with fifty other vessels of various sizes, their ship had waited for the right weather conditions for their voyage to South America. This day brought the easterly winds necessary to propel them from the Mediterranean Sea on the 6,000-kilometer voyage to the Southern Hemisphere and their destination, Rio de Janeiro, the capital of the Portuguese colony of Brazil.

The son of a Bavarian doctor, Spix was born in 1781. Awarded his Ph.D. at the age of only nineteen, his early academic career included studies in theology, medicine, and the natural sciences. He qualified as a medical doctor in 1806. In 1808 he was awarded a scholarship by King Maximilian Joseph of Bavaria to study zoology in Paris, at the

time the world's leading natural sciences center. Here the young
Bavarian mixed with the leading biologists and naturalists of his day,
including the French naturalist Jean-Baptiste Lamarck, the intellec-
tual giant who proposed a mechanism of evolution that would challenge (unsuccessfully, it turned out) the theory of natural selection
developed some decades later by Charles Darwin.

In Paris Spix's abilities as a scientist grew. In October 1810 the
king once again acknowledged his growing reputation, this time
with an appointment in the Bavarian Royal Academy of Sciences,
where he was charged with the care and study of the natural history
exhibits. Martius was a gifted academic too. Thirteen years younger
than Spix, his interests were mainly botanical, especially palms.

The two scientists found themselves aboard one of two Brazil-
bound ships as members of an expedition mounted in the name of
the Emperor Francis I of Austria, whose daughter was to marry the
son of John VI of Portugal. King John had been forced to live in
Brazil following the invasion of his homeland in 1807 by Napoleon
Bonaparte of France. The Austrian emperor had invited a group of
Viennese scientists to join the royal party that was to travel to
Brazil. Maximilian had agreed that two members of the Bavarian
Royal Academy of Sciences should go with them.

Spix was to concentrate his efforts on animals, the local people,
and geological recording, including the collection of fossils. Martius
was to devote his energies to botanical investigation, including soil
types and the study of how plants spread to new lands. The king
was a bird collector in his own right and hoped that the two men
would bring him novel and unique prizes from their expedition in
the New World.

"After everything possible was got ready, and the books, instru-
ments, medicine chest, and other travelling equipage sent off direct
to Trieste, we set out from Munich on 6 February 1817, for Vienna."[1]

At Trieste they joined the ships, two naval frigates, the *Augusta* and the *Austria*. Both were substantial vessels equipped with forty-four guns and a crew of 240 sailors.

On June 29 they crossed the equator and on July 13 Cabo Frio was sighted, "and soon after the noble entrance of the bay of Rio de Janeiro." The arrival in South America made a big impression on the travelers.

Towards noon, approaching nearer and nearer to the enchanting prospect, we came up to those colossal rock portals and at length passed between them into a great amphitheatre, in which the mirror of the water appeared like a tranquil inland lake, and scattered flowery islands, bounded in the background by a woody chain of mountains, rose like a paradise full of luxuriance and magnificence . . . at length the capital of the infant kingdom, illuminated by the evening sun, lay extended before us.

A sensation, not to be described, overcame us all at the moment when the anchor struck the ground at another continent; and the thunder of the cannon, accompanied with military music hailed the desired goal of the happily accomplished voyage.

The travelers decided to spend some time initially in the relative cool and comfort of the southeast of the country, first in Rio de Janeiro and then in São Paulo and Curitiba. Spix and Martius explained:

. . . It seemed most expedient to journey first to the southern Captaincy of S. Paulo, mainly to acclimatise ourselves gradually to the hot conditions we would encounter during our travels and acquaint ourselves with this more temperate southern zone. From the Captaincy of S. Paulo we planned to travel through the interior of Minas Gerais to the S. Francisco River and Goyaz, before continuing either down the Tocantins to Pará or across the interior to Bahia and the coast, where we would arrange transport of our collections to Europe before penetrating the interior of the Captaincies of Piauhy and Maranhão to arrive finally at Pará, the goal of our desires.

To a twenty-first-century traveler such an itinerary would be demanding enough, entailing a journey of thousands of kilometers, mainly on rough tracks and by river. Although the Bavarians enjoyed the small luxury of letters of recommendation from the Portuguese/Brazilian government that would help smooth their path with colonial administrators, they could carry only basic equipment, much of which was for scientific purposes rather than their personal comfort. They had incomplete maps, primitive medical supplies, and could rely only on mule trails and rivers to cover the vast distances that lay ahead of them. In those times natural history exploration was a hazardous business. Disease, attack from native people or wild animals, climbing and firearms accidents, starvation, and even the use of dangerous chemicals for scientific purposes, such as arsenic—all took their toll on the early naturalists.

Despite the dangers, it was with great enthusiasm and apparently little thought for their impending discomfort that on December 9, 1817, Spix and Martius set out from the coast for the interior of Brazil. Although misgivings about their venture were expressed by Brazilian friends, the Bavarians happily set off with a team that included a guide hired in Rio de Janeiro, a mule man, a drover, a "newly bought Negro slave," and eight mules, two for riding and six more for their bags and equipment.

They met several early setbacks. In addition to being assailed by a huge variety of fleas, ticks, flies, mosquitoes, and other biting and disease-carrying insects, the scientists lost their guide when he decided to go his own way. He left one night when everyone was asleep, never to be seen again. He had taken most of their valuables. Spix and Martius were forced to recruit new help and to replace stolen equipment before they resumed their journey through the recently colonized landscape.

The countryside was sparsely settled, but in some places the clearance of the native vegetation was already well under way. They wrote that "From Ytú we advanced N.W. by the side of beautiful thick woods, and enjoyed a delightful view of the valley of the Tieté, which is now entirely cleared of the forests, and planted with sugar cane, beans, maize and so on." It was in this area that their slave decided to follow the example of the guide and make an unscheduled departure himself.

According to Spix and Martius, the slave "did not know how to appreciate our kind treatment of him, and embraced the first favourable opportunity to abscond." He was, however, brought back to them the next day by professional runaway slave hunters the men had engaged locally. The naturalists wrote: "We followed the advice of our host, treating him, according to the custom of this place, very kindly . . . giving him a full glass of brandy."

In addition to the departure of their staff, flooded roads, swollen streams, and cold mist dogged their progress. But despite the difficult conditions, the two scientists earnestly persisted with their scientific work. "If in the evening we at length met with an open shed, or dilapidated hut, we had to spend the greater part of the night in drying our wet clothes, in taking our collections out of the chests and again exposing them to the air." On drier days they would spend twilight and hours after dark "writing notes in the journals, in preparing, drying and packing our collections." Despite the hardships, they recalled how "This simple mode of life had its peculiar charms."

To early Portuguese visitors, Brazil was known as the land of parrots. Spix and Martius came across plenty of them as well. In August 1818, in the region of Januária in Minas Gerais in the upper reaches of the river São Francisco, the Bavarian travelers happened upon what were almost certainly Hyacinth Macaws in a "magnificent forest of buriti palms." The large cobalt blue birds circled over the travelers in pairs with their croaking calls echoing in the still and peaceful surroundings. A few days later, Martius and Spix briefly split up. Martius set off into the dry semi-arid forests that fringe the river São Francisco. Here he found forests of indajá palms, which, because of the much drier conditions, were the first palm groves that they had found "where we dared to roam around with dry feet and safe from giant snakes and alligators."

Martius observed with fascination how the local Hyacinth Macaws greedily ate the palm fruits. "The large nuts of these palms with their very fine rich oil make them the favourite trees of the large blue macaws which often flew off in pairs above us. As beautiful as this bird's plumage is, its hoarse penetrating call assaults even the most insensitive of ears and if it had been known in ancient times, would have been regarded an ominous bird of deepest foreboding."

For the Hyacinth Macaw the arrival of the Europeans was indeed a compelling omen of ill fortune. Martius's party themselves captured some of the birds. He later remarked, "[T]he small menagerie of these quarrelsome birds, which we took with us chained to the roof of a few mule loading platforms, played a special role in that their continuous noise, which could be heard from afar, indicated the location of the caravan, which we usually left far behind in our forays to investigate the region."

Martius and Spix most likely knew about the Hyacinth Macaw before they arrived in Brazil. That species had by then been described to science by a British ornithologist, John Latham. He had spent years cataloging museum collections, including the birds collected during Cook's eighteenth-century voyages in the Pacific. In

1790 he was the first to grant a scientific name to the giant blue parrots. But the two Bavarians were the first to note the relationship between these magnificent blue birds and different kinds of palms, upon the fruits of which they dined.

By November Spix and Martius reached the coast of eastern Brazil and the town of Salvador in Bahía. The grinding travel schedule had taken its toll, so they rested there until mid-February 1819 to recover their strength. They then set out north through the harsh drought-prone northeast of Brazil. They suffered extreme hardships, notably lack of water, and often traveled in uninhabited country. By May they had reached the banks of the river São Francisco at Juàzeiro.

Along the north and south shores of the great river they found the thorny caatinga woodlands. This dry country stretched in all directions to the horizon and beyond. It was sparsely settled and mainly used for sheep and cattle pasture. In this strange dry land Spix spent some time collecting birds.

It was here that he shot a magnificent long-tailed blue parrot for their collection. The bird was taken from some curious woodlands found along the sides of creeks seen in that part of the caatinga. The specimen of the parrot was tagged and brief notes were made about it. Spix recorded that "it lives in flocks, although very rare, near Juàzeiro in the region bordering the São Francisco, [and is] notable for its thin voice." Spix didn't realize that he had just taken the very first specimen of a bird that would one day symbolize how human greed and ignorance were wiping countless life forms from the record of creation.

From Juàzeiro the pair traveled through the parched woodlands north along the river Canindé to Oeiras in Piauí, close to the modern city of Floriano. Martius wrote: "The caatingas mostly consisted of sparse bushes and in the lowland areas, where there was much more water, the carnauva palms formed stately forests, the sight of which was as strange as it was delightful. Blue macaws, which live in the dense tops of these palms, flew up screeching above us." It seemed that the travelers had happened on more Hyacinth Macaws or perhaps their rarer and smaller cousins, Lear's Macaws—two of the "four blues" exhibited in Berlin in 1900 (see chapter 4).

By the end of 1819 Spix and Martius had worked their way inland about 3,000 kilometers farther west, mainly by river, penetrating deep inside the seemingly limitless rain forests of the Amazon basin, and then they traveled farther into the vast interior of South America. They finally arrived nearly 3,000 kilometers farther downstream at the port of Belém in Pará at the mouth of Amazon on April 16, 1820. Their collection of specimens and live animals was loaded aboard the *Nova Amazonia* and they set sail for Lisbon. They traveled through Spain and France to arrive back in Munich on December 10, 1820, nearly four years after they had left.

Throughout their extensive travels Spix and Martius made careful observations on the wildlife they encountered. They were also careful to note details of the local economy in the places they visited, especially mining and agriculture, and in so doing they painted a picture for those who would follow of investment, trading, and other commercial opportunities. It is no coincidence that the greatest concentration of German industry anywhere in the world today is still in the Brazilian super metropolis of São Paulo. Certainly this fact is linked to the historical relationships between the two countries and the information provided by early travelers. Thus began centuries of encroachment into the world's biologically richest and remotest places—a process that continues today, only now hugely accelerated and more often with the aid of remote sensing from spacecraft than with the assistance of mules.

Spix and Martius recorded their travels in three substantial volumes published in 1823, 1828, and 1831 in which they dedicated their great scientific achievements to their royal patron: "Attachment to Your Majesty and to the sciences was the Guardian Genius that guided us amidst the danger and fatigues of so extensive a journey, through a part of the world so imperfectly known, and brought us back in safety, from that remote hemisphere to our native land." But only the first volume was a joint venture. Martius completed volumes two and three alone following the death of Spix in 1826. Spix was forty-six and had never really recovered from extremely poor health that resulted from the privations and sickness he experienced in Brazil. Martius went on to write a classic work on palms that he completed in 1850. He died in 1868.

Not only was the account of what they saw of great importance; their collection made a substantial contribution to the Natural History Museum of Munich. They brought back specimens from 85 species of mammals, 350 species of birds, 116 species of fish, 2,700 insects, and 6,500 botanical specimens. They also managed to bring back live animals, including some parrots and monkeys. Many of their specimens were from species of animals and plants new to science.

Among the treasures brought home to Bavaria was the blue parrot shot by Spix near Juàzeiro. Since it was blue with a long tail, it seems that Spix believed he had taken a Hyacinth Macaw.

It was customary by this time for all species to be assigned a two-part name, mainly in the then international scientific language of Latin—but also Greek—following the classification system proposed during the eighteenth century by the Swedish naturalist Carl von Linné, better known as Linnaeus. The idea was to avoid the confusion often created by the use of several different colloquial names by adopting a common international system. The first part of the name denoted the genus—that is, the group of closely related creatures or plants to which the specimen belonged. The second half of the title was to identify the particular species.

Whether he knew about Latham's name for the blue parrot or simply used the name in ignorance (this occurred quite commonly in the early years of natural history classification), Spix called the little blue caatinga macaw *Arara hyacinthinus* in his volume called *Avium Brasiliensium Species Novae* published in 1824–5. He also had specimens of the larger and similarly blue Hyacinth Macaws that he proposed be renamed "*Anodorhyncho Maximiliani*." "*Anodorhyncho*" was a new name proposed by Spix to denote the genus of large blue macaws to which it belonged, and "*Maximiliani*" was in honor of the king who had sponsored his explorations in South America.

Spix's misnaming of his blue parrots was quite understandable. Unlike modern naturalists, Spix was not able to rely on a glossy field book that succinctly set out with accurate color pictures, maps, and clear descriptions the birds he might encounter on his travels through the interior of Brazil. Even now, at the start of the twenty-first century, there is still no handy field and identification guide for Brazilian birds, although Helmut Sick's 1993 *Birds in Brazil* provides a comprehensive overview of birds occurring in the country. It is worth noting that many dozens of guides are available for the birds of Europe, a portion of the globe with far fewer endangered species.

With no manual to rely on, it was not a straightforward business for Spix to recognize new species, let alone ones that had already been collected by other museums or expeditions. For a start, any naturalist seeking to catalog a vast and diverse country like Brazil, even a relatively obvious and distinctive group of animals like birds (even large blue parrots), would need a basic understanding of what had already been collected and what typical geographical variations might be expected over different species' sometimes vast ranges. Such knowledge in early nineteenth-century Bavaria was, as elsewhere, extremely scarce.

It was not until 1832, six years after Spix's death, that the magnitude of his error became apparent. The blue parrot he had collected in the caatinga, and so carefully transported all the way back to Munich, was utterly unique, unlike anything else ever cataloged: Spix had found a new species. It later emerged that not only was it a species new to science, it was a representative of a whole "new" genus.

Spix's mistake was noticed first by another Bavarian naturalist, his assistant, Johann Wagler. Wagler, a professor of zoology at the University of Munich, realized that the bird collected by Spix was smaller than the birds previously described as Hyacinth Macaws and was a different color too. It had a grayish head, black bare skin on its face instead of the yellow patches seen in the Hyacinth, and it had a smaller and more delicate bill than the bigger Hyacinth Macaw and its relatives.

In his *Monograph of Parrots*, published in 1832, Wagler paid tribute to the bird's collector in the naming of a "new" species after him; "*Sittace Spixii*," he called it—a name basically meaning "Spix's Parrot." Wagler, like Spix, completed his bird book just in time. That same year Wagler was involved in a shooting accident. He peppered his arm with small shot while out collecting birds. He contracted blood poisoning, amputation was fatally delayed, and he died in the summer, aged thirty-two.

Following Wagler's realization that a species new to science had been found, the French naturalist Prince Charles Bonaparte proposed in the 1850s that it be placed in a new genus called *Cyanopsittaca*. Bonaparte, the son of Napoleon Bonaparte's brother Lucien, was a passionate ornithologist who had a special interest in parrots. Since this bird was unlike the other blue macaws in several important respects, Bonaparte believed that a whole new genus of parrots was warranted. He took the Greek word for blue, *Kyanos*, and the

Latin for parrot, *Psittacus*, to denote a new genus literally meaning "blue parrot."

In the 1860s in a monograph of parrots compiled by the German ornithologist Otto Finsch there is an everyday German name that translated means "Spix's Blue Macaw." Finsch wrote that the small blue macaw was easy to distinguish from the Hyacinth Macaw because of its smaller size and more bare skin on its face and around its eyes. He concluded that it was "An exceedingly rare species and found in few museums. Discovered by Spix on the river São Francisco at Juàzeiro." Significantly, he wrote that "Other travellers do not mention it at all."

Three decades later, the Italian zoologist Count Tommaso Salvadori compiled the *Catalogue of the Parrots in the Collection of the British Museum*. Salvadori completed his two-year task in 1891. He retained Spix's bird in a genus called *Cyanopsittacus*. The fact that no other birds quite like it had been discovered meant that it remained in the genus on its own, thereby signaling that it was quite unique with characteristics seen in no other bird.

The second half of its scientific name was *spixii*. From now on the bird collected in 1819 by the river São Francisco would be known in its scientific Latin form as *Cyanopsittacus*—or more commonly today, *Cyanopsitta spixii*—and in English as Spix's Macaw.

The fact that the species was now officially recorded was, however, to prove a mixed blessing. It intrigued not only scientists, but also conservationists and collectors, the former seeking to save the species, the latter to own and possess the most sought after of all birds. But the blue caatinga parrots were to prove an elusive quarry for all concerned.

Astonishingly, Spix's Macaw effectively disappeared from the eyes of naturalists and travelers and was not observed in the wild for eighty-four years after Spix first encountered one. The fact that Spix's Macaw was a rare bird was not lost on the early catalogers and naturalists. Indeed, no European recorded one alive in the wild again until the start of the twentieth century, when Othmar Reiser saw Spix's Macaws during an expedition of the Austrian Academy of Sciences to northeastern Brazil in June 1903.

He wrote: "As I knew that Spix had discovered this rare and beautiful parrot in the area of the river São Francisco near Juàzeiro, I made sure to keep an eye out for it in the area described. Unfortunately without success. Any enquiries made to the local people were also negative." Finally, at the lake at Parnaguá in the state of Piauí, more than 400 kilometers west of Juàzeiro, Reiser and his companions were rewarded with two sightings of the elusive blue bird. They reported one sighting of three birds and another of a pair. "They arrive apparently from a long distance and the thirsty birds at first perch, calling, on the tops of the trees on the beach to survey the surrounding area as a precaution. After flapping their wings for a few times they fly down to the ground with ease and drink slowly and long from pools or the water at the bank."[2]

Reiser tried to approach but found the birds nervous and not tolerant of people. His attempts to shoot the macaws in order to obtain a specimen failed. "So it was that the parrot species most desired by us was the only one to be observed, but not collected," he lamented. The only other encounter with Spix's Macaw noted during this expedition was a captive bird shown to the party in the town of Remanso. Reiser tried to buy it, but it was not for sale.

Other Spix's Macaws were for sale, however. Despite the lack of scientific observations by naturalists working in the field, the blue parrots were being taken out of Brazil to a life in captivity overseas.

In 1878 the Zoological Society of London at Regent's Park had obtained a live bird for its collection from Paris. It died and so the zoo set out to get hold of a replacement. In November 1894 a second bird was procured for the Society by Walter Rothschild: That one lasted until 1900. A third was held at the London Zoo from June 1901 but expired after just a year. These individuals were among a steady trickle that by the late nineteenth century were being exported to meet a growing demand. As with other rare species, when these birds died they were often included in museum collections. Following the bird's demise, the skin of the first Zoological Society specimen was preserved and placed in the collection held by the British (now Natural History) Museum at Tring in Hertfordshire. The second London bird's skin is now kept in the American Museum of Natural History in New York. And it wasn't only the large zoological institutions that were interested in owning them. In late Victorian England, as in other parts of the world at the time, aviculture was growing in popularity.

In the December 1897 issue of *Avicultural Magazine*, a journal for serious bird keepers, the "Honourable and Reverend" F. G. Dutton from Bibury in Gloucestershire, England, wrote: "Have any of our members kept a Spix? I have seen only two—one that our zoo acquired some years ago from the Jardin d'Acclimatation [in Paris], and one bought by Mr Rothschild. . . . They were both ill tempered: but as the first had a broken wing, it had probably been caught old. I was greatly tempted by the offer of one from Mr Cross the other day, but there are so many calls on a parson's purse, that he cannot always treat himself to expensive parrots. I ought to have been keeper at the parrot-house in the zoo." Although he does not mention a price, it is clear that even in the late nineteenth century Spix's Macaws were the preserve of the more discerning and wealthier bird collectors.

After Dutton had published his request for details on any Spix's Macaws kept in Britain at that time, Henry Fulljames of Elmbourne

Road in Balham, London, came forward. Dutton soon paid Full-james a visit at his house to view his parrot collection. Dutton wrote: "Lastly, the most interesting bird was the Spix's Macaw. . . . It was very tame and gentle, but not, as regards plumage, in the best of condition. I never can see a bird in rough plumage without longing to get it right. And so it has been arranged between Mr Fulljames and myself that I should have the Spix at Bibury, and try what a lit-tle outdoor life might do for it." Although Dutton had hatched an apparently foolproof plan to have a Spix's Macaw for free, at least temporarily, Henry Fulljames's housekeeper put an end to the scheme. She was very reluctant to lose sight of the Spix's and the bird stayed where it was.

Dutton persevered, however, and by September 1900 he had ac-quired a Spix's Macaw of his own. "My Spix, which is really more a conure than a macaw, will not look at sop of any sort," he wrote, "ex-cept sponge cake given from one's fingers, only drinks plain water and lives mainly on sunflower seed. It has hemp, millet, canary and peanuts but I do not think it eats much of any of them. It barks the branches of the tree where it is loose, and may eat the bark. It would very likely be all the better if it would eat bread and milk, as it might then produce some flight feathers, which it never yet has had." He later wrote that his Spix's Macaw, which lived in his study, was learning to talk.

Dutton was not the only one to wonder if Spix's Macaw might not be closer to the conures than the other macaws. Conures are slender parrots with long tails. They are confined to the Americas and are mainly included in two genera: *Aratinga* and *Pyrrhura*. Sev-eral writers repeated Dutton's conjecture, but given the many macawlike characteristics of *Cyanopsitta*, it is safer to assume that it is a macaw.

By the early twentieth century, Spix's Macaws were well known among bird keepers—at least from books. In Arthur G. Butler's 1909 *Foreign Birds for Cage and Aviary*, the author refers to the earlier published claims that Spix's Macaws are bad-tempered birds. "As all bird keepers know well," Butler wrote, "it is impossible to be certain of the character of any species from the study of one or two examples only. Even in the case of birds which are generally ill tempered and malicious, amiable individuals may occasionally be met with. Moreover circumstances may alter cases, and a Parrot chained by the leg to a stand may be excused for being more morose than one in a roomy cage." Butler, in common with previous commentators, remarked that Spix's Macaws were extremely rare.

Another famous aviculturist in the early part of the twentieth century was the Marquis of Tavistock. In his book *Parrots and Parrot-like Birds in Aviculture*, published in 1929, he remarked that "This rather attractive little blue macaw was formerly extremely rare, but a few have been brought over during recent years. It is not noisy, is easily tamed and sometimes makes a fair talker. There seems to be little information as to its ability to stand cold or as to its behaviour in mixed company, but it is probably neither delicate nor spiteful. . . . In the living bird the feathers of the head and neck stand out in a curious fashion, giving a peculiar and distinctive appearance."

While birds occasionally turned up in collections, attempts to find Spix's Macaws in the wild were repeatedly frustrated. In 1927 Ernst Kaempfer had been in the field with his wife collecting birds in eastern Brazil for two years. Although the Kaempfers had managed to ship some 3,500 bird specimens back to the American Museum of Natural History in New York City, the Spix's Macaw still eluded them.

Following a search on the north shore of the river São Francisco near to Juàzeiro, Kaempfer wrote:

The region is one of the ugliest we have seen on the whole trip. No forest or anything alike; the vegetation is a low underbrush and open camp where grass only grows. The river is very large here forming on both shores large strips of swamp; the latter ones without any particular bird life besides small *Ardeidae* [heron family] and common rails. Owing to the character of the country the collection we could make was small only. All questions about *Cyanopsitta Spixii* that Spix discovered here a hundred years ago were fruitless, nobody knew anything about such a parrot.

The only Spix's Macaw that Kaempfer was able to track down was a captive one that he saw at the Juàzeiro railway station, another bird taken locally from the wild and about to embark by train on the first leg of a journey to lead a life in distant and obscure captivity.

In the early twentieth century the only certainty surrounding Spix's Macaw was its scarcity. As Carl Hellmayr, an Austrian naturalist studying the birds of South America with the Field Museum of Natural History in Chicago, put it in 1929: It is "one of the great rarities among South American parrots." Indeed, during the entire first half of the century, the only other possible record of the species in the wild, apart from Reiser's in 1903, was a vague mention from Piauí before 1938.[3] This report, from the extreme south of the dry and remote state, was from an area of deciduous woodlands that comprises a transition zone between the arid caatinga and the more lush savannas of central Brazil.

The species was not heard from again in the wild until the 1970s. Various collectors and zoos, however, owned Spix's Macaws. Living birds were exported from Brazil to a wide variety of final destinations. Several went to the United States, where one was, for example, kept in the Chicago Zoo from 1928 for nearly twenty years. Others finished up in the U.K., where several private collectors and zoos, such as Paignton in Devon and Mossley Hill in Liverpool, kept them. In all, there were up to seven in the U.K. in the 1930s. At least one was kept in Ulster during the late 1960s; a recording of this bird's call is in the British Library of Wildlife Sounds. Spix's Macaws were also kept in the Netherlands at the Rotterdam Zoo and in Germany. One spent some time at the Vienna Zoo during the 1920s, while at least a pair had been imported to Portugal from Paraguay.

Spix's Macaws were also supplied to collectors in Brazil itself, and at least one was successful in breeding them. During the 1950s a parrot collector called Álvaro Carvalhães obtained one from a local merchant and managed to borrow another from a friend. They fortunately formed a breeding pair—by no means a foregone conclusion with fickle parrots—and after several breeding attempts, young were raised. Carvalhães built up a breeding stock of four pairs that between them produced twenty hatchlings. One of these later finished up in the Naples Zoo. The rest remained in Brazil, where they were split up with another breeder, Carvalhães's friend and neighbor, Ulisses Moreira. The birds began to die, one by one, as time passed, but the final blow that finished off Moreira's macaws was a batch of sunflower seeds contaminated with agricultural pesticides. This killed most of the parrots in the collection, including his Spix's Macaws.

Although there was evidently a continuing flow of wild-caught Spix's Macaws during the 1970s, to meet international demand in bird-collecting circles, the openness with which collectors declared the ownership of such rare creatures sharply declined in the late 1960s. At that point, the trade in such birds was attracting the attention of agencies and governments that were increasingly concerned about the impact of trapping and trade on rare species.

Brazil banned the export of its native wildlife in 1967[4] and the

Spix's Macaw became further prohibited in international trade under the Convention on International Trade in Endangered Species (CITES) in 1975.[5] Effective July 1 that year, all international commercial trade in Spix's Macaws between countries that had ratified the Convention was illegal, except in cases where the birds were involved in official captive-breeding programs or were being transferred for approved educational or scientific purposes.

This new legal protection didn't stop the trade, however; it simply forced it underground. Because the trafficking was increasingly secret, the volume of commerce and the final destinations for birds being captured was unknown to anyone but a few dealers, trappers, and rare parrot collectors. Despite the increasingly clandestine exploitation of wild Spix's Macaws and a near total lack of details about its impact, it was becoming ever more clear that the species must be in danger of extinction in the wild. The blue parrot first collected by Spix would come to symbolize a bitter irony: People's obsessive fascination with parrots was paradoxically wiping them out.

CHAPTER 3

Parrot Fashion

P arrots are surprisingly like people and can bring out both the best and worst in humans. From love and loyalty to greed and jealousy, the human qualities of parrots can provoke the most basic of our human responses in their keepers. Perhaps that is why for centuries parrots have been our closest and most cherished avian companions.

There are hundreds of kinds of parrot. The smallest are the tiny Pygmy Parrots of New Guinea that weigh in at just 10 grams—about the size of a wren or kinglet. These minuscule parrots creep like delicate animated jewelry along the trunks and branches of trees in the dense, dark rain forests of New Guinea. The heaviest parrot, the rotund nocturnal Kakapo (*Strigops habroptilus*) of New Zealand, grows up to 300 times larger. This great flightless parrot, camouflaged so it resembles a huge ball of moss, can weigh up to 3 kilograms.[6]

Some parrots are stocky with short tails, others elegant with long flowing plumes. The smaller slender ones with long tails are often known as parakeets (the budgerigar, *Melopsittacus undulatus*, is one), while it is the stouter birds that most people would generally recognize as "parrots." The mainly white ones with prominent crests are called cockatoos and the large gaudy South American ones with long tails, macaws. Despite this remarkable diversity, all of them are instantly recognizable, even to lay people, as members of the same biological family. The unique hooked bill and unique feet, with two toes facing forward and two backward, identify them straightaway.

Where the parrots came from is a baffling biological question. Many different ancestries have been suggested, including distant relationships with birds as diverse as pigeons, hawks, and toucans. Even with modern genetic techniques it has not been possible to unravel the ancestral relationships between parrots and other modern birds. What *is* known, however, is that parrotlike birds have been around for a very long time.

The oldest parrot known is from a fossil found by a Mr. S. Vincent in 1978 at Walton-on-the-Naze in Essex, England. The tiny fragile clues that these diminutive birds ever existed were painstakingly investigated by scientists who identified the species as "new": They named the creature *Pulchrapollia gracilis*. "Pulchrapollia" translates literally as "beautiful Polly," and "*gracilis*" means slender.

This ancient parrot was small and delicate—not much larger than a modern-day budgie. Its remains were found in Early Eocene London Clay deposits dated at about 55.4 million years old. More remarkable is the suggestion that parrots might have been around even earlier. A fossil bird found in the Lance Formation in Wyoming might be a parrot too. If it is, it would demonstrate the presence of such birds in the Late Cretaceous, more than 65 million years ago, thereby confirming that parrots coexisted with the animals they are ultimately descended from: the dinosaurs. Awesome antiquity indeed.[7] To place this ancestry in perspective, the earliest modern humans (*Homo sapiens*) are believed to have appeared only about 200,000 years ago.

Across the eons of biological time since the first parrots appeared, the group has evolved into one of the world's largest bird families. Of the 350 or so species of parrot known today, some are widespread, others confined to tiny areas. In either case, most species are found in the warm tropical latitudes. Some do, however, brave freezing temperatures in high mountains in the tropics—for example, the high Andes—or extend into cooler temperate areas such as New Zealand and southern South America. The Austral Conure (*Enicognathus ferrugineus*) for example toughs out a living in the raw cool climate of Tierra del Fuego, while the Antipodes Parakeet (*Cyanoramphus unicolor*) occupies the windswept outpost of Antipodes Island and neighboring rugged islets in the Pacific well to the south of New Zealand. The Andean Parakeet (*Bolborhynchus orbygnesius*) has been recorded on the high montane grasslands at over 6,000 meters in the high Andes.

The majority of the world's parrot species are found today in South America, Australia, and New Guinea. The single country with the most species is Brazil, with over seventy different kinds. In mainland Asia from Indochina to Pakistan and in Africa there are remarkably few. This uneven distribution appears to be linked to the breakup of the ancient supercontinent of Gondwanaland.[8] Whether people have as yet documented the existence of all living parrots is an open question. Four species of parrot new to science have been found since the late 1980s.[9] All are from South America and amazingly have waited until the Space Age to be noticed, let alone studied.

Though we still know little of these birds' place in nature, parrots have become uniquely familiar to humans and have been

closely associated with people for centuries. The oldest document in
the literature of the Indian subcontinent is the Rigveda, or Veda of
the Stanzas, of about 1400 B.C. This ancient work, written in San-
skrit, remarks on the great fidelity of parrots and records how in the
mythology of that time they were symbols of the moon.

The Ancient Greeks were also well aware of parrots. The historian and physician Ctesias traveled widely in the East around 400
B.C. As well as holding the great distinction of producing the first
published account of unicorns, he also brought news to Europe of
curious humanlike birds kept by the natives in the lands he visited.
Aristotle wrote some hundred years later about a parrot, but he may
not have seen it himself because he described it, presumably on the
strength of its hooked bill, as a kind of hawk.

During his conquests of the fourth century B.C., the Macedonian
general Alexander the Great marched through Afghanistan to the
Indus Valley in modern-day Pakistan. There his men acquired parrots that were later brought home with their other spoils of war.
Alexander was probably the first person to bring live parrots to Europe. They were medium-sized green parakeets marked with black
on the face and maroon patches on the wings. They had long tails
and a shrill cry. They are today known as Alexandrine Parakeets
(*Psittacula eupatria*).

After Alexander's conquests, the expansion of trade between the
Greek city-states and the Orient ensured that Europeans would
soon become more familiar with parrots. In the second century B.C.
the earliest known picture of a parrot was produced in a mosaic at
the ancient Greek city of Pergamum.

The Greek historian Diodorus Siculus wrote in 50 B.C. about parrots he had seen in Syria. Since no parrot is native to that country
today, they were most likely imported—probably from Africa. In
A.D. 50 Pliny described parrots that he said were discovered by ex-

plorers sent to Egypt. Although these birds are not known to occur naturally in Egypt now, they might have been imported from the savannas beyond the desert, or it might have been that the desert was less extensive than it is today. Other accounts of the same birds gave their origin as India. Since there is only one parrot in the world that has a natural distribution that embraces both Africa and India, it is very likely that these birds were Ring-necked Parakeets (*Psittacula krameri*). This species is one of the most widespread, adaptable, and common parrots in the world today, and has a long history of living with people.

Ring-necked Parakeets were prized, for example, in Ancient Rome, where they were kept as pets. So valuable did they become that they were often sold for more than the price of a human slave. Demand was intense, so a brisk trade built up with birds brought into Europe in large numbers. They were kept in ornate cages made from silver and decorated with ivory and tortoiseshell. Noblemen carried the birds through the streets of Rome as a colorful accessory. The statesman and philosopher Marcus Cato wrote: "Oh, wretched Rome! What times are these that women should feed dogs upon their laps and men should carry parrots on their hands." Some parrots, however, found a less fortunate fate in Rome. During the rule of Emperor Heliogabalus from 222 to 205 B.C. they became a table delicacy. Not only that, but they, as well as peacocks, were fed to his lions.

With the decline of Rome and its excesses, parrot keeping faded in Europe. A few Ring-necked Parakeets made it back with Crusaders and merchants during the Middle Ages and Marco Polo came across cockatoos in India, although they are not native to the subcontinent and presumably had made their way there on the trade routes from farther east. Today the most westerly distributed naturally occurring cockatoos are found in islands in the Moluccan

Sea and in the Philippines. French sailors also found African Grey Parrots (*Psittacus erithacus*) in the Canary Islands. They had been imported there from West Africa. These parrots were found to be excellent talkers and by the middle of the fifteenth century a steady flow of birds to the islands had been established from Portuguese trading posts along the African coast.

Popular, colorful, and in short supply, parrots once again became expensive status symbols. During the fifteenth and sixteenth centuries—the great age of exploration—the fact that parrots were fashionable, in big demand, and valuable meant that sailors traveling to new lands in tropical latitudes were on the lookout for them.

When Columbus returned to Seville in 1493 from his first expedition to the Caribbean, the parrots he brought back were displayed at his ceremonial reception. He had obtained the birds from natives who had tamed them. A pair was presented to his royal patron, Queen Isabella of Castile. These parrots were probably the species of bird from the genus *Amazona* that remains native to Cuba and the Bahamas today, the Cuban Amazon or Cuban Parrot (*Amazona leucocephala*).

As the conquistadores pressed their explorations throughout the islands and deeper into the mainlands of Central and South America, they found the practice of taming and keeping parrots was commonplace among the local populations. There is every reason to believe that the indigenous peoples of the tropics have kept parrots for thousands of years, and certainly for a lot longer than Europeans, a practice that many tribal societies continue to this day. Forest-dwelling peoples with an intimate knowledge of their surroundings took the colorful birds to the heart of their culture, where they became prized and revered possessions. Small-scale collecting by indigenous people for local trade was, however, very different from the approach of the Europeans. The foreigners had wholeheartedly embarked on their globalization adventure and wanted volume supplies for the mass markets back home.

The parrots and the forest people were to have a lot in common. One was to face biological oblivion, the other, cultural genocide. There is a story from 1509 in which the tame parrots belonging to local villages raised the alarm about an impending attack. Perched in the trees and on huts around a village, the birds screamed and shouted at the approach of Spanish soldiers, thereby enabling the local population to escape from their assailants into the forest. But the alliance of birds and "Stone Age" humans was no match for muskets and axes. They did not resist the might of the colonial powers for long. The birds and the forests were soon victims of an unprecedented age of plunder.

In the 1500s the plumage of brightly colored birds became fashionable for personal ornamentation. Taxes levied on the Indian populations recently subjugated by European armies were partly paid in macaw feathers. The long plumes of these birds were naturally collectable and desirable—exotic and beautiful. European consumers wanted them and would pay handsomely. Feathers were one thing, whole birds quite another. As the voyages of novelty-hungry explorers penetrated more and more remote localities, so the variety of parrots brought home increased. In 1501 Portuguese sailors brought the first macaws back to Europe from Brazil. The birds were known to the local people as *macauba* and were probably Scarlet Macaws (*Ara macao*). Such birds were to become among the most desirable of all parrots to cage and own. Later on, a blue one would also enter the trade. That creature, the Spix's Macaw, would become the most valuable of all.

In 1505 parrots were imported to England. They were an instant success and became fashionable accessories. In addition to his six wives, Henry VIII kept one (an African Grey) at Hampton Court. A portrait of William Brooke, 10th Baron Cobham, with his family painted in the middle 1500s hangs at Longleat House in Wiltshire, England. It portrays a family dressed in typical Tudor clothes seated around a meal table. A parrot stands among the dishes of food. It looks like some species of Amazon but is not any bird we know today.

Being vegetarian and able to thrive on a diet of seeds and fruits,[10] parrots could endure the long sea voyages that would kill most insectivorous birds. The trade became more regular and grew increasingly lucrative as the birds' popularity soared. The establishment of Portuguese and Dutch colonies in Asia would soon ensure a supply of birds from the East too.

Mass-produced metal cages meant that the birds became more widespread in captivity as the ever-expanding supply of wild parrots brought down prices. When zoological gardens were opened in European cities during the nineteenth century, the cheeky, colorful parrots were an instant hit with the public. London Zoo was the first scientific zoological garden in the modern world. It was founded in 1828 and opened its gates on the fringes of the green expanse of Regent's Park as a means to fund the scientific work of the London Zoological Society. Parrots were a big draw; so a special building, the Parrot House, was opened.

The redbrick Parrot House at the zoo today is an essential part of the gardens' character and stands as a monument to the popularity of parrots during Britain's imperial age. Many of the parrots that have passed through there are among the rarest, most beautiful, and most coveted creatures in the world. Spix's Macaws were fleetingly among them, but in an age when the fragility of our world was undreamed of, little or no thought would have been spared for the precariousness of these birds' existence.

In those times the complete disappearance of entire species

through collecting must have seemed a most unlikely prospect. During this colonial age in which collecting was obsessive, the accumulation of animals would not have seemed very different from amassing, cataloging, and displaying inanimate objects. Today we know better. While our forebears took precautions to safeguard paintings, statues, and other works of art for posterity, they could not fully understand the implications of hoarding these precious living creatures.

Even though the individual feathered treasures could not be preserved indefinitely, the rise of zoological gardens contributed to the growing familiarity and popularity of parrots to the point where such birds gradually took on symbolic values. Parrots came to stand for exotic places, tropical forests, color, and intelligence. These aspects of the birds' appeal were in turn ruthlessly exploited by advertising and marketing executives.

The earliest example of parrots being used for sales purposes was in ancient India, where high-class prostitutes carried a parrot on their wrists in order to advertise their profession. In the age of mass media these birds have reached vast audiences to sell a wide array of products. One television advertisement had an Amazon parrot playing the role of a talkative companion to a pirate. This was to sell rum-flavored chocolate.

Other parrots appeared in promotions for fruit drinks and tropical holidays, while a major British food retailer in 2001 adopted the Blue Parrot Café brand for a range of children's foods, featuring a blue macaw chosen for its friendliness and intelligence, and the sharp eyes it would need to select the very best ingredients. Gaudy Scarlet Macaws are the symbol of a Central American airline based in El Salvador: The fact that such birds are now extinct in that country has not deterred the marketing people. For obvious reasons, parrots also have been featured repeatedly in promotions for telecommunications and copier products. This promotional use of parrots further elevated their popular familiarity, inadvertently stimulating demand for the birds as pets.

Today a large majority of the world's different species of parrot are held somewhere in captivity. One estimate is that between 50 and 60 million of them are kept worldwide. Hundreds of parrot, parakeet, cockatoo, and macaw clubs and societies exist for enthusiasts. They have hundreds of thousands of members drawn from the many millions who keep parrots of some sort.

The most widespread parrot in captivity today is the humble budgie. These pretty little green parakeets were first brought back from Australia in 1840 by John Gould, and since then have been effectively domesticated. The word budgerigar appears to be derived from the name given to the bird by Australia's Aboriginal people. Budgies are probably the most common pets after dogs and cats, and have been bred in captivity for hundreds of generations into a variety of color variants, including white, blue, and yellow.

It wasn't, of course, simply the convenience of parrots' ability to tolerate long sea voyages that led to their popularity in captivity. Of the thousands of bird species alive today, parrots have emerged as our most popular and valuable feathered companion. Animal traders and pet shops seldom stock seagulls, herons, or thrushes; beautiful as these birds are, there is little or no demand for them as pets.

One reason why parrots are so hugely engaging compared with most other birds is that they can manipulate objects. In their natural forest homes, parrots clamber through foliage using their beak like a grappling hook, swinging in all directions to reach the finest fruit, nectar, and seed delicacies at the tips of even the thinnest twigs. Once they have procured their favored feast, they need great dexterity in manipulating tricky food items with their feet, bill, and fleshy prehensile tongues.

This acrobatic ability and "hand"-eye coordination makes these birds' behavior instantly charming to dextrous humans who can see aspects of themselves in the brightly colored and inquisitive birds. And like people, individual parrots show a distinct preference in the use of one or other of their reptilelike feet for manipulating objects. One study of South American Brown-throated Conures (*Aratinga pertinax*) revealed that about half habitually used their right foot and half the left.

On top of this, though, surely the principal reason why we find parrots so irresistible is because of their ability to copy the human voice. From earliest times, the capacity of parrots to "talk" has fascinated us. After thousands of years, it is still their most famed and demanded attribute. The talent for mimicry has impressed people down through the ages. Parrots were, for example, allocated roles in various Indian fables and plays. The Hindu sex manual the Kama Sutra sets out no fewer than sixty-four achievements that a man must strive for—one was to teach a parrot to talk. Four centuries before Christ it was perhaps more surprising for Ctesias's European readers to learn of a bird that could talk than the mythical one-horned unicorn that he wrote about. His writings in *Indica* about a Blossom-headed Parakeet (*Psittacula roseata*) he saw in the East included an account of its ability to copy the human voice. The bird belonged to an apothecary he had met on his travels, and Ctesias said it "could speak an Indian language or Greek, if it had been taught to do so." Pliny's description of parrots included the observation that they "conducted clear conversations and that, in order to teach them to speak, they must be given a few raps with a small stick on the head, which is as hard as their beak."

Although in Ancient Rome it was often the responsibility of the household slave to teach the parrot to talk, professional parrot teachers offered a service too. Presumably this skilled job would have been well paid and highly regarded. Certainly the best modern-day animal trainers who teach animals to perform in zoos and for film and television shows can earn a good living. But being trained by a professional teacher to be a good talker didn't guarantee a long and comfortable life in captivity. The tongues of talking parrots were eaten as a cure for speech impediments.

Later on, parrots like African Greys that could talk very well were revered in Europe. It was believed by the Roman Church that these birds' ability to speak elevated them in the hierarchy of creation. A parrot belonging to a Venetian cardinal undoubtedly reinforced this impression; his bird could faultlessly repeat the Lord's Prayer. Although today we use the phrase "parrot fashion" as a derogatory figure of speech to denote unthinking repetition, modern science has recently suggested that the medieval church might in fact have had a point. It seems that parrots don't simply copy: They use words to communicate specific meanings.

One famous African Grey Parrot called Alex has worked for years with American psychologist Irene Pepperberg. Alex has been intensively trained under laboratory conditions to use sounds in relation to their meaning and as a form of communication with people. Alex has demonstrated the ability to use words to describe dozens of objects, colors, and materials, and uses commands such as "Come here" or "I want." Alex has also begun to communicate with words that he has not been taught but has overheard and put into the correct context. He also picked up the idea of "no"—a conceptual breakthrough. He would say "No" to his keepers when he wanted to be left alone. Although a long way from being able to hold conversations, Alex does interact with people via human speech.

Pepperberg's work suggests that parrots, like people, are biologically primed to learn, socialize, and communicate. It seems that in common with human children, parrots need to learn from their peers and elders which sounds are significant and worth remembering. The fact that this kind of social learning goes on in the wild is demonstrated by the fact that different flocks of parrots develop their own "dialects." These "language" differences have emerged in studies of geographically isolated populations of parrots and show how their use of sound is not instinctive but learned and cultural. In captivity, where the parrot's normal feathered companions are instead replaced by human "flock members," the significant sounds are the ones "taught" by people or those that seem to elicit a strong response from their human companions. Since the sound of a telephone or the beep of a microwave oven sends the owner (flock member) running to them, these sounds acquire importance and the parrot will therefore reproduce them.[11]

Alex's achievements in mastering aspects of human communication are quite staggering. It is worth considering that while parrots have learned our language, we humans have so far failed to communicate with these birds in the whistles, squeaks, and squawks that are comprised in their native tongues. It is also worth dwelling for a moment on the question of who is mimicking whom. The next time a parrot says "Hello" and you return the greeting, remind yourself who said it first. There is every impression that some parrots seek attention by talking to people. They use the words that experience has shown them will get a response. The bird says "Hello," the human responds. Following this most humanlike introduction, the bird acquires the social contact, attention, and stimulation it craves. Most people can identify with that.

Despite parrots' legendary ability to talk, it is remarkable how little is understood of their use of sound in the wild. It was not until 1993, for example, that there was firm evidence of vocal mimicry of wild African Grey Parrots.[12] What does seem ever clearer, however, is that their sophisticated use of sounds is more than simply an ability to duplicate. It appears to be a reflection of these birds' capacity to process and exchange information, and is linked to their behavioral and mental flexibility.

One reason parrots need such mental abilities is because, like people, they are social animals. Their brains and instincts are those of creatures that interact at an individual level. Most species live in flocks, at least outside the breeding season. Throughout the year and especially when they are nesting, individual parrots maintain a strong bond with their partner. What goes on in their minds, what emotional dimension there is to the bond between pairs of birds we can only guess at. Like people, however, it seems that the attachment between a pair goes very deep. Where "love" meets instinct we cannot know, but considering the intelligence of parrots we should not rule out the possibility that an emotional state comparable to that found in humans might bind pairs of these birds together.

Many species pair for life and will only change partners if theirs dies. The pair bond is reinforced by various behaviors, including mutual preening and feeding. This aspect of their makeup explains why in most species males and females are similar in size and color. Sexual dimorphism is most marked in mammals and birds where the males are polygamous and compete with one another for the attentions of several females. In monogamous breeding systems the need to show off with bright plumes and displays is less necessary and for that reason (in the majority of parrots) the sexes look alike.

A close bond has great value. Birds that have bred together generally get better at it as time goes by. Rather like first-time human parents, new pairs of parrots can get into difficulties while older and more experienced birds appear to cope much better. Some species might also benefit from a close monogamous relationship in being instantly ready to breed when conditions permit. Many parrots have no defined nesting season and begin their breeding cycle when conditions are suitable; some of the Australian grass para-keets are notable in this respect. The budgerigar, for example, quickly nests after unpredictable rains, when it lays up to eight eggs. The birds wander in search of areas where rain has fallen and are triggered into breeding condition when such an area is located. The chicks mature fast and leave the nest after only a month. The establishment of a year-round monogamous pair bond is an advan-tage under these conditions since it saves time when the unpre-dictable rains fall. The search for a partner and the formalities of courtship are dispensed with and any possible delay in the birds' ability to make the most of abundant food to feed their chicks is avoided—again, an advantage that many humans will identify with.

Even when the birds are forced to be less sociable and to spread out to take advantage of widely scattered nesting sites or food sources, in most species of parrot the family group forms a tight so-cial unit. When the young are fledged from the nest, they fly with their parents to learn the feeding techniques and skills of vigilance and predator recognition and avoidance they will need to survive.

In their various levels of social organization, there are hierar-chies, peer groups, families, and breeding partners. To cope with such a complex social environment parrots must recognize individ-uals and know their place in the social order. That in turn requires memory and the ability to learn and to communicate. And such abilities are of premium value to creatures that live a long time. The longer they live, the more they can learn. Longer-lived birds can pass on more information and wisdom to their offspring, thereby improving the young birds' chances of survival in the unforgiving world of the forest.

Parrots are almost legendary for their longevity. There are many stories of parrots living in excess of a hundred years and of birds that have become family heirlooms passed down from one generation to another. Certainly there are birds that have been in families for many years, but the oldest documented birds have not lived beyond their sixties.[13] By the time macaws reach their fifties they often have cataracts and arthritis, and are approaching senility. Some other birds live for a long time—members of the albatross family, for example,[14] but the longevity of parrots is quite exceptional nonetheless.

Their humanlike traits give parrots a unique personality and character. What other birds have so consistently managed to grab tabloid newspaper headlines? There have been stories about parrots that wolf-whistle at blondes, a parrot that swore at wild birds when it got stuck up a tree in the garden, a parrot that told the firemen to rescue him before putting the fire out, and the ship's mascot that yelled "Arse" and "Bollocks" from a cupboard during an important speech by an admiral and told the enlisted man to "fuck off" when asked to be quiet. There was another story about a parrot that telephoned the police when its owner was locked out.

Tens of millions of years of quite separate evolutionary advance lies between people and parrots. Yet the psychology of these birds and humans has uniquely converged. Parrots are the most humanlike of birds, which has made them irresistible to human curiosity. And the appeal seems to go both ways. Parrots can build long-term relationships not only with other parrots, but also with other long-lived sociable creatures—people.

Rosemary Low knows all about that. She has kept parrots for more than forty years. Starting with budgies when she was twelve, Low progressed from there to larger and more demanding species. She has a vast published literature to her name, including a seminal work on the care and breeding of parrots printed in three editions.[15] She has looked after some of the world's largest parrot collections and has an impressive track record of breeding the birds in captivity. In the early 1960s, at sixteen, she acquired an African Grey via a friend's father who was a bank manager in Nigeria. She says it was her first real parrot and gave her many insights into the challenges of keeping the birds in captivity.

Low believes that parrots' ability to mimic human sounds and to interact emotionally with people has been their downfall.

> This is why the African Grey is so popular, but it is a tragedy. They are among the most sensitive birds and there is probably no parrot species less suited to a life in captivity. They have so many behavioural problems when caged. You practically need a degree in psychology to understand grey parrots. They are very clever birds. Like cockatoos they soon learn to manipulate people. The owners can't cope with them any more so they get passed on from one place to another. It would be like a child finding itself in a new home every eighteen months or so. If it was a person it would be enough for it to end up in a psychiatric hospital.

Captive-bred parrots make better companions but cost at least twice as much. Until very recently there was little interest in breeding the likes of the more common species of Amazon parrots, cockatoos, or macaws for the pet market because they were so cheap and readily available from the wild. And cost aside, captive breeding is not as straightforward as it sounds.

With the larger and more intelligent parrots in particular, one of the main issues in captive breeding is compatibility. As is the case with humans, it is not sufficient to put a male and female parrot together and expect them to produce and rear young. A pair of birds randomly selected by human keepers can sit together for years and do nothing, but if provided with a partner they like, will nest immediately. Although it can be worth leaving birds together for a period to see if they will finally accept one another, placing parrots with incompatible partners can also lead to stress and emotional damage—something else humans can relate to.

The natural commitment to one partner can translate into close relationships with parrots' human keepers and has given pet parrots a reputation for devotion, faithfulness, and affection. But the fact that parrots choose those they will or will not bond with can also be a source of disappointment for parrot owners. Having bought a bird, the new keeper can sometimes find that it decides to bond with another member of the human family or a friend. And parrots can also demonstrate fierce jealousy in taking a dislike to individuals whom they regard as competitors for the affections of their human "partners." Such selective bonding and expression of choice leads Low to believe that parrots are capable of almost human emotions.

The combination of this humanlike emotional sophistication, an instinct for loyalty, the ability to mimic speech—and even to communicate with words—added to their astonishing and vivid beauty has paradoxically proved a curse to the parrots, making them extremely valuable. This market value has sucked down some species to the very brink of extinction.

Although most rare parrots are protected from trade under international law, as well as, in most cases, national legislation in the countries where they are found, the clandestine traffic in rare birds flourishes. Parrots today are part of an illegal trade in wildlife that ranks second in value only to the multibillion-dollar drug and arms black markets.

Even though the rarest and most protected kinds must often be kept in secret for fear of detection by the authorities, for the collectors there is still the irresistible allure of possessing birds that other people in their circle do not. The parallels with stolen works of art are surely apposite. The "owners" enjoy the birds' beauty and uniqueness with the added kick of having exclusive control of an object passionately sought and admired by others. The fact that other underground collectors know (or believe) that they have them adds to the attraction. This is a shadowy world of rumor, double-dealing, and half-truths.

For some of the leading parrot collectors the challenge of breeding is important. Many also rationalize a conservation motive into their passion for rare birds, and in this respect a minority are sincere. But in the end it is rarity that is the sharpest spur. As in Ancient Rome, parrots are potent symbols of civilization, wealth, and high living; they remain in demand as expensive accessories of the rich and powerful. In this close-knit world, birds like Spix's Macaws are the epitome of quality and grace; they are the true elite.

At this end of the market, large sums of money change hands. Many thousands of dollars are routinely paid for a single rare parrot. But even though the resale value of birds and their offspring can be considerable, for the majority of these specialists cash is not the primary motivation. Some collectors spend fortunes on their parrot-keeping facilities and there is no way they could regain their costs from the sale of birds. A small number are much more businesslike and breed rare parrots on a commercial basis.

And where there is valuable property and jealousy, there is theft. Rare parrots are frequently stolen from their owners. The rarest and most endangered parrots are most at risk. Puerto Rican Parrots (*Amazona vittata*) are one of the most endangered of all species. Some of these birds are kept in breeding aviaries run by the U.S. Fish and Wildlife Service at the Luquillo National Forest on their native island. In April 2001 bird thieves broke in and took several birds, much to the despair of the biologists who had been working for decades to save them from extinction.

Until as recently as the late 1980s, the effect of trapping on many of the rare and collectable species in the wild was unknown. The driving force behind the demand for the birds was rarity in captivity. Parrots weren't considered as real wild birds with natural habitats. So familiar a commodity had they become to the collectors that the idea of them disappearing from their native forests was not seriously considered. Even when the obvious rarity of some parrots was acknowledged and the impact of trapping seen as a threat, most enthusiasts denied they were connected to the plight of parrots in the wild. Collectors preferred to blame poor farmers clearing forests or the governments of developing countries rather than face the consequences of their own obsession.

But by the end of the twentieth century it was clear that many of the main target species taken for the elite collectors' market were getting into serious trouble. They now comprised some of the rarest and most endangered birds in the world. Many of the worst-affected species occupied tiny ranges in the wild, often only a single small island.

When the Convention on International Trade in Endangered Species (CITES) came into force in 1975 (see page 31), banning trade in some of the most threatened parrots, the smugglers tried every means possible to circumvent the treaty's protective measures. Rare-parrot laundering via countries with more open borders or less strict regulations, document falsification, disguising rare species as common ones, and straightforward smuggling have all occurred and still do.

Even in countries that had the will to enforce the Convention, the means used by the traders to evade detection grew ever more sophisticated. Parrots have been packed inside sections of drain-pipe, hidden inside vehicles' spare tires, and put in plastic bottles to smuggle them past customs officials. Rare parrot eggs have been taken on planes strapped against the bodies of smugglers to keep them warm, hatched in incubators, the babies hand-raised, and the birds sold for a fortune. Where detection of smuggling in some places has improved, the trade routes have shifted to exploit the next weakest point of entry.[16]

During the second half of the 1980s, the scale of the disaster about to overtake the world's most familiar and popular birds finally became clear. One man was devoting his working life to the matter: Nigel J. Collar at the International Council for Bird Preservation (ICBP), a network of bird conservation groups from around the world headquartered at Cambridge in England.[17] He had been writing about endangered birds for years and was the world expert on the subject. Collar had accumulated a vast global network of museum curators, academics, and ornithologists who helped him piece together a picture of what was happening to the world's fast-disappearing birds.

The results of this sifting through old manuscripts, field reports, and collections was the compilation of so-called Red Data Books. Collar's great tomes systematically set out the situation faced by individual endangered species so that action to save them could be properly directed and prioritized. Basing his research on the collections and journals of the early natural history explorers such as Spix and Martius, the fieldwork of top ornithologists, and bird records compiled by different societies and academic bodies, Collar coordinated research that in 1988 led to the publication of *Birds to Watch*. It showed that more than one thousand species of bird out of a total of about ten thousand were in danger of disappearing for good.

One family was doing worse than any others—the parrots. Some 71 out of the 350 known species were then listed as at risk of extinction. Collar found that the principal reasons for this catastrophic decline were collection of birds for the pet and collector markets and destruction of the birds' forest homes.[18]

Collar's findings demanded that there be a change in the one-sided relationship between people and parrots. Hundreds of years of trapping and deforestation had taken their toll: There wasn't much time to spare. Some of the most beautiful parrots were already at the very brink of extinction; for them the endgame was now in play. Just a few last moves were left as a final prelude to more than 50 million years of evolutionary memory being wiped away for good.

The group of parrots nearest to the edge was the blue macaws. Once seen in the flesh, it is obvious why this group of spectacular blue parrots above all others should attract special attention from the trappers, dealers, and collectors. Outstanding among even the parrots for charisma, charm, and visual impact, the blue macaws—Spix's among them—have been doomed by their unique qualities to be among humanity's most prized possessions.

CHAPTER 4

The Four Blues

Visitors to the Berlin Zoo in 1900 enjoyed a unique spectacle. The crowds filing past the cages didn't know it, but they were the only people in history to have seen all four species of the spectacular blue macaw alive together. In addition to the rare Spix's Macaw, captive Hyacinth, Glaucous, and Lear's Macaws were then held in the Berlin aviaries. All had been imported from South America. These highly coveted zoological treasures would never meet again.

Today these three large and similar-looking blue macaws are included in the biological genus *Anodorhynchus*, from the name coined by Spix. These macaws are larger than the *Cyanopsitta* macaw first collected by Spix. They also differ from Spix's in having a proportionately larger bill and curious patches of bare yellow skin at the base of the beak and around the eyes. The function of the bright startling highlights is unknown but could be to aid recognition—

some form of adornment that is important for bonding and breeding—or a means to reduce their temperature when the birds get too hot. The large black hooked bill of the *Anodorhynchus* macaws is uniquely adapted for eating the fruits of various palms. The largest nuts eaten by the largest species, the Hyacinth Macaw, are about the size of a golf ball. Even with a big hammer or heavy-duty bench vise, it is impossible for a person to break them open. The macaws are, however, experts. They rotate the nuts in their bill, manipulating where necessary with tongue and foot to place the tough objects in exactly the correct positioning for peeling. Once they have removed the tough external skin, the birds make perfect transverse cuts with the heavy square chisel at the cutting edge of the lower half of their bill that enables them to split the nuts in two. Inside is the prize, a nutritious fatty kernel.

As the palm trees evolved tougher and tougher shells to prevent their seeds being eaten, so the big blue macaws advanced larger bills to crack them. And so it went on—an ecological arms race that produced surely the most impressive of all bird bills. Remarkably, the huge and powerful bill of these macaws is rarely used in anger. Despite having the potential to remove fingers easily, the birds are the gentle giants of the parrot world.

Fieldworkers studying Hyacinth Macaws have described the effect of their work on palm nuts as resembling that of a machine tool or laser rather than that of a bird's bill. Once opened, the coconut-like flesh of the nut is crushed into a paste that the birds find absolutely irresistible. Hyacinth Macaws are clever when it comes to cracking such tough nuts. One German aviculturist noticed that when his macaws were given *Acrocomia* nuts brought home from a visit to South America, the birds used small pieces of wood to help grip the fruits firmly in their beaks. His macaws would shave a small piece of wood 3 to 4 millimeters long from their perch, position it inside the upper half of their bill, and use it as a wedge to keep the smooth nuts in place for easier opening.

These big blue macaws (the Hyancinth, Lears, and Glaucous) can eat other food, but their ecological niche is very much dependent on palms. Since they eat so many of the nuts, they need lots of palm trees to keep them going, so they live around types of palms that grow in communal clumps. They need palms that produce the right-sized nuts, and nuts that permit the extraction of the nutritious flesh. These exacting requirements are paramount in determining the distribution of these spectacular birds.

The largest of the three big blue macaws, the Hyacinth Macaw, is the largest parrot in the world. The intelligence, huge size, striking coloration, dramatic appearance, and pure charisma of these parrots make them exceptionally collectable. Their top-heavy appearance—a third of their muscle weight is concentrated in their large head to operate the massive beak—gives them a unique identity.

Hyacinth Macaws have a comical expression, particularly when they're flying—their features appear overemphasized. In some respects they resemble clowns, and to the first-time observer it is as if nature has made some amusing mistake. They are very inquisitive, engaging, and usually have quite a laid-back disposition. It is no wonder that ever since they were first seen they have been in demand. Rosemary Low sums up the Hyacinth's appeal: "It is just such a charismatic creature, even if you don't have the faintest interest in parrots you look at one and it just knocks you out. They are incredible birds, not just their colour but their behavior, their character—it is extraordinary."

Although there is undoubtedly more to it, color plays a big part in the attraction. Blue land animals are rare. There aren't any blue mammals and there are very few blue birds. Since earliest times people have placed a great value on blue and gone to great lengths to manufacture the color. The plant woad (Isatis tinctoria) yielded a blue dye called indigo that once held great ceremonial importance. Later on, this plant attained considerable commercial value. Until the advent of synthetic dyes, woad was cultivated in great plantations that were for a time a mainstay in some colonial economies. Indigo was, for example, the main export of El Salvador until coffee took over in the 1870s.

Among the parrots there is only a handful of species that are naturally mainly blue and very few that have completely blue or bluish plumage; the four blue macaws are the most spectacular. The least known of the trio of larger blue macaws is the Glaucous Macaw (Anodorhynchus glaucus).

The Glaucous Macaw

Europeans visiting South America made their first references to this bird during the late eighteenth century. Travelers to the southern part of the continent made their long journeys to the interior principally by river. It was in the middle reaches of the great rivers Paraguay, Paraná, and Uruguay in southern South America that early chroniclers saw a large long-tailed blue parrot. Its general plumage was pale powdery blue but brighter—almost turquoise— above. It had a heavy grayish tinge on the underparts and head, and in certain lights could appear nearly green. Sánchez Labrador, a Spanish priest dispatched by the Jesuits to work as a missionary with the Guaraní Indians in the region of what is today northern Argentina and southern Paraguay, was one of the first to write about a bird that was probably of this species.

Labrador worked there from 1734 until his return to Europe in 1767 following the expulsion of the Jesuits from the continent by the Spanish and Portuguese colonial authorities. He was a passionate naturalist who spent long hours documenting the wildlife in the many places he visited. Much of his writing remains unpublished and apparently languishes unedited in the archives of the Vatican. One manuscript on the fish and birds of Paraguay written in 1767 has, however, been printed. In it are some of the very few details from that era about the Glaucous Macaw.

The priest used the local Guaraní Indian name for the bird, *Guaa obi*. *Guaa* is the onomatopoeic name for macaw and *obi* (or *hovy*) describes a color between blue and green. He wrote about one of these macaws that he met in the village of La Concepción de Nuestra Señora:

When a missionary arrived from another mission, the macaw would go to his lodging. If it found that the door was shut, it would climb up . . . with the help of its bill and feet until it reached the latch. It then made a sound as if knocking and often opened the door before it could be opened from the inside. It would climb on the chair in which the missionary was sitting and utter 'guaa' three or four times, making alluring movements with its head until it was spoken to as if thanking him for the visit and attention. Then it would climb down and go into the courtyard very contented.

If it did anything untoward to other tame birds, the missionary would call it. It would approach submissively and listen attentively to his accusation, the punishment for which was supposed to be a beating. When it heard this it lay on its back and positioned its feet as if making the sign of the cross and the missionary pretended to beat it with a belt. It lay there quietly . . . then it turned over, stood up and climbed up the robe to the hand of the missionary, who had pronounced the punishment, to be stroked and spoken to kindly before leaving very satisfied. . . .

There are very many of these birds in the woods of the eastern
bank of the Uruguay River, but they occur rarely in the forests
along the Paraguay River.

Other travelers to the region also came across the Glaucous
Macaw but recorded very few details about its natural history. Félix
de Azara lived in South America from 1781 to 1801. His 1805 account of his travels mentions a blue-green macaw that he saw on
the Paraná and Uruguay rivers in Argentina and northward to just
inside the south of modern Paraguay. He said that the "*Guaa-hovy*"
was a common bird along the banks of these rivers. Apart from a
few details on its distribution, no more was noted.

The French explorer Alcide Dessalines d'Orbigny traveled in
southern South America between 1827 and 1835. He found the
species on the Uruguay River, probably on both the Uruguayan and
Brazilian sections, also in Argentina on the Paraná River. Besides
making passing references to this species in his travel journals, he
ate one, but found it very tough and the taste disagreeable. He
noted that it was not a very common bird. More significant than details about the culinary potential of the Glaucous Macaw, however,
was his observation of the vast swaths of yatay palms that grew on
the rich soils that flanked the broad watercourses. These palms
made a big impression on d'Orbigny. In his journal for April 23,
1827, he wrote:

There I saw for the first time, the palm tree known by the local
people under the name "yatay," which had given the locality the
name of Yatayty. . . . This palm does not grow to a great height,
the trunk of it is thick and covered with old marks where the
leaves had been attached, in which grew several figs which finish
by smothering the tree. The leaves of this palm are elegantly

curved and the green-blue of their fronds directed towards the sky, contrast pleasantly with the surrounding vegetation.

But d'Orbigny correctly saw the implications of colonial development for the fate of these beautiful palm forests:

> In the past the yatay palm covered all the sands in these places, but the need to develop the land for cultivation, or the appeal of the pleasant foodstuff that the heart of the tree offers, had necessitated such exploitation that, since the time of the wars, it can no longer be found on foot in other than very small numbers, sad and last of what is left of the handsome forest, of which they formed part, and which before long must disappear entirely.

Later that year and in early 1828, d'Orbigny recorded more details about the fate of the splendid forests. On January 4 he noted:

> I was leaving Tacuaral, so as to go to Yatayty, without doubt the most productive land in the entire province of Corrientes. . . . All the inhabitants of other parts of the province come to settle in the middle of these woods, cutting down the palm trees and planting the lands. . . . It is also to be feared that they will destroy the palm trees, which will no longer grow back in the inhabited regions, and will finally disappear completely.[19]

D'Orbigny also recorded some of the very few details collected at the time about the habits of the Glaucous Macaw. Of the river Paraná he wrote: "All along the cliff, one saw scattered pairs of macaws of a dull blue-green, from which the woods echoed repeatedly the incessant shrill cries. Each pair appeared either at the edge of huge holes they had dug out of the cliffs in order to lay down their brood, or perched on the hanging branches of trees which crowned the banks."

Other reports of these birds, or reports of parrots that might have been Glaucous Macaws, during the middle part of the nineteenth century, were few and far between. After 1860 no new wild specimens were added to museums and only a very few were procured by European zoos. There were three in the Amsterdam Zoo during the 1860s; several in Hamburg and Antwerp zoos during the 1870s and 1880s, respectively; two in London between 1886 and 1912; one in Berlin from 1892 to the early twentieth century; and one in Paris from 1895 to 1905. Another one was reportedly kept in the Buenos Aires Zoo until as late as 1936, but was said to be an old bird that was by then forty-five.

From the early twentieth century, even reports of captive Glaucous Macaws became less frequent, while reports of birds in the wild virtually came to an end. Indeed, after 1900 there were only two records that *may* have been of living wild birds—one from Uruguay in 1950, where a single bird was seen on a fence post, and another from Paraná in Brazil in the 1960s, where locals said they lived in the steep banks that flanked the Iguaçu River. The locality where the macaw on the fence post was seen was later turned over to a eucalyptus plantation. They were not reported again on the Iguaçu. By the late 1970s, the Glaucous Macaw seemed to be extinct.

Then, in June 1991, a British newspaper made the remarkable claim that parrot breeder and collector Harry Sissen had a Glaucous Macaw among the birds he kept at his farm in Yorkshire, England. As it turned out, the claim was wrong. It was a similar-looking but quite different species, a Lear's Macaw. But the report was one among persistent and continuing rumors that the birds still existed in the wild and were still being supplied to bird collectors in the U.S.A., Brazil, and Europe. Another parrot enthusiast who was more concerned for the birds' conservation was Tony Pittman. He believed the Glaucous Macaw could still exist and decided to go and look for it.

Pittman had been interested in parrots for years and his special enthusiasm was for the blue macaws. He and his associate, Joe Cuddy, planned to trace the routes of the explorers, naturalists, and writers who visited South America during the eighteenth and nineteenth centuries. They used research assembled by endangered bird expert Nigel Collar to find all the manuscripts and early accounts of the Glaucous Macaw that they could lay their hands on.

The firm records formed a circle covering Corrientes and Misiones provinces in northeast Argentina, Artigas Province in northwest Uruguay, and portions of the southernmost states of Brazil. Collar was convinced that the species might yet survive, and Pittman and Cuddy were determined to look for themselves. In June 1992 they set off for Buenos Aires en route to search in the places where the birds had been reliably reported, in some cases more than two hundred years before.

They assumed that the original habitat of the bird was gallery forests along the main rivers from which the birds would foray into palm groves to feed. They also had good reason to believe that the Glaucous Macaws once nested in the steep cliffs and banks along the main rivers. With these likely habitat preferences in mind, they looked in the most promising areas.

Pittman remarked that "driving through the countryside where the Glaucous Macaw was found in the eighteenth century is just like driving through parts of southern England. There is no way a bird that size could be around with no one noticing it. It's very bare of trees and heavily ranched." In addition to large-scale cultivation and ranching in the areas where the yatay palms once grew, there was modification or flooding of large sections of the river valleys by huge engineering works, such as the Salto Grande hydroelectric complex on the river Uruguay. The men spoke to the locals but could find no one who knew of the Glaucous Macaw. Not only that, but they encountered genuine astonishment from people at the idea that such a bird could possibly still exist.

Disappointed, Pittman and Cuddy returned with no evidence that the bird survived. But in 1997, following new information, they went back, and this time they did find someone who knew of the blue macaw they sought. While in the vicinity of the little town of Pilar that lies on the Paraguayan bank of the river Paraguay, Pittman was introduced to Ceferino Santa Cruz, a ninety-five-year-old cotton farmer who lived in a little village.

The old man spoke only the local Guaraní Indian language, so Paraguayan friends had to translate his words into Spanish. He told them that he had been born there in 1902. His father had moved to the place in 1875 following the devastating War of Triple Alliance with Argentina, Brazil, and Uruguay. This bitter conflict ruined Paraguay, killing 90 percent of the country's adult male population. Ceferino's father was among the survivors. Although the old man had never himself seen the blue macaws, his father had told him about them. His father had said that the parrots fed on fresh green palm fruits. This interview, across generations through the Indian tradition of storytelling, provided perhaps the only direct link that remained with the Glaucous Macaw. No one else in the world seemed to know anything about it.

The inescapable conclusion was that the Glaucous Macaw was extinct, and probably had been for some years. The most likely reason for its disappearance was degradation and disappearance of its habitat, especially the yatay palms on which it probably fed. One analysis found that yatays are the only colonial palm species occurring where these birds once lived with a nut of the right size and type. Ornithologists examining the bird's likely diet concluded that "There has been no palm regeneration in the range of this extinct macaw, and the remnant palm groves are more than 200 years old."[20]

The reason for the palm's disappearance was the introduction of European agriculture. The colonists soon learned that the places where the yatay palms grew indicated the richest soils, and naturally that was where the farmers first settled. The region was accessible by river and a substantial population grew up in early colonial times. The city of Corrientes that lies in the heart of the bird's historical range was founded in 1588, the year the Spanish Armada sailed on England, so the impact of an advanced European society had, by the time of Pittman's visit, already lasted more than four hundred years.

Even in areas where the birds' favorite palms might have survived the onslaught of plowing, their eventual loss was assured by extensive cattle grazing. Ranching was already an economic mainstay by the end of the eighteenth century, and the effective regeneration of sufficient palms for the macaws to survive did not occur; their staple food plants were nibbled away by the cattle before they had a chance to grow or produce fruit, and eventually died out. Indeed, several species of palm in the genus *Butia* (to which the yatay belongs) are themselves listed as threatened with extinction. The trapping of birds for captivity certainly hastened the macaw on its way, but to what extent this pressure was complicit in its disappearance cannot be known.

It seems that the last living Glaucous Macaw reliably identified by a scientist was the one kept in the Paris Zoo (Jardin d'Acclimatation) for ten years from 1895. Whatever the reasons for its rapid slide into oblivion, the Glaucous Macaw—a large and conspicuous blue parrot—had become extinct, and no one had noticed until decades after the event. Indeed, one leading parrot expert blithely described the species as "rare" even in the late 1970s, by when it had not been seen for certain in the wild for more than a century. Certainly no visitors to the Berlin Zoo in 1900 would have realized that they were gazing upon a doomed species.

The Lear's Macaw

In the 1970s, ornithologists believed that a similar fate awaited the gorgeous blue Lear's Macaw (*Anodorhynchus leari*). This parrot was known to Victorian naturalists as a similar-sized species to the Glaucous Macaw (although a little larger at 71 centimeters) and the two were obviously close evolutionary relatives. The Lear's was, however, darker, deeper blue, and more glossy; in some respects it was more like the Hyacinth Macaw, from which it was distinguished not only by size, but by a curious facial expression created by the oval bare yellow skin patches around the eyes that made the birds look a bit sleepy.

The English name "Lear's Macaw" came from the title conferred on the species by French biologist Prince Charles Bonaparte—the nephew of Napoleon—who in 1856 wrote the first scientific description of the species. The Englishman Edward Lear, much better known for his nonsense verse, had illustrated the macaw in his book *Illustrations of the Family of Psittacidae, or Parrots*. The first installment of this work appeared in 1830. Lear was then a promising young artist who had begun work on painting parrots at a time when their popularity was soaring. Despite the care Lear devoted to his work, in common with others he mistakenly believed that his painting of the blue macaw was of a Hyacinth. Although he had the "wrong" species, he did produce an excellent painting and the name stuck and remains with us today, alongside the bird's other common English name: Indigo Macaw.

But during the nineteenth century, Lear's Macaw was even less well documented than its enigmatic cousin the Glaucous. Very few specimens were added to museum collections following the deaths of birds in zoos, but their natural origin was quite obscure. Although odd ones turned up in the U.S.A. and Europe in consignments of Hyacinth Macaws from Brazil, they were also rare in captivity. Scarcity and mystery added to their collectability; the rarity and obscurity made demand for them greater, not less.

In February 1907, the journal of the Avicultural Society carried an item on the Lear's Macaw by the Reverend Hubert Astley. Astley, who had several of the birds, wrote: "[M]y Italian servant said about the Lear's Macaw I have in Italy, 'è proprio un papagallo signorile,' a real gentleman amongst parrots, an aristocrat." Astley evidently took great pride in his Lear's Macaws and found the species to be especially clever. One particular bird was his favorite. He wrote that "He loves a game with a handkerchief. It is thrown right on to his head, covering it completely up, upon which he proceeds to dance up and down with great glee, and at last either dances it off, or else pulls it off with one claw, holding it, and then laughing loudly and in a most human way: waiting for the fun to be commenced all over again."

Sadly for Astley's macaws, their natural preferred food of palm nuts was not on the menu. "He likes sun-flower seed chiefly, with apple, banana or pear in the morning, and at five o'clock tea he always has some 'Albert' or 'Marie' biscuit, soaked in hot milk, and given not too moist." The bird might have seemed to enjoy this fare, or more likely ate it from lack of choice. At the time, where the birds came from was not known, let alone what they ate. Astley remarked, "It is a curious fact that none of the authorities in Europe seem to know from what part of South America the Lear's Macaw is bought. It is probably somewhere in Brazil, for they are brought from the ports of Bahía, Santos and Rio de Janeiro. . . . So they probably inhabit some of the great forests in the heart of Brazil, and a few young birds are reared from the nest, and carried to the ports on the coast."

Indeed, the failure of ornithologists to locate a wild population of Lear's Macaws had moved Dutch ornithologist K. H. Voous to suggest that it was not a proper species at all. Examinations of the few museum specimens of Lear's Macaws and a comparison between those and a few Glaucous and Hyacinth skins led Voous to propose in 1965 that it might be a crossbreed between the other two. At the same time as controversially suggesting that it was not a proper species, Voous threw down an ornithological gauntlet. He challenged someone to draw up accurate distribution maps for *Anodorhynchus* macaws—in other words, to find Lear's Macaws in their natural habitat. He added the understated rider that this "may prove a hard task."

One man ready to take on Voous's challenge was the German-Brazilian scientist Helmut Sick. He'd arrived in Brazil as a young man from Germany just before the outbreak of the World War II. He traveled there with a colleague to study birds in the Atlantic rain forests in the eastern coastal state of Espírito Santo. The trip was scheduled to last three months, but during that time, in September 1939, Germany invaded Poland and war broke out in Europe. Sick decided to stay where he was.

Because he was a German national, Sick was kept in captivity by Brazil, which had a stance of neutrality. During the war years he developed considerable expertise on termites, one of the very few animal groups lending themselves to convenient direct study by a prisoner in the tropics. When the war ended, Sick resumed his career as a professional zoologist and became one of Brazil's foremost bird experts. He traveled widely in pursuit of his ornithological passion, making many new discoveries.

He had read Voous's writings but was convinced that the Lear's Macaw was a distinct species and that, although rare, it still lived somewhere in a remote part of Brazil. He set out to prove it. He had been interested in the bird since 1954, but all of his efforts to locate it had come to nothing. He found it incredible that a giant blue parrot with a 1.2-meter wingspan could have gone unnoticed for so long. Dozens of scientific expeditions had by then crisscrossed Brazil; Sick had been on many of them himself. Still no one had found the Lear's Macaw—it seemed to many a nonsense bird, worthy of the man who had given his name to it.

There was one clue though. It came from the town of Juàzeiro on the river São Francisco, the town near where Spix collected his blue macaw. There, in 1950, one of Sick's colleagues had seen a tame captive Lear's Macaw that he believed had been caught nearby. Sick also had a hunch that it was in this arid and remote region that the birds would be found. He began searching in earnest in 1964, but the region of northeast Brazil where he thought the birds might be was larger than France. After four exhausting expeditions during the 1960s and 1970s, Sick began to narrow his options. He decided in 1978 that the place to look was the Raso da Catarina, a remote region of the caatinga. He described the place as "a rugged dry area, a great white patch on the map far away from civilisation." There were no roads, no towns and few rivers, only a vast area of thorn bush, cacti, rocks and dry cliffs. The single reason the place was notable at all was for its traumatic and violent past.

The Canudos hills on the south side of the Raso da Catarina had been a refuge for revolutionaries and bandits during the nineteenth century, and the place had been scarred by conflict and war. In the Canudos war of 1896 to 1897 a group of religious zealots revolted against the republic. Thousands of the rebels perished. More than a thousand soldiers, including elite government troops, also died there, many from thirst. It was into this tragic "Lost World" that Sick was to venture next in his decades-long search for the enigmatic blue macaw.

Sick and his two field assistants arrived at the Raso da Catarina in the height of summer 1978. Traveling along tracks and trails in the driest and most inhospitable part of the vast caatinga, they found, on December 29, the first evidence that they might be close. A hunter told them that several months before he had killed a bird like the one in the pictures the scientists had shown him. The man had eaten it but kept some of the long blue feathers. As it happened, Sick had made a special trip to San Diego in California the previous year to study live Lear's Macaws kept there in the city's zoo, and he had also devoted time to making careful measurements from museum specimens, so he knew what he was looking at when the hunter produced the bird's remains. The feathers were from a Lear's Macaw. Elated at this find, they decided to search the local area.

Sick's four-wheel-drive diesel Toyota, the most robust off-road vehicle available in Brazil, had found the going too tough. Buried up to its axles in sand, it had to be abandoned in favor of a tractor and then horses. And Sick, no longer a young man, was in bad shape too. He wrote a letter to his family about the rigors of the search:

Three days before departure I noticed that I was developing a hernia. It soon got worse. . . . Wherever possible I pressed it in with my hand while walking, holding a weapon and other things with my other hand. Endless riding on pack animals, not on a saddle, but on a wooden frame for attaching loads to and without stirrups, so that one's legs hanging without support over the sharp edges went "to sleep" and the blood vessels in the upper thigh became squashed. It was a miracle that my prostate did not play up, which was my greatest concern. On the very first day I suffered a malaria attack as well. My assistants frequently had fever, diarrhoea, sunburn and injuries because of plants and allergies and so on.

But on December 31, 1978, Sick's team got their reward. They found wild Lear's Macaws, the first ever recorded by scientists. Observed flying high above the caatinga, they were on their daily commute to feed on palm nuts. The birds' exceptionally long wings and deep wingbeats helped distinguish them from any Hyacinth Macaws that might have wandered into the region. The blue macaws swooped and dived over the cliffs and canyons of the rugged Raso.

Sick wrote to his family: "I have succeeded in solving the greatest mystery in the ornithology of South America (not only of Brazil)— the discovery of the origin of the Lear's Macaw, a magnificent large blue macaw . . . which until now was only known from specimens in captivity." They were found in a remote dry canyon where they roosted and nested on inaccessible cliffs. It was the only species of macaw to occur there, and this remote rocky area appeared to house twenty-one of them. Sick shot one in order to prepare the first properly documented museum specimen of the species collected from the wild. It went to the museum in Rio de Janeiro.

Sick's letter reflected on the experience of finding the macaws:

On my birthday (I was sixty-nine on 10 January) I sat in one of the macaw canyons and observed the birds arriving to roost, at least fifteen through the new telescope, provided to me a few days before my departure by the Brazilian scientific service and imported after years of struggle from Zeiss in East Germany. The viewfinder encompassed a pair of the splendid birds. . . . They were surrounded by a dense cloud of insects and sometimes scratched themselves on the head. It was certainly the most memorable birthday of my life.

Professor Helmut Sick returned to Rio with a double hernia, but was soon fixed up and back to work.

Scientific papers about the amazing find were published, and interest in the macaw was intense.[21] Carlos Yamashita, one of Brazil's leading parrot experts, picked up the baton. In 1983 he visited the Lear's Macaws to determine more details about their habits so that they might be more effectively conserved. He found that the parrots nested in burrows dug into the soft sandstone cliffs; this was also where they spent the night. The macaws would leave the cliffs at dawn and come back after sunset. Yamashita followed the birds and found that they were flying to palm groves in the cattle pastures that lay some distance from their canyons. The most important palm that the macaws visited was the licuri (*Syagrus coronata*), a species named by Martius, Spix's traveling companion.

The palms grew up to two meters high and produced the hard nuts the birds adored. The nuts were small—about the size of a British pound coin, one euro, or a U.S. quarter, but very hard. Yamashita saw that they fed in groups of two or three. They would take nuts both from the ground and directly from the trees, but in either case there would always be a sentinel perched high up in a tree with a commanding view so that the alarm could be raised at the first sign of danger.

Yamashita confirmed Sick's belief that the macaws lived only in the Raso, a compact area of 15,000 square kilometers. He estimated the total population at only sixty birds. And this tiny nucleus was threatened by hunting for the pot and trapping of live birds for the international collectors' market. Longer term, the birds were also at risk from the loss of the palm trees. Although local ranchers had left palms so that cattle could feed on the fruits, whether there would be enough for the birds to eat, especially in severe drought years, was another question. The nuts were also collected for people to eat and were vulnerable to dry-season fires set by ranchers to improve their pastures.

Another hazard threatening the macaws' survival was the risk of a landslide at their roosting sites. The cliffs they had decided to live in were highly fractured, and the extreme daily temperature variation created periodic landslides and collapses. One occurring at night or in the breeding season would have disastrous consequences for such a tiny population.[22]

Why there were so few of the birds was not obvious when Sick found them—and still isn't. But like the Glaucous Macaw, the Lear's tiny population could be a relict—the last survivors from a time when the species was much more widespread. D'Orbigny's observations of the Glaucous in the nineteenth century suggested that, like the Lear's, it was also a cliff-nesting species. This, along with their outward similarities, in turn points to some quite recent (in evolutionary terms) separation of the two species, perhaps the result of a more widespread ancestor declining to the point where only two isolated populations remained, the Glaucous in a few river valleys in the south of the continent, the other, the Lear's, at its arid outpost in the northeast.

What drove the Lear's Macaw into its last refuge? There could be several possibilities—farming, trapping, climatic changes, or perhaps the breaking of an ecological relationship with some long-extinct creature. These birds once shared their palm savannas with sabre-toothed cats, giant armadillos, and great ground sloths. Yamashita thought it might be that the ground sloths that once walked the South American plains passed palm nuts in their dung, digested off the hard outer coating, and thus provided a relatively easy source of food for the macaws to exploit.

Whatever the reason for its long-term rarity, the most serious immediate danger to the Lear's Macaw was trapping for the live parrot market. Ever since its discovery by scientists in 1978—and certainly before then, too—the relict population of Lear's Macaws has been subject to capture for commerce. The main method used by the trappers is to wait until the birds have gone to roost in their traditional cliffs and then, after dark, to lower nets down in front of their holes. When the birds wake before dawn and try to leave for their morning food, they become entangled in the mesh. They are hoisted up, crated, and shipped out to the rich buyers who will pay a fortune for them.

Although other groups of Lear's Macaws have subsequently been discovered in other remote canyons of the Raso da Catarina, the upper population estimate is still tiny. The initial estimate of about sixty was revised upward to about 120 with the discovery of a new population. More groups were subsequently found, pushing the total number of wild birds to 246 by 2001. Given these changes to the total known population, any estimation of the proportion of birds trapped and traded is very problematic. But from this tiny group of very slow-breeding birds, and in spite of the best efforts of underresourced conservation workers, it is certain that dozens have been trapped and traded.

The dealer who was notorious for catching Spix's Macaw also specialized in the supply of Lear's Macaws. He boasted about capturing some forty or fifty of the birds. He said that for one of the first pairs of Lear's Macaws he supplied he was paid $13,000 and given a new car too.

In 2000 information collected by scientists observing the cliff-nesting macaws suggested that of the 43 suspected breeding pairs in the study area, only three produced young. Thus, at the start of the third millennium, with trapping still a constant problem, the fate of the Lear's Macaw hangs in the balance.

The Hyacinth Macaw

The Hyacinth Macaw is doing better—at least comparatively speaking. The range of this truly magnificent parrot is vast compared to the Lear's and Glaucous Macaws, embracing large swaths of the interior of Brazil. Three main population centers exist—one in the drier transitional rain forests of the southern Amazon basin, one in the dry Gerais region of central Brazil, and one in the vast Pantanal wetlands of southwest Brazil, from where its range spills over into neighboring parts of northeast Bolivia and marginally to northern Paraguay.

Nevertheless, like the Glaucous Macaw centuries before, these parrots are under pressure from the conversion of palm savannas to agricultural production. Huge areas of the interior of Brazil have been turned over to large-scale farming, and the macaw's range has shrunk. Proposals to drain large parts of the Pantanal wetlands, the one place where these birds still have an apparent stronghold, are a constant threat. Even where total conversion of the habitat has been avoided, the macaws still suffer from the loss of large trees. These huge parrots depend on the few species of leguminous trees that are large enough to provide them with nesting holes; otherwise they may not reproduce. In the Pantanal big trees are taken for building materials or cut down to deny shelter for vampire bats that suck the blood of the cattle there.

In the north of their range in the southern Amazon basin, the macaws are hunted by the Indians for feathers to make into headdresses and other adornments. Although this traditional practice was not a problem historically, it became so as the tribal people increasingly came into contact with tourists and traffickers willing to pay substantial sums for spectacular souvenirs containing the long feathers of ten individual Hyacinth Macaws. And in common with most large animals in rural Brazil, they were widely shot for the pot.

All of this had by the 1980s drastically reduced the population of wild Hyacinth Macaws. But despite the best efforts of wildlife campaigners and enforcement agencies, the traffickers had by the late 1980s ensured that there were quite a lot more Hyacinth Macaws in captivity than there were in the wild. Some were smuggled directly out of Brazil to international markets; others were taken from the interior via private airstrips to Bolivia and Paraguay. Once there, the macaws were "laundered" either as captive-bred or as captured in those countries where wildlife exports were still legal until the 1980s, or they were simply smuggled into markets with no attempt to falsify documents or cover up the birds' true origin.

These parrots' habitual use of particular trees for roosting or nesting, their daily routine of visiting particular favorite palms, their curiosity and relative fearlessness made them easy prey for the trappers. Even in the early 1980s, when trade was still "legal" from the point of view of international law, a single bird would fetch up to $2,000 in the United States.

But the scale of the trapping could not be sustained. One estimate suggested that some 10,000 were taken from the wild during the 1980s alone. This was from a species that did not breed every year and, even when it did, usually reared only one, less often two, young.

So intense was the trapping that in 1987 a special survey was commissioned of the Hyacinth Macaw in the wild.[23] The results suggested that between 2,500 and 5,000 Hyacinth Macaws remained in their native palm forests—as little as half, or perhaps only a quarter, of the birds taken for trade during the 1980s alone. This reckoning was enough to convince the world's governments later that year immediately to ban trade in Hyacinth Macaws. With that decision, cross-border commerce in all blue macaws became illegal under international law.

In the face of the trade ban, not only did massive demand remain—it grew. In 1998 British macaw enthusiast Tony Pittman set up a Web site dedicated to blue macaws and their conservation. The most frequent unsolicited e-mail inquiry received over the three years to 2001 from the thousands of people visiting the Web site from sixty-eight countries, was, according to Pittman, "Where can I buy such birds and how much do they cost?" The Hyacinth Macaw was already known in smuggling circles as a rare bird, and the fact that commerce was now banned had the effect of pushing up prices. This meant that catching the birds was more lucrative than ever before, and the trade intensified. The smuggling involved not only trappers and dealers in South America, but leading figures from the world of aviculture and parrot conservation in North America and Europe too.

One was Tony Silva, an American from Illinois with a worldwide reputation for breeding parrots. Silva had strong views on parrot conservation and had acquired a high profile in the debate on how to save the blue macaws from extinction. He had published several large books on parrots and their conservation, including *A Monograph of Endangered Parrots* and *A Monograph of the Macaws*. His expertise in aviculture was widely regarded, and his track record in parrot keeping included a spell from August 1989 to January 1992 when he was the curator of birds at the largest and most spectacular collection of parrot species anywhere in the world: Loro Parque in Tenerife.[24]

Following a four-year undercover investigation code-named Op-

eration Renegade by the U.S. Fish and Wildlife Service's Special
Operations Branch, Silva and some of his coconspirators were arrested in 1994 for breaking the requirements of the U.S. Endangered Species Act. Taped telephone conversations, surveillance
reports, and the penetration of smuggling operations by federal
agents revealed how, between 1985 and 1992, Silva and his mother
imported hundreds of endangered and protected birds and other
wildlife into the U.S.A.

Among the birds involved in the illegal trafficking were shipments of Hyacinth Macaws, including one consignment of fifty and
another of seventy-nine birds. With a retail value of up to $15,000
each, a shipment of fifty could fetch three-quarters of a million dollars. Other illegally shipped items seized by the authorities included an elephant tusk and a parrot-feather headdress made by a
tribe of Amazonian Indians.

When Silva's illegal shipments of live birds arrived in the U.S.A.,
they were laundered into the avicultural world with forged documents. In order to determine the sex of the endangered parrots he
imported, Silva paid a vet to undertake surgical examinations of the
birds in a motel room in a Chicago suburb. Anesthetized and
opened with a scalpel, the birds were processed rather like the victims of latter-day backstreet abortionists meeting demand for their
dangerous and sordid trade away from the gaze of the authorities.

Other rare parrots involved in Silva's smuggling operation included the endangered and very beautiful Queen of Bavaria
Conures (Guaruba guarouba),[25] endangered Blue-throated Conures
(Pyrrhura cruentata) and several rare Amazon parrots. So confident
was Silva that he could get away with his illegal trafficking that he
took out ads for some of the birds in American Cage Bird Magazine.

The U.S. authorities also suspected that Spix's Macaws were imported as part of Silva's smuggling operations.[26] Whether such par-

rots were shipped by him into the United States was never proved in court, but it is possible that they were, especially considering that Silva's operation was assisted by overseas suppliers who had also played leading roles in the saga of the Spix's Macaw. One was Silva's codefendant Ann Koopmann from Asunción in Paraguay. She was the daughter of a former Paraguayan military officer who was himself arrested in 1987 for trafficking two young Spix's Macaws (see chapter 7). Her role was to arrange shipments of birds caught illegally in Brazil to the U.S.A. via Mexico. She and Silva used various code words to foil eavesdropping enforcement agents; their word for Hyacinth Macaws was "blues"—a rather weak disguise that did not fool the federal agents for long; if anything, it helped them.

Another coconspirator named in court was the Filipino aviculturist Antonio de Dios. He had obtained Spix's Macaws and supplied various species of smuggled wildlife to Silva in the United States from his base in the Philippines. Among them were the Red-vented Cockatoos (*Cacatua haematuropygia*), one of the world's most threatened species.

Silva's expansive writings on rare parrots recorded, among other things, how the Hyacinth Macaw was "worth its weight in gold"; having imported more than one million dollars' worth of these birds into the U.S.A., he would surely know. In 1989 he also committed to print the story of a Paraguayan wildlife dealer who in 1972 received 300 young Hyacinth Macaws taken from wild nests; 99 percent of them died. Silva also divulged details about a Brazilian trapper who, with the aid of a single assistant, took some 200 to 300 Hyacinth Macaws from an area that they worked for two to three years. With insights like these Silva was uniquely placed to reach the conclusion that "Unless all of the pressures [including illegal trade] are brought under control, this species may be unable to survive in the world to greet the twenty-first century."

Silva knew exactly the consequences of what he was doing, and the authorities were well aware of that fact. U.S. Attorney Burns said, "It is unconscionable that a person of Mr Silva's stature in the avicultural community would contribute, ultimately, to the illicit process that threatens these exquisite creatures with extinction." In 1996 he was sent to prison for seven years. It was the longest sentence ever handed down for bird smuggling. His mother got two years. Silva was also convicted of tax evasion.

In the face of growing awareness about the plight of the blue macaws, neither increased rarity nor crackdowns by the wildlife trade enforcement authorities diminished demand for the birds in captivity. There was a ready market and many collectors would pay handsomely to own all four of the blue macaws if they possibly could. But no matter how determined the efforts of Silva and the other traffickers, or how good their contacts among the trappers and dealers, the zoological spectacle unwittingly staged in Berlin in 1900 could not be repeated. Strive as they might in their search for a full set of all four blue macaws, the parrot El Dorado eluded the collectors. One of the four, the Glaucous Macaw, could not be found and was probably extinct. The trade had taken a tragic toll on the Hyacinth Macaw and threatened the Lear's with imminent extinction.

In early 1990 it was not known if the fourth and most coveted of all the blue macaws—the Spixes—still hung on in some remote palm groves like the Lear's or had, like the Glaucous, already been exterminated. Many believed that the Spix's Macaw was now lost. Others were not so sure.

CHAPTER 5

What Are You Looking For at the End of the World?

B y early 1990 there was serious doubt that the Spix's Macaw existed in the wild any longer. One person most interested in learning its fate was Nigel Collar. One chilly morning in February, he called me into his office. I had joined the staff at the International Council for Bird Preservation to assist in the gathering campaign to save the world's most threatened birds. As the worsening plight of the parrots had become clearer, ICBP had decided to hire someone to focus solely on that most endangered group—I was that person. The most threatened species of parrot at the top of my list was unquestionably the Spix.

Collar's little office was upstairs in the middle of a Victorian house called The Mount in the Cambridge suburb of Girton. Every available surface in the little room was covered with piles of papers, reports, scientific journals, and notes. It looked like chaos but was the background research for another work that would chart the worsening fortunes of endangered birds—an eleven-hundred-page volume entitled *Threatened Birds of the Americas*. Collar said that I should know about a very important development with the Spix.

A couple of green folders had been removed from one of his bursting filing cabinets and placed beside a pile of reports and letters on the table. The contents of the files detailed the inexorable decline of Spix's Macaw. Collar knew the history of this enigmatic species very well, including how rumors and misinformation had made it extremely difficult to determine what was actually going on. The bird had been seen only a handful of times since it was first found by Spix in 1819, and was mainly known from a few moth-eaten museum specimens and a few captive birds. But a newly arrived fax had given Collar fresh cause to hesitate before declaring the Spix extinct. He suggested I read it too.

The fax was from a distinguished Brazilian wildlife photographer, Luiz Claudio Marigo. Marigo said the rare blue parrots had been seen twice the year before in the Chapada das Mangabeiras, a range of hills in the cerrado woodlands of the Gerais, a rugged area of the interior where the states of Piauí, Goiás, Maranhão, and Bahía meet. To a naturalist, the discovery of wild Spix's Macaws would be more valuable than a gold strike, marking the chance to conserve a critically endangered species. Not only that, the new information offered me the tantalizing opportunity to see one of the world's rarest creatures. Persistent, if unsubstantiated, rumors of birds still being offered for sale had continued to circulate. If there really were some at liberty, then it was vital to find them before the trappers finished them off. If the Spix could be found, perhaps it could be saved.

A budget to cover expedition expenses was cobbled together and a team comprising four Brazilians and myself was formed. Marigo, who would be joined by Francisco Pontual, a passionate young conservationist also from Rio, would lead the effort. Carlos Yamashita would come too; the São Paulo-based parrot specialist who had worked on Lear's Macaw would bring invaluable expertise. The team would also have the ornithologist Roberto Otoch from the northeastern city of Fortaleza. He knew the dry interior well and said that he had seen the macaws himself in the area where we planned to look.

I busied myself in the ICBP offices unearthing all the material I could find to shed light on the possible state of the Spix's Macaw and where we might locate it. There really wasn't a lot of information about the species in the wild. The few reports following Spix's discovery of it were separated by huge intervals. More than eighty years separated the first specimen from the next sighting by a scientist, and from then on it was hardly reported at all in the wild.

One of the few more recent sightings—itself sixteen years old—had been made by the veteran ornithologist Helmut Sick.[27] He and his field assistant, Dante Teixera, fleetingly saw some Spix's Macaws in 1974 near Formosa do Rio Prêto, a little town in the northwest of the state of Bahía. Sick had recorded two parties of birds there—one of three macaws, the other of four—flying over buriti palms (*Mauritia flexuosa*). Sick and some other ornithologists believed that Spix's Macaws, like other kinds of blue macaws, fed on palm nuts, and speculated that they specifically preferred the fruits of buriti palms.

Sick also gleaned details from bird trappers that extended the possible range of the Spix's Macaw to embrace the northeastern part of the state of Goiás and the southern part of the state of Maranhão. This information, supported by a couple of other sightings from reliable ornithologists by then coming in from other parts of Piauí, extended the possible range of the Spix's Macaw to a vast area of the dry interior of northeast Brazil.

Collar had not been the only one to wonder where to start. The same question had occupied Paul Roth, a Swiss ornithologist working in the biology department of the University of Maranhão at São Luís, Brazil. In June 1985, with a $2,000 grant from ICBP, Roth had set off for the remote northeast on the first of five expeditions in search of Spix's blue caatinga parrots. Roth had tried to improve his chances of finding the birds by focusing on the three general areas where the earlier reports of Spix's Macaws suggested they formed little clusters: One was in southern Maranhão and neighboring parts of Piauí, the second along the banks of the middle reaches of the river São Francisco in northern Bahía, and the third in the Gerais region. The place we planned to look, the Chapada das Mangabeiras, was in this last area.

Roth crisscrossed these huge tracts of rugged country looking for signs of the mysterious blue birds. During his first expedition he met a bird trapper from Piauí who knew a lot about parrots. He told Roth to go to Curaçá, a little town about ninety kilometers northeast of Juàzeiro, near the place where Spix found the first known specimen. In April of the following year, 1986, Roth was able to confirm that there were indeed Spix's Macaws about thirty kilometers south of Curaçá. But there were only three, a pair and a single bird, the trio with which our account began in chapter 1; two others had recently been trapped. It was later to emerge that two birds were exported from Brazil that year via a trader in Paraguay and were sent to Europe accompanied by a forged export permit. It is possible that these two were those in question (see chapter 7).

Roth found the elusive birds in an area of woodland bordering the Melância Creek, one of the many watercourses that drained the otherwise dry country during the wet season. He made close observations of the birds and found they preferred the bigger caraiba trees that grew by the creek for nesting and as lookout posts. It was

Roth who learned what a problem the aggressive African bees were for the Spix's Macaws, and he also confirmed that these parrots, like any other bird or animal large enough to be worth a round of ammunition, were seen as fair game for the pot.

But despite these disturbing new details, it was clear that the real and present danger was trappers. To help protect the few birds he had tracked down in that vast dry area, Roth arranged for contacts of his in Munich to pay a few of the locals to guard them. Having done what he could to safeguard the trio in the Melância Creek, he set off again in search of the other flocks he was convinced were out there somewhere. Roth's confidence stemmed from his conviction that the trappers must have led him to the three birds at Curaçá while they got on with capturing some other Spix's Macaws that he didn't know about. He set himself the task of finding these other populations before the traffickers finished them off.

The news of Roth's guards at Curaçá spread far and wide. The trappers became wary of Roth and briefed one another on how to deal with his endless questions about where to find more of the blue parrots. Convinced that he was being fed misinformation by people who would rather he didn't find the location of any more Spix's Macaws, he nonetheless persisted with his one-man mission to scour the interior of Brazil.

He conducted more searches in the remote wilds of Piauí, he looked in Maranhão along the Parnaíbinha River, and went to the Gerais region where Sick had seen the birds. He traveled thousands of kilometers across the interior searching and asking wherever he went for evidence of other families of the elusive blue parrots. In the Gerais his battered car had been no match for the vast swamps and dense forests dissected by the rugged high plateaux. An additional hazard was the presence of armed men, called *pistoleiros*, hired by local ranchers to help "settle" land ownership disputes. With a real danger of violence and a vehicle not up to the job, Roth's search had been superficial. He had not found the birds, but he believed they might well be there. And so the new information from Marigo was especially intriguing.

While Roth had been conducting these far-flung searches, the situation at Curaçá had gone from bad to worse. He returned to the Melância Creek in May 1987 to pay the guards and check on the last three birds. By the time he arrived there were only two left: A month earlier another one had been caught. For all his searching, Roth could say with certainty that in the wild he knew of just a single pair of Spix's Macaws. Disaster followed. On Christmas Eve 1987 Roth was called by his local contacts to be told that a trapper had returned and taken the last female. The bird trader and his entourage of bullies had not been gentle in their theft. Knowing that a few of the locals were working for Roth to protect the parrots they had arrived with armed accomplices.

The robbers had chosen their moment well. Because of the Christmas holidays Roth could not make contact with the Brazilian wildlife enforcement authorities and it was not until early in 1988 that the alarm was finally raised in official circles. By then the bird had been quietly spirited into the underworld and was on its way to a wealthy collector. In January 1988 Roth received news that even the last one had gone too, taken by the trappers. It seemed that it was the end of the story for the birds at the Melância Creek. The Curaçá population had been wiped out forever.

Roth remained convinced that the Spix's Macaw still lived somewhere in the vast wilds of the interior. He believed that there must be another population being plundered by the trappers, but where it was he didn't know. The task of the 1990 expedition was to find it. With a potential search area of 300,000 square kilometers, a territory larger than Great Britain, to find a parrot was considerably

more challenging than searching for a needle in a haystack. At least
we had a strong lead: Marigo's fax about the sightings in the Gerais
and the remote hills of the Chapada das Mangabeiras.

At dawn on June 9, 1990, I arrived at the Rio de Janeiro international airport. Unlike Spix and Martius, I'd spent just eleven
hours crossing the Atlantic from Europe. It was impossible not to
think of the sixteenth-century navigators who had first come here
from Portugal aboard frail wooden ships, propeled onward under
billowing sails at the mercy of the winds, with only the stars for
guidance, not knowing where they would land or when they would
get there. Impossible too was not to contemplate how different was
modern travel and how profound were its consequences in acceler-
ating the rapid shrinkage of our planet.

On leaving the airport terminal, the modern traveler is struck by
the smell of cane alcohol. In some ways the smell sums up Brazil's
environmental situation. Because of the worsening economic crisis
caused in part by vast external debts owed to Western banks and official agencies such as the International Monetary Fund, there has
been a government program of import substitution. The idea was to
help balance the country's accounts by conserving foreign exchange
through avoiding imports, including oil. As part of this policy, many
of the vehicles in Rio have been converted to run on alcohol dis-
tilled from sugar cane grown in Brazil rather than gasoline or diesel
imported from abroad. Of course, sugar cane needs land, so forests
have been cleared to make space to grow it. Brazil's ecological dilem-
mas can be smelled in the penetrating aroma from the car exhausts.

That evening—in the glamorous city of Copacabana Beach, the
"Girl from Ipanema," and Sugarloaf Mountain—brought a vivid
demonstration of the social inequalities that had driven a wedge
through the heart of Brazilian society. In the middle-class suburb of

Gavea, right next to the comfortable house of a couple of English friends in this pleasant neighborhood, was one of Rio de Janeiro's largest favelas, an informal settlement where the homeless, landless, poverty-stricken, and excluded were washed up at the tidemark of polite society.

Thousands of human souls were squeezed into a shantytown of makeshift dwellings that clung to the steep hillside. Its inhabitants, many coming from the rural areas of the northeast, scratched a living from scavenging, intermittent work, or crime. The brutal existence was ruled by drugs and violence. Even the police rarely ventured in. It was a product of a deeply divided society, failed economic policy, and corruption. So desperate was Brazil to deny this aspect of its nationhood that this great scar was not even marked on city maps; neither were several other large shantytowns.

Although many people in the developed nations regard Brazil as a Third World country, it has the planet's eighth largest economy. I was soon to learn that widespread poverty is more a reflection of the great inequality caused by corruption, debt, and institutional failures than the absence of national wealth. In the face of such enormous social problems it was painfully obvious that the conservation of rare species was not a top priority.

In Gavea several of Brazil's leading ornithologists had gathered that evening to discuss the Spix's Macaw and the chances of finding some in the wild. It was there that I first met the dark-bearded Marigo, whose fax had first encouraged the expedition, the dashing young Francisco Pontual, and the 81-year-old Helmut Sick. We exchanged pleasantries and sipped cold beers in the humid warmth of early evening. Sick explained why he believed the Spix's Macaw was a bird of buriti palm groves and set out his views on where such birds might still be found. He made comparisons with the other blue macaws and advised that the search team should target their efforts around buriti palm groves in remote areas of the Gerais. Marigo in turn explained the source of his new lead.

I finished the evening impatient to leave for the northeast. But a couple of days' wait in Rio, while vehicles were prepared and the other expedition members arrived, was unavoidable. To make use of the time, a few of us decided to visit the notorious wildlife market at Duque de Caxias in the hope that valuable information could be gathered from the animal dealers there. Right under the noses of the Rio police, macaws, anteaters, crocodiles, and monkeys, including the very rarest species, were available for sale on the street. It was all illegal, but no one attempted to interrupt the traders.[28] Dozens of endangered animals and birds were for sale. Some of the more common species of parrot had had their tails trimmed and their feathers colored with hair dye to resemble more valuable species. The crude imitations would not fool the more discerning collectors, but they were a demonstration of the value of such exotic species. And it showed how few rare parrots there were—no blue ones were there, fakes or otherwise.

In Rio, you could buy almost anything—girls, boys, drugs, guns, you name it—if you had the money. All you had to do was go to the right part of town and ask the right people. As far as rare wildlife was concerned, most of Brazil's rarest creatures could be ordered from here. But not, it seemed, Spix's Macaws. A few discreet enquiries revealed no one able to supply such a bird. But Rio was a long way from the northeast and not known as a trafficking route for such parrots. That no one claimed to be able to supply them did not mean no one was trapping them.

With the arrival of Yamashita, a compact Japanese/Brazilian parrot expert, and the large-framed Otoch in Rio the next day, it was time to set off on the three-day drive to the northeast. Two four-wheel-drive vehicles were loaded up. One was a battered old Toyota that belonged to Helmut Sick. This veteran vehicle was the one he'd abandoned in the caatinga during his successful search for the Lear's Macaw back in the 1970s. The paint was gone here and there, but what remained was, appropriately, blue. The other was an ageing white Land Rover belonging to Pontual. Getting hold of spares from England was a hellish problem, but Pontual thought the aggravation was worth it.

We chugged off north toward the moist coastal mountains that flanked Rio de Janeiro. Once clothed with dense rain forests, the coastal strip was now largely bare. Cultivated, ranched, logged, and mined, the thick lush wall of green that greeted the first Portuguese sailors in the 1500s had been all but obliterated. It used to stretch in an unbroken 3,000-kilometer-long belt from the state of Rio Grande do Norte in the north along the coastal lowlands and mountains to northern Argentina in the south. About 2 percent of the original forest is left. These woodlands are priceless. Separated from the expanse of rain forests in the Amazon basin by the dry interior, thousands of unique species have evolved there in isolation, several now endangered parrots among them. The clearance of the forests pushed many species to the brink of extinction and an unknown number over it. Even the protected areas were not safe from fire, sometimes set deliberately to clear yet more land.

Crossing the coastal mountains and reaching the plateau of the interior, the forest fragments that were still left became drier. In the state of Minas Gerais (Portuguese for "General Mines") smelting operations had for centuries depended on a ready supply of charcoal. The forests were the source. Truck after truck spewed out stinking clouds of diesel fumes en route to the region's many ironworks. Where the natural forest once stood was either completely denuded or, at best, replaced with vast sterile plantations of eucalyptus or acacia to feed the foundries.

North toward the interior, the drier cerrado woodlands replaced the wetter forests of the coast. The cerrado is the second largest vegetation type in Brazil after the rain forests of the Amazon. Mostly evergreen, there were patches of more seasonal woodlands where limestone came to the surface and made conditions more arid. But along the route of the road, most of the tree cover had gone. From horizon to horizon, the forest had been annihilated. The wholesale destruction of the cerrado had been brought about in part by logging of hardwood trees. Some of these were even more prized than the valuable woods taken from the Amazon; the rest had been turned into charcoal. The cleared areas were now either abandoned, converted to sanitized wood farms, or turned over to cattle grazing. Vast open-cast mines had taken their toll too—not only for iron ore, but gold and other minerals. It was an ecological disaster zone.

After two days of constant driving, the vehicles reached the capital, Brasília. North from there the landscape was more broken and rugged. Dramatic red sandstone escarpments carved a jagged edge across the skyline. Although less densely settled, the environmental impacts seen to the south were evident here too. In the flatter areas the rusty-colored soils that had once supported native forests had been turned over to huge soybean and sugar cane plantations.

The soy, like the sugar, was part of another grand scheme to balance Brazil's economy. The land was cheap, and for this reason so was the soy. The plan was to grow vast quantities to sell on the international market to earn foreign exchange. There was huge demand in Europe where the soy was fed to cattle. In Europe taxpayers funded vast farm subsidies that made the soy an even cheaper source of animal feed. This in turn encouraged farmers to raise more cattle, thereby contributing to Europe's overproduction of food. The soy thus helped to create Europe's so called "milk lakes" and "beef mountains." Some of this surplus was then dumped on world markets, undercutting developing-country farmers, putting many of them out of work, including Brazilian ones.

Many of the small farmers who lived there before the arrival of large-scale mechanized production had left. Some moved to virgin forest areas where more forest was cleared for farming. Several of these mass migrations had been assisted with funds from international agencies such as the World Bank. The people who stayed behind remained very poor and often had no land. The huge farms belonged to absentee landlords who harvested the profits from the massive plantations. Ten years earlier, the great blocks of forest there had been largely untouched.

These insane and self-defeating attempts to balance the national accounts flew directly in the face of numerous speeches and promises about the government's commitment to conserving the environment. The vast soy and sugar cane farms were just the most obvious examples of how Brazil's precarious economic situation fed worsening environmental devastation. It was the end point in a process of deforestation, the early stages of which had been documented by Spix and Martius when they passed through the region more than 170 years earlier.

On the fourth day we drove across the border from Goiás into northwest Bahía; the dirt roads made the going slower. The little town of Barreiras was at the agricultural frontier. Half-built houses and newly cleared woodland with burned areas and recent plantations of bananas and maize showed that people were moving into some of the moist valley bottoms. In places heavy machinery had been used to clear large areas for cattle pasture. This was the front line of deforestation, and it was moving north frighteningly fast. Every day another swath of forest was consumed in the insatiable lust for agricultural land, one of the few commodities in Brazil that might keep long-term value in the face of hyperinflation.

Despite the recent agricultural incursions, buriti palm groves still grew in profusion in some of the flat areas flanking the rivers. This was the kind of environment where Spix's Macaws might still hang on. The habitat was similar to that where Helmut Sick had recorded his sightings of the birds. But our frequent stops to scan the woods and conversations with locals revealed no trace of them.

North of Barreiras on a dirt road the radiator of the Toyota failed. There was no choice but to stop in Formosa do Rio Prêto while it was repaired. The little two-street town straddled the clear swift river Prêto. We moved into the local guesthouse, a little white one-story building. Part of the back wall was missing and chickens wandered in and out of the bedrooms as they pleased. But it was comfortable and served good food—always eggs and fruit for breakfast and a combination of beans, rice, chicken, and beef for dinner.

While marooned there, Yamashita and I studied maps in an attempt to identify likely search areas. Marigo busied himself seeking out local knowledge. He wanted to speak to the village pharmacist and an associate of his who had been mentioned to us by Sick, who had stayed at his house in 1974, at the meeting in Rio. They were birdwatchers and might have some recent news. One of them said he knew that there were Spix's Macaws near the place we planned to search. When asked by Marigo why he believed the parrots could be found there, the pharmacist said Sick had told him so. It was the only trace. One solitary repetition of what Sick had said more than fifteen years before confirmed there was no new information to be had. With the Toyota repaired, it was time to move on.

On the track to the north lay the border with the poverty-stricken state of Piauí, and to the west, the border with northern Goiás, the Gerais, and the Chapada das Mangabeiras, the area where our search team expected to locate Spix's Macaws. Heading north, we found that more large farms, some irrigated from the waters of the São Francisco, had recently replaced the natural forest. Huge expanses of sugar cane, maize, and soy flanked the road to the horizon.

In this desolate land a lone police officer had established a traffic checkpoint. With a hand hovering over his pistol he waved the vehicles to a halt. He wanted to know why four-wheel-drives with Rio number plates were in this remote place, evidently suspecting that drugs trafficking might be the reason. Once Marigo explained, the policeman soon relaxed, and it turned out that he owned a farm just nine kilometers from the Santa Isabela ranch where the Spix's Macaws had been reported. He certainly had a good knowledge of the local parrots that lived there and could describe them with some accuracy, including Hyacinth Macaws. But he had no experience of Spix's.

Pressing on, we drove into the rugged Gerais and finally approached our destination. The vegetation was less disturbed and wilder. In contrast to the new farmlands we'd seen to the south, colonization was still in its early stages. Chunks of intact forest clothed the sides of the ridges. But people were moving in, mainly poor landless people, including drought refugees from the caatinga in the east who had been driven here by the punishing climate to scratch a subsistence living from the land.

In a small settlement composed of half a dozen shacks strung out along the dirt track, people scattered in all directions at the arrival of our unfamiliar vehicles. A small blond-haired child with a deep dark tan, perhaps the descendant of some long-since-dead Dutch or German colonists, was the only one to remain at the trackside. Wearing only a pair of dirty ripped shorts, he chewed on a stem of sugar cane. The poor rural people believed that rubbing sugar cane on young teeth helped to clean them. The child's teeth were already black.

Marigo got out of the Land Rover and looked around for someone to talk to. In his khaki trousers and gray field jacket, he appeared to the locals rather like the *pistoleiros* who came and threatened violence as a prelude to taking control of the land. The frontier of large-scale mechanized farming was nearby and any flat land that could handle big machinery was in demand. The clearance of peasant farmers from their small holdings by gunmen working for city-based land speculators was a routinely brutal activity.

The poor farmers who had arrived there from some other even worse predicament had no official title to their farms. They couldn't even read. The police weren't interested in their problems, so they had to fend for themselves. The best they could do was to cower in their rough little huts and hope that they wouldn't be beaten up or have their homes burned down in another cruel attempt to move them on.

Despite their poverty and endless vulnerability, caatinga people are generally friendly and welcoming. They often greet strangers with a question. "What are you looking for at the end of the world?" Marigo and Pontual told them. The inhabitants of the nameless little hamlet found it difficult to believe that five men had driven from Rio de Janeiro to look for a parrot; one had even come from England! But despite their nervous incredulity, they tried to be helpful.

A man invited us indoors. He asked if we would like to share his water, dispensed from a tall and unglazed earthenware vessel. He carefully ladled the precious fluid into a chipped china cup. We took it in turns to drink.

The locals relaxed as they realized we were not joking and really were looking for a parrot. There was some discussion but no recognition of the blue bird in the photographs. A little confused, the people in the small settlement came outside and bade farewell to their odd brief visitors. Amid a cloud of dust, the two vehicles swayed off deeper into the bush.

Toward the Santa Isabela ranch the dirt road gave way to sandy tracks that in turn were replaced by barely discernible mule trails. The odd wooden-framed hut plastered with mud and covered with palm fronds was the height of civilization in this forgotten place. It was getting dark, so we pitched camp. Marigo walked a few hundred meters to a nearby dwelling to let the locals know what was going on lest any more fear and confusion be caused by our presence. Reassured, the couple who lived there said that for a tiny price they would provide hot coffee in the morning. With hammocks secured we went to the river to swim, to be refreshed by the cool clear water and to contemplate the staggering beauty of the sharp starlit sky.

Before dawn, the local couple appeared in the middle of the mule track. They squatted on the ground and made a fire. A blackened coffee pot was produced and a brew made. The dark liquid was almost unrecognizable; like most other items of value, Brazil's best coffee beans were exported. The dark potion was gratefully consumed all the same; then we asked for some more.

Yamashita took out a packet of Lucky Strikes and tapped one of the cigarettes on the outside of the red-and-white box. He looked thoughtfully around at the trees now visible in the early morning light and shook his head. "There are no Spix's Macaws here," he said in a barely audible voice. The rest of us pretended not to hear his unwelcome analysis. Although we all knew birds well enough, Yamashita was the one who really knew about Brazilian macaws. "These woodlands are all wrong," he explained. "This is not the caatinga forest they prefer. There are macaws here, but not Spixes," he added. On cue, macaws appeared high overhead—a couple each of Green-winged (Ara chloroptera) and Blue-and-gold Macaws (Ara ararauna). They croaked gruffly as they made their way off to breakfast in some fruit trees. "No, not here," repeated Yamashita, drawing on the cigarette and shaking his head.

Marigo and Otoch would not be swayed, however: They believed that the expedition's information was reliable and insisted that the Santa Isabela area be properly researched. Yamashita gave a shrug of indifference and smiled. I was concerned. Had I really traveled to the other side of the world and spent thousands of dollars in a vain search for a bird that no longer existed?

Moving deeper into the wild palm swamps, rugged hillsides, and dense cerrado woodland, we found the going got very slow. The Toyota became stuck in a sandy depression. As we struggled to free it, two mules led by a young boy came past. Laden with crates filled with bottles of Coca-Cola, the little caravan passed by on its leisurely way toward some outlet for the fizzy drinks even more distant from the tarmac road. Although there was no running water, sanitation, or electricity, Coca-Cola's reach extended to even the remotest settlements. Once Coca-Cola had arrived, how far behind would be the ecological obliteration and social dislocation that came in the guise of "development"?

A couple of hours of sweating and cursing followed as we struggled with the Toyota before we resumed our trek. A little further and contact was made with the local cowboys who worked on the Santa Isabela ranch. They were lean men with dark skins who, half starved and overworked, looked older than their true years. They listened politely to our request for details on any blue parrots nearby and were well aware of the value of big macaws. But they had no knowledge of the Spix's, just the blue-and-yellow ones that flew high overhead most days. They spoke with some amusement about those birds. They had evidently tried to catch them, but failed; a grudging respect for the creatures' guile was in their faces.

From a new camp we prepared to conduct several days of early morning and evening searches of the area around the Santa Isabela ranch. Rugged escarpments that gave way to elevated tablelands flanked the broad valleys where the cattle were grazed. The landscape resembled the backdrop to a Western film; only the flat-topped hills were covered with cerrado woodland. In the wetter areas of the valley bottoms grew lush groves of buriti palms.

The palm fronds made dense tufts at the top of their tall bare stems, providing sparse but welcome shade in the otherwise open grassy areas. Some parts of the ranch had been lightly burned to improve the pasture, but otherwise the place remained beautifully wild. Despite the remote location, the search revealed only a few of the more common parrots, including darting flocks of little green Red-bellied Macaws (*Orthopsittaca manilata*), a kind of *maracana*. Yamashita's mutterings became more convincing: "The information we have is for the little green macaws. In some lights they look bluish. It's a mistake—there are no Spixes here."

Lacking any positive leads, we decided to invest in the services of a local guide to better chart the few routes that penetrated deeper into the rugged landscape. On our fourth day in the Gerais, while struggling at walking pace along a sandy track, our vehicles came upon a man on a bicycle with three little cages strapped to his rickety machine. The rider was a bird trapper heading south. He was friendly and seemed happy to take a break from his journey so as to have a chat with us.

He explained that his general routine was to visit a network of small farmers who would supply him with young parrots taken from nests on their land. In this way the most valuable species were sucked from even the remotest corners of the interior. Most would be sold to dealers, although he would obtain the rarer birds to order for individual collectors. His usual itinerary was to travel south with several cages loaded on his bicycle before he passed the birds on to dealers in the towns. The man was very open about his illegal work. He seemed pleased that anyone was interested and cheerily discussed his business. He quite obviously regarded the risk of arrest and prosecution as negligible.

Strapped to the bicycle in the cages were three Blue-fronted (*Amazona aestiva*) and a couple of Yellow-faced Amazon parrots (*Amazona xanthops*). These, he said, would be exported from the country; a handful of songbirds he would sell locally. But it was what he knew rather than what he transported that was of most value to us. When shown a photograph, he instantly identified the bird pictured in it. "Spic Macaw," he called it. He assured us it could be found only far to the east, by the river São Francisco near to Juàzeiro, more than 600 kilometers away. This, he insisted, was the only place it lived. Yamashita smiled and nodded.

There seemed to be little point in continuing the search around the Chapada das Mangabeiras. No one in the area knew of Spix's Macaws there, and the only person who seemed to know what he was talking about had said we should go to Juàzeiro, the same place where Spix himself had found the birds more than 170 years before. The search in the Gerais was abandoned in favor of heading toward Juàzeiro.

In the drier lands to the east, the clearance of the forest to make way for cattle had caused catastrophic soil erosion. The grazing animals had eaten most of the vegetation, leaving the bare earth vulnerable to the effects of the rare but heavy rains. Deep gullies scarred the land. Little grew. There were few trees, fewer birds, and no parrots. It was a ruined and ecologically bankrupt landscape supporting only a few skinny cattle.

A brief diversion was made to search around Parnaguá, where Reiser's Austrian expedition had reported the birds in 1903. There was still some natural woodland left and contact was made with some experienced hunters who knew the place well. They were certainly aware of the local parrots, but no one could recall little blue macaws with the long tails.

We pressed on toward Juàzeiro rather subdued. Our leads had failed to turn up any Spix's Macaws and we were all very well aware that the only known birds near Juàzeiro, the ones found by Paul Roth at Curaçá in the mid-1980s, had all been trapped. Since we had few leads in these easterly lands, we decided to visit the owner of the farm where the three Spix's Macaws had lived. He had a town house in Petrolina, a city on the opposite shore of the river to Juàzeiro, and was happy to meet us.

It quickly became clear that he was very familiar with Spix's Macaws. He insisted the birds lived only in tall trees by creeks, sometimes coming down to drink but otherwise staying in the high branches. The gallery woodland habitat at his farm, he maintained, was very rare. Tall trees grew in very few places in these dry lands. His belief was that the remaining ribbons of caraiba woodlands were a remnant of the primeval caatinga that once fringed the valley of the São Francisco River. He finished off by casually remarking that Spix's Macaws still lived there. This was stunningly unexpected news.

The little town of Curaçá lay about 90 kilometers farther down the river, northeast of Juàzeiro. The countryside between Juàzeiro and Curaçá was very different from the places we had searched in the west. Instead of dense woodlands there was dry thorny scrub, cacti, and open, bare dusty areas. In this degraded and drought-ravaged land the places with better soils near the river valley had been converted from overgrazed caatinga to vast irrigated farms growing maize, soy, and sugar cane.

Our search party scanned left and right for signs of the tall trees and the ribbons of gallery woodland that might still support some Spix's Macaws. There was only one place where the tall caraiba trees came near to the road that ran parallel to the river on its south shore. It was a place called Riacho Barra Grande. *Riacho* was the local word for "creek" and the woods along its fringes formed a precious green oasis in the midst of a vast expanse of low thorny scrub and colossal desolate irrigated fields. Just beyond lay Curaçá.

Curaçá was a backwater compared to the larger upstream cities. A settlement of around 10,000 souls, the town was a transit point for the long-distance buses and trucks that bounced over the unmade roads of the interior, and a supply and market center for the scattered rural settlements that lay around in the caatinga. The broad channel of the São Francisco lay on the north side of the town, which supported a few shops and bars and a couple of hotels.

Lunchtime saw Marigo propped up at the bar in a small restaurant looking at his bird book. Otoch, Pontual, and I were seated at a table with a cold beer each; Yamashita smoked a cigarette and sipped his iced Coke. We were quiet and thoughtful. A man approached. He was curious to know what strangers were doing in town—was it something to do with birds?

Marigo by now had a well-practiced explanation. He mechanically showed the man pictures of the macaw. Surprisingly, the newcomer nodded and said that he would be back in a few minutes. He soon returned with a Polaroid photo. It was unmistakably a picture of a Spix's Macaw. The bird was in a wire-fronted crate. The man explained that he had taken the photo a few years ago near a farm about 30 kilometers from town. He had heard that the bird had been sold to a collector in Recife. We learned that the picture was taken at the Concordia farm, the same one where Roth had found the birds, the same farm we planned to visit. Because of the timing of the capture and where the bird had been sent to, Yamashita was convinced that the photo was of the last female captured in 1987.

It transpired that the man with the photo was a land-use planner who owned a farm to the south next to a little range of lime-stone hills called the Serra do Borracha. He had a good knowledge of the local area and was aware that the creeks with the tall trees were unique. He spoke of how he used to see the macaws in the trees at Riacho Barra Grande. Birds used to visit there from the Melância Creek, he recalled. These two creeks were the best places he knew to find the tall caraiba trees that were so liked by the macaws. The planner explained in some detail that very little of the creekside woodlands remained, estimating that a total of about 2,500 hectares in the Barra Grande Creek and its tributaries and a further 1,000 hectares in the Vargem Creek system downriver from Curaçá were all that remained.

The owner of the Concordia farm, the place where yet another witness now claimed the birds could still be found, had graciously offered us one of his vacant buildings to stay in. The alternative—the tents—was not an attractive option in the heat of the dry season. The building on offer was a partially complete farmhouse—small, but compared to most people's dwellings nearby quite comfortable. It lacked water or power but was cool in the day and there were fixtures for our hammocks. A few meters away was the dwelling of a cowboy and his family.

The leather-clad cowboy was called Binum. He was slight but wiry and strong. He was a native of the caatinga, and like the animals and birds, well adapted for the rigors of life there. He worked for the farm owner and with the aid of dogs and horses looked after his few dozen cattle. His family also kept a few sheep and goats of their own, and grew a few crops nearby. The cowboy's wife agreed to cook for the search party while we stayed at the farm.

The cowboy's family home comprised a small kitchen and a bedroom that for now doubled as a storeroom for a pile of little wizened heads of harvested maize. In the bedroom four children slept on mats and in hammocks. The cowboy and his wife had a corner of the little kitchen. She was pregnant once more, and cooking for the strangers would provide a welcome financial boost. However, although she could evidently produce miracles from primitive facilities, cooking for another five adults would not be easy. The only source of water was a rudimentary well, and extra firewood would be needed for the stove. The only sign of the twentieth century was an old battery-powered transistor radio.

The house was a day's ride on horseback from Curaçá, so their isolation was nearly complete. This family, like most rural people in the caatinga, lived on its wits. There was no social safety net, no one to fall back on in hard times—just the brutal heat of the caatinga and its ever-present threat of prolonged drought followed by even worse destitution.

Otoch said he would take the Toyota to town the next day so the woman could buy the supplies of flour, coffee, and other basics that would be needed during our stay. The cowboy's wife pointed toward a little brown and white goat that grazed nearby. Since she had nothing else ready, it would be slaughtered for dinner. Marigo agreed to a daily rate for cooking services and passed some folded banknotes to the woman so she could buy the necessary supplies in Curaçá.

The woman was sturdy and healthy-looking. As she stood outside her little house and conversed in Portuguese with Marigo, I mulled over the survival prospects in this place for the weak and sick. As I sensed the conversation was coming to an end, Marigo suddenly looked shocked—his eyes wide and mouth open. The wife had casually mentioned that she had seen one of the blue macaws that day. She spoke as though the macaw was a daily part of her life and taken completely for granted. Despite the complete poverty of her surroundings, it seemed she could claim one treasure that no rich person could match: She had shared her day with a wild Spix's Macaw.

The two farm buildings were right next to the Melância Creek. It was like no other place that we had visited during the previous four weeks of constant searching. The tall caraiba trees formed a long thin green gallery through the otherwise dry and spiny caatinga. These trees had been given their scientific name of *Tabebuia caraiba* by Martius. The Bavarian explorers had certainly seen the caraiba woodlands when they passed this way—indeed, many of the older trees now stood exactly where they had then. I wondered if one of these magnificent craggy trees might be the one in which Spix shot his bird.

Caraiba trees are not a rare species; they occur widely over the drier parts of South America and south to Paraguay. But here in the caatinga they formed unique ribbons of woodland that the macaws evidently preferred and that seemed to be found nowhere else than along the creeks that flanked the São Francisco River over its middle reaches. In that respect they were the key element in a unique habitat confined to only a small part of the dry interior. What, if any, relationship the macaws had with buriti palms was not obvious: There didn't seem to be any.

The bed of the creek was composed of deep fine sandy soils. In places it was wet, and here and there were little pools. Even in the dry season there was groundwater near the surface; this sustained the distinctive parklandlike vegetation. Amid the lush green growth there were a number of dead or partially dead trees whose bare branches reached aloft like thin white fingers.

We searched the banks of the Melância Creek until dark, but found nothing. I was now edgy and impatient, frustrated that yet another sighting might prove illusory or mistaken. I was tired and suffering from diarrhea, the novelty of being in these wild lands was wearing off, and I was beginning to wonder if it was all worth it. I yearned for the bright lights and comfortable bars of Rio de Janeiro.

The next day, July 8, 1990, at 4 A.M., Yamashita woke me from shallow slumber in my hammock. It was time to resume the search. We silently climbed into the vehicles. It was too early to expect any coffee so we set off bleary-eyed and still half asleep. By dawn, equipped with binoculars, a telescope, long camera lenses, and a video camera, our little troupe hid on a bend in the creek. We had decided to follow the advice of the cowboy's wife, who insisted the blue macaws could often be seen there.

As the first light of day pushed back the shadows cast by a low yellowish moon, the creek began to come to life. Some distance away a parrot called. It cried a resonant, rolling "*Kraaa kraaa kraaa.*" It was neither harsh and gruff like the call of the big macaws seen in the cerrado, nor shrieking like that of the smaller ones that had apparently been mistaken for Spix's. This sound echoed the tape recordings of Spix's Macaw that Yamashita had brought with him. The cry grew louder, then louder still. Finally the source of it came into view. Its blue plumage was visible in the first proper daylight. With a pale head, a distinctively long tail, and deep wingbeats, there was no doubt what it was. We had found a Spix's Macaw. It flew closer with a flock of the smaller, mainly green *maracanas*[29] and set-tled in a nearby tree. Hidden in the bushes by the creek, we had an uninterrupted view. We were speechless as we simply stared at a creature we had come to regard as almost mythical.

The blue parrot perched and nervously looked round. It was alert, apprehensive. Its keen senses probed the shadows.

Whoever had told Paul Roth that all of the Spix's Macaws from the Melância Creek had been captured was mistaken. Spix's Macaw was not, after all, a dead parrot. It was not extinct.

Our excitement was intense.

"Christ, we found it," I muttered.

Yamashita grinned. "Spix's Macaws only live here, nowhere else, just a little strip of woodlands by the river, that's all," he whispered.

Marigo and Pontual with their cameras trained on the bird babbled excitedly in Portuguese. Shutters clicked and videotape rolled. I stared at the bird through my heavy East German binoculars. Fearing the parrot might disappear as suddenly as it arrived, I tried to memorize every detail of its form, color, and behavior. As my eyes flickered over its blue feathers, noted its sharp yellow iris, long tail, pale head, and black bill, I knew that the majestic wild blue bird had made an impression so vivid and powerful that it would remain with me for the rest of my life.

In the vastness of the dry Brazilian interior we had located a wild Spix's Macaw; 60 centimeters of blue feathers, flesh, blood, bones, and instincts, a tiny vessel of unique existence in the sprawling thorn scrub. To have searched the length of this vast country and to have found this bird was nothing short of a miracle.

We were desperate to find other Spixes. Frantic searches up and down the creek and into the contiguous Barra Grande Creek were hastily organized. During the day, the one bird was seen or heard a few times, but there were no traces of others. Nonetheless, its discovery was a cause for celebration.

That evening we drove into town for dinner and drinks and to discuss how to spend our time in the coming days. There were some clear priorities. The first was to search for more Spixes in other areas where the caraiba trees still grew by the creeks. There was every reason to believe that Spix's Macaws had a strong preference for the gallery woodlands where those trees grew. Another was to do a quick survey of the habitat to see if it could be established what made it especially unique and so important for the parrots.

The following day the team split up; Pontual and Marigo would go to the creek before dawn to erect a hide near to the bird's favorite tree; from there they would film and photograph the parrot and any companions. Otoch, Yamashita, and I would head farther down-river toward the Vargem Creek to see if another population of Spixes could be found in the caraiba trees there.

Finding the Vargem Creek was easy, although the roads to it were not good. A few houses were scattered along its tree-fringed course. Yamashita and I knocked on doors to ask the locals if they knew of any blue macaws there. "It has a long tail and a shining eye," reported one old man, who also gave a very convincing imitation of its distinctive call. He said the birds had always been rare and when he had seen them it was among the caraiba trees by the creek. Another local who knew of the bird repeated that it was very rare and that he had not seen any at all lately. A third recognized the Spix by its pale head—a sure sign of an eyewitness—but had not seen the birds for fifteen years. All three said trappers had taken them away.

Encouraged by the thought that the macaws had perhaps been there until recently, we decided to survey the creek. Yamashita and I found that close to the confluence with the São Francisco River, the Vargem Creek was broad with a braided channel; caraiba trees were scattered across its course. Farther away from the main river, the creek narrowed and the trees became more concentrated, like the gallery woodlands along the Melância Creek. It was very similar to where we had found the single bird. But the search brought no sightings or trace of any kind that the Spix's Macaw still lived there. We were compelled reluctantly to deduce that trappers had cleaned it out.

The discovery of a second suitable habitat that could have supported Spix's Macaws might explain the rumors of other birds in trade that could not have come from Curaçá. Further evidence that the species had been there came from a farmer interviewed on the way back to the Concordia farm. He said that he had only ever seen the long-tailed blue macaws in the Vargem Creek. They were always very scarce, he said, but could often be seen perched in the bare branches at the tops of the tall trees. He added that he hadn't seen such birds for years.

Back in the Melância Creek the team exchanged notes. The news from the Vargem Creek was tantalizing, but it seemed we had arrived there a few years too late. The photographic work had gone well but no other Spix's had been seen. The lone macaw we had found was unsurprisingly very nervous. Repeated attempts had, after all, been made to trap it and the sight of any people sent it into panic. Its natural suspicion was what had kept it alive.

Next morning, we began a detailed survey of the Melância Creek, to describe in a more systematic manner the preferred habitat of the Spix's Macaw. We estimated tree heights, recorded trunk diameters, noted bare branches and possible nest holes, and described the soils and the distance the tall trees grew from the creek edge. We also noted where nest holes had been opened with saws and axes and observed how several of the caraiba trees had recently been climbed. There were nails hammered into the smooth bare trunks and fallen branches had been propped up beneath some of the lower nest holes to enable the trappers to make closer inspections.

Aside from the evidence of trapping, the habitat survey soon revealed another critical threat. There were no young caraiba trees. Most of them were large, old, and partially dead, with hollows and bare boughs. Although the macaws liked holes to nest in and bare perches to sit on, the dying habitat was a disaster. A clue to what had happened was found next to the farm buildings. In the moist creek bed by the cowboy's house, the family had planted some maize. To prevent the goats and cattle eating the crop, a rough wooden fence had been erected round it. Inside, among the maize plants, were thousands of tiny seedlings—caraiba tree seedlings. They had germinated from seeds dropping from the huge trees that grew at the shady edge of the creek. They had survived in the exclosure where they were protected from the grazers, but outside the animals had eaten the lot. You couldn't blame the poor creatures: In the dry season there was little of anything to eat. A succulent young tree would be a real treat.[30]

On finding the young tree seedlings, Yamashita reflected for a moment and then retired to the shade, where I was already writing notes. We had both realized what this discovery portended. The logic was inescapable. The habitat of Spix's Macaw was clearly the special caraiba gallery woodlands. It wasn't a palm specialist like the other blue macaws after all. That theory had turned out to be an erroneous guess based on the habits of the other blue macaws; the search during the previous month had demonstrated that, as had Roth's work. There was, in fact, no photographic evidence or specimens of the Spix from any other habitat apart from these gallery woodlands—everything else was based on rumor and hearsay, or seemed the result of misidentification, including that in Helmut Sick's record. The remaining fragments of caraiba woodlands were now confined to just a couple of small patches by the São Francisco River; the rest of it had gone, either logged and grazed out of existence or more quickly swept aside to make way for the vast irrigated farms. The pressures on the special vegetation meant that not only was the bird rare, so was its habitat.

Once we had worked this out, we chose to study intensively the single blue parrot in an attempt to determine why Spix's Macaws were so dependent on those curious and obviously rare woodlands. Close observation of the macaw revealed that it had paired with one of the little green *maracanas*. The two birds flew together all day. The larger Spix's would accompany a flock of the *maracanas* but would always be close to one bird in particular. At times they were seen alone together. The *maracana* appeared nervous and flighty, suggesting that something was desperately wrong, but did not resist the advances of the bigger blue bird. We were baffled by why it had accepted such a partner. Perhaps the bigger bird was better able to drive off predators than its own kind. Whatever the reason, they sat together and flew together and we even saw and filmed the Spix trying to mate with the smaller macaw.

The blue bird seemed impelled by deep instincts. His unstoppable urge to socialize, win companionship, and find a mate had found its outlet with one of the little *maracanas*. They were a quite different species, but close enough in the Spix's mind to trigger behavior that under other circumstances would only be initiated by a partner of his own species. We had already surmised that the Spix pictured in the Polaroid photo we had seen in town had been his mate. She had been captured more than two years before, and despite the fact that he was a strong flier and that his call could travel great distances over the serene flat caatinga, it seemed that the one wild bird we had discovered had found no other parrot like himself. In a desperate bid to preserve the material substance of his being his reproductive instincts had driven him to pair with a different species. No endangered species could possibly face a more desperate state of affairs than this.

It hadn't taken vast powers of deduction to work out that the single macaw found in the creek was most likely the last survivor of the trio found by Roth. The other two—the single male and the partner of this last wild bird—had both been captured in 1987, one in April and one at Christmas. Somehow this one had managed to outwit the trappers, who were still evidently after him.

With this thought came the realization that not only were we in the presence of the last Spix's Macaw at Curaçá—it was the last wild

Spix's Macaw anywhere. After searching all the gallery woodland habitat that remained we had found just one bird. And that was it. The awful conclusion was that the world population of wild Spix's Macaw contained just a single example. The last of the little group of macaws found at Curaçá was the sole representative for an entire genus of unique birds.

Unlike all other mortal creatures that one day must face the inevitable reality of their own demise, the death of this bird would mark the end not only of himself, but of his entire kind. The Spix's Macaw would have perished completely, become extinct.

CHAPTER 6

The Legions of the Doomed

The Spix's Macaw and the other species of imperiled parrots heading fast toward their final showdown with the forces of extinction are not alone. They are just one group among countless irreplaceable life forms being driven to destruction by environmental change of unprecedented speed, set in motion centuries ago during the great age of European exploration.

The tentacles of Europe's imperial powers rapidly spread across the world during the sixteenth century. The adventurers and entrepreneurs who set forth in search of fortunes and new worlds found remote places that had remained untouched by external influences for millions of years. The Europeans happened upon ecosystems so remote and fragile that the disruption they brought caused the natural fabric of those places to unravel completely.

One of the best-known examples was the Mascarene Islands. Lying between about 1,000 and 1,500 kilometers east of Madagascar inside the southern tropic in the Indian Ocean, the islands of Réunion, Rodrigues, and Mauritius had evolved a unique flora and fauna. Borne of millions of years of isolation, these volcanic outposts had given life to species of birds, animals, and plants seen nowhere else. In common with the wildlife species on hundreds of other islands, the ancestors of these distinctive life forms had arrived by chance. Some of the accidental immigrants thrived, gradually changing over time and ultimately evolving into new species under the unique conditions found there.

When Portuguese and then Dutch sailors arrived in the Mascarenes in the sixteenth century, they were greeted by rich green forests that clothed the islands' towering volcanic peaks. The bountiful wildlife seemed a gift from God. Dozens of varieties of tasty meat and fruit were set out for the taking. Because these human voyagers were the first land predators to reach this remote part of the ocean, the islands' birds were tame and defenseless. They had no reason to be naturally wary and lacked the means to escape or fight when threatened. Mass slaughter ensued.

One species became symbolic of the plunder. It was a flightless member of the pigeon family. With no predators to worry about and abundant food on the ground, these curious-looking creatures had lost the power of flight and grown large—larger than a turkey. They became known by a comic-sounding name—the Dodo. There might have been several species of dodolike birds found in the Mascarenes. The Mauritius Dodo (*Raphus cucullatus*) disappeared first, gone by 1670.

When Europeans first put ashore in 1505, at least twenty-eight birds lived in these islands and nowhere else; the three dodos were simply the most famous emblems of this irreplaceable ecosystem. The great majority were quickly plunged into oblivion. Among these ecological casualties were several species of parrot. One was a

rather beautiful blue bird that flew among the forest trees on Rodrigues. This parrot belonged to the genus of *Psittacula* parakeets
that were popular in Ancient Rome. But unlike its cosmopolitan
cousins that ranged naturally from the Atlantic coast of Africa
across Asia to central Burma, it lived on just one tiny Indian Ocean
island. Not only was its total population confined to that minuscule
portion of the earth's surface, it also had the distinction of being the
only other wholly blue parrot known to humankind.

In the 1870s two specimens of these birds were shot, preserved
in alcohol, and shipped to England. These same artifacts today con-
stitute the total earthly remains of a gorgeous bird we now know as
Newton's Parakeet (*Psittacula exsul*). They are kept in the bird collection at Cambridge University's Zoology Museum.

Safely stowed in an old mahogany cabinet, they are not on public display and have to be specially fetched by the museum's meticu-
lous curator for inspection. The skins are irreplaceable, and no one
is left unaccompanied with them. The parrots' remains reek of
mothballs and shed a fine dust when handled. These last shreds of a
bright thread cut from the fabric of life are in good condition and
give an idea of what the living birds once looked like. They are remarkably similar in color to Glaucous Macaws—a dull greenish blue
with brighter turquoise highlights. The specimens are from a male
and female—both long and slender birds about 40 centimetres from
bill to tail tip. These stiff, still, and lifeless remains aside, their kind
is gone forever.

The original labels are still attached to the birds' now stiff dry
legs. The male's says in ancient ink "Rodrigues 14 August 1875." The
female was collected a little earlier. Her label is made from a fragment of card that was previously part of a dinner party invitation.
On one side are her details, written by a long-gone museum curator;
on the other it reads "Mr and Mrs W. H. Thompson request the

pleasure. . . ." The label speaks of a time when a card was treated as a valuable commodity. In those days forests were abundant and our means to process them primitive. Today the situation is dramatically different: Natural forests are everywhere disappearing while our ability to convert them to wood, card, and paper, which we largely waste, is hugely advanced. The disappearing forests are, of course, where most of the world's endangered birds live.

Why Newton's Parakeet died out is not known for sure, but educated guesses can be made. These birds apparently tasted good and were shot for food. Others were caught for pets; not only did they look very attractive but they could talk well. One tame bird apparently mastered both Flemish and French words. The settlement and clearance of the native forests from Rodrigues and their replacement with maize, coconuts, sugar, and other crops would have considerably hastened the parakeets' demise. And not only was their habitat removed, as with the similarly fated Seychelles Parakeet (*Psittacula wardi*), the arrival of agriculture brought the persecution and destruction of the birds as crop pests. Parrots ate grain and fruit, and for this they were mercilessly shot.

The English naturalist Slater described in a letter to Alfred Newton how on September 30, 1874, he had sighted one of the parrots in some forest at the southwest end of the island. In 1875 the second of the two surviving specimens was collected. By 1876 the little blue parrots of Rodrigues were scarce. One observer said in that year that they were unapproachable. Perhaps by then they had learned to fear the two-legged newcomers. But it was too late. These passing references are the last evidence of surviving Newton's Parakeets.

Several other parrots quickly disappeared from the islands of the dodos. One was the impressive Mascarene Parrot (*Mascarinus mascarinus*). A large light brown bird with a lilac head, black face, and great red bill, it was common on Réunion (and possibly Mauritius) when the Europeans came. The establishment of the plantations of coffee, bananas, maize, vanilla, and sugar sealed its fate. By the early part of the nineteenth century it had disappeared in the wild. The last known living bird was housed in the collection of Spix's patron, King Maximilian of Bavaria, where it died during the 1830s. Like the Spix's Macaw it was unique—the only species included in its genus. When it disappeared, another piece from the jigsaw of evolution was lost with it.

The Broad-billed Parrot (*Lophopsittacus mauritanus*) was probably flightless and today a few bones are its only legacy. It lived on Mauritius but was extinct very soon after the arrival of the Europeans. The Rodrigues Parrot (*Necropsittacus rodericanus*) was referred to in a few manuscripts, but also soon disappeared. Both these birds had massive bills, but given the rather weak structure it seems likely that they ate soft foods.

These parrots often fell victim to animals introduced to the islands, including pigs and goats set free by sailors to provide food for ships that would drop anchor there later on. Monkeys and rats also became established. These animals played havoc with the cavity-nesting parrots, preying on eggs and young and adult birds.

But if the rats and monkeys were one problem, the people were something else. Willem Bontekoe van Hoorn visited Réunion in 1618. Reflecting on his experiences there, he wrote: "The most amazing thing is that when we catch a parrot or other bird and pinch it a bit so that it shrieks, all the others that were in the neighbourhood come by as if they wanted to free it, and were therefore taken. We went back to the ship with a load of feathered food."

Only one species of parrot survived the colonial onslaught against the Mascarene Islands' wildlife—the pretty green Echo Parakeet (*Psittacula echo*). It still lives on Mauritius, where it feeds on the seeds and fruits of indigenous trees. But because of the near total clearance of the island's native forests and the effects of non-native animals, the Echo had by the late 1980s declined to under ten individuals, and most of those were males. This tiny remnant population clung to existence in the last 2 percent of remaining native forest.

A similar fate befell the parrots living on the islands in the Caribbean. After Columbus had firmly placed the West Indies on the Europeans' world map, a free-for-all began. The imperial powers vied with each other to claim new possessions before a competitor country staked its claim. Britain, France, Holland, and Spain were quick to establish colonies. The islands became a source of cheap commodities; sugar, tobacco, hardwoods, and coffee among them. There were also the native peoples, a source of slaves, at least to begin with, before they were killed off through brutal treatment and newly introduced diseases, including smallpox.

The West Indies were rapidly settled and soon of great economic importance. The colonial governments back home found not only new sources of tax revenue, but also new export markets for consumer goods. By the 1640s there were about seven thousand French and over fifty thousand English colonists in the West Indies. Later that century they would be joined by many thousands more, and then hundreds of thousands of slaves brought from Africa. The plantation economy and the plunder of natural resources that followed transformed the islands.

When Columbus first charted the West Indies, there were unique parrots on most of the main islands. Many would not last long. Across the more than 2,000-kilometer-long chain from the Lesser Antilles adjacent to the coast of Venezuela in the south through the larger islands of Cuba, Hispaniola, Jamaica, and Puerto Rico in the center to the Bahamas in the north, many unique species were doomed. In addition to trapping, trade, and hunting, habitat loss undoubtedly played a part in the demise of most, if not all, of the Caribbean parrots. The forests were ransacked for their valuable hardwood trees and cleared to make way for crops. For some parrots, so total has been the removal of material evidence of their existence that we know of them now only from a few remarks handed down in contemporary manuscripts. In this category are several species of macaw.

The accounts of colonists, explorers, and naturalists suggest that as many as five (and perhaps more) kinds of macaw lived on the Caribbean islands. All have vanished. One was reported from Dominica in the Lesser Antilles. It was green and yellow and was apparently eaten and collected as a pet. It was not seen alive after the 1790s. Another green-and-yellow species apparently lived in the mountains of Trelawny and St. Anne's on Jamaica. A specimen was collected from the Oxford Estate but does not survive today. It is presumed that this species, too, was hunted to extinction, probably by the early nineteenth century. Jamaica also had a red macaw, but this was probably extinct by the end of the eighteenth century.

Another species, the Lesser Antillean Macaw, was found on the French islands of Guadeloupe and Martinique. This one was violet-blue and placed in the genus *Anodorhynchus* alongside the Hyacinth Macaw of South America. Whether it was native to the islands or actually descended from Hyacinth Macaws imported from the mainland that had gone wild we shall never know. The birds were trapped, traded, and eaten, and by 1760 were rare. They disappeared soon afterward, leaving no surviving specimens. Another macaw, known only from a single bone found on the island of St. Croix, remains shrouded in mystery.

The Caribbean macaw that survived longest lived on the largest island, Cuba, and possibly Hispaniola as well. It also occurred on the Isle of Pines, Cuba's little neighbor. A splendid red-bodied creature with a golden yellow nape, a darker crimson back, and intense blue in the tail and flight feathers, it would today be priceless. It was hunted for food, taken for a pet, and its nest trees were felled to get hold of young birds. The last one to be shot was taken in the Zapata Swamp on the south side of Cuba in 1864. It was extinct in the wild by 1885. A few survived in captivity. Berlin Zoo had some up until the turn of the century. The Cuban Macaw could have been seen there alongside that other unrepeatable show—the four species of blue macaw.

The accidental extermination of the Caribbean parrots embraced a beautiful purple and green Amazon parrot from Guadeloupe and another from Martinique. The naturalist Labat, in an account published in 1742 about the Martinique bird, remarked, "[T]he parrot is too common a bird for me to stop to give a description of it." He took its abundance too much for granted: Within sixty years it, too, had gone forever.

The little islands and secluded bays of the Caribbean made perfect hiding places and bases for the English, French, and Dutch buccaneers who preyed on vessels returning home with colonial bounty. The badge of office for practitioners in this industry was a parrot or macaw. Sitting on their masters' shoulders issuing oaths and foul language, the parrots later became symbolic of the region in the age of exploration. One of the characters in Robert Louis Stevenson's *Treasure Island* was a parrot. It was a female bird called Captain Flint and she belonged to Long John Silver. Stevenson didn't give too many details about the bird, but he probably meant it to be an Amazon parrot. Such was the importance of her role that this fictional bird uttered the last words in his classic novel: "Pieces of eight! pieces of eight!"

During the pirates' heyday in the late sixteenth century through the middle of the eighteenth, some captains, it must be safe to presume, had aboard their ships birds that are now extinct. Red Cuban Macaws, the violet parrots once found on Guadeloupe, and the yellow and green macaws from Jamaica would no doubt have once graced the quarterdecks of boats flying the Jolly Roger. If some of those birds had survived, the modern pirates who collect rare parrots today would undoubtedly pay a fortune for them. The privateer captains could not have guessed that the most precious plunder of all was perched on their shoulder.

In spite of the litany of woes that fills the stories of parrots from the tropical islands of the New World, happily some did survive, albeit more by accident than design. The parrots that do remain are mainly confined to the last remote fragments of forest that cling to the sides of volcanoes and mountains. From these remote outposts about a dozen species of Caribbean parrot greeted the third millennium. Most of them are included in the genus *Amazona*, and no fewer than ten of them are in immediate danger of extinction.

In common with the parrots of the Mascarene islands, these birds evolved into their present unique forms following the arrival of their ancestors on the islands at various times in prehistory. The parrots that gave rise to the birds we know today may have been blown from the mainland by the Caribbean's frequent hurricanes. Indeed, the species found on the Greater Antilles (Cuba, Hispaniola, Puerto Rico, and Jamaica) do resemble some of their cousins in Central America and appear to be quite recent descendants of birds found there now. By contrast, those in the smaller Windward Islands to the south are very different from any other modern-day parrots in Central or South America, suggesting that their ancestors arrived on their islands long ago. Whatever their origin, the result is spectacular. The four species of Amazon parrots found in the Lesser Antilles are among the most impressive parrots anywhere.

The little island of Dominica is blessed with two of them: the magnificent Red-necked Parrot (*Amazona arausiaca*) and the truly majestic Imperial Parrot (*Amazona imperialis*). The Imperial Parrot is one of the largest parrots alive today. It is a dark, thickset iridescent purple and green bird that dwells in the wet forests that clothe the brooding volcanic peak of Morne Diablotin, the island's biggest mountain. The parrots retreated to higher and higher altitudes as their native forest habitat was claimed by banana plantations and as continued persecution took its toll. In 1975 the population was estimated at up to 250 birds; by 1983 its numbers had dropped to barely 60. Its cousin the Red-necked Parrot fared a little better with a population of a few hundred. Both are utterly vulnerable to disasters such as a direct hit from a powerful hurricane. The number of Red-necked Parrots was halved by such events in 1979 and 1980.

St. Lucia and St. Vincent have unique parrots too. The amazing-looking creature from St. Vincent occurs in two broad color schemes: brown or green. Both are striking with white heads, blue faces, and bright shocks of yellow in their wings and tails. In the early 1970s about 1,000 of these birds were estimated to be hanging on. By the late 1980s the population was believed to be about half that. The St. Lucia birds did worse still. In 1950 this breathtaking beauty, a great green parrot with an iridescent blue face and scalloped black and red breast, was believed to have a population of about 1,000. A survey in 1978 estimated that only about 100 survived.

It almost goes without saying that all four of these rare, chunky parrots are highly collectable and valuable.

Many other parrot species were wiped out after the colonial settlers arrived. They became a symbol of how, in the quest for wealth and new lands, people's disregard for wild nature led to the destruction of beautiful life forms and unique habitats. Indeed, most of the species of bird that we know to have gone extinct during the last 500 years lived on small islands.

There is now a new emergency. It seems that the rash of extinctions seen in island life forms is set to overtake the continents too. It is now clear that the processes initiated in the 1500s that altered the course of biological history on hundreds of islands are now shaping the destiny of the larger landmasses too. Today dozens of parrots found in continental areas are at risk of extinction. In addition to the Glaucous Macaw, the classic example of a parrot that speaks of the shape of things to come is the Carolina Parakeet (*Conuropsis carolinensis*).

In the 1880s a bird of this kind came into the possession of the Cincinnati Zoo, where they named him Incas. When he died on February 21, 1918, he was widely mourned. The little green bird with a lemon-yellow hood and orange forehead had arrived at the zoo with his mate, Lady Jane, in a crate of the birds captured from the wild. At that time they sold for about $2.50 each. As the years went by and the birds' impending fate in the wild became more obvious, the zoo's few birds became hugely valuable: $4,000 was at one point offered for their last pair. According to Colonel Stephan, the general manager at the zoo, the cause of Incas's death was grief at the loss of his partner of three decades: She died a few months before his own demise. There was no way she could be replaced, for there were no more to replace her with.

The Carolina Parakeet was a common species when colonists arrived in the lands we know today as the United States, occurring in large flocks east of the Great Plains. They ventured into open country to feed but preferred river valleys with dense forests filled with mature trees. These parrots fed on a variety of native seeds and fruits, but their favorite was the tough-shelled seed of the cocklebur. When cultivation and orchards arrived, the birds naturally also turned their attention to crop plants. This was to be their undoing.

John James Audubon, who would later gain worldwide fame for his illustrations of the birds of North America, wrote about the parakeets in 1831. "The stacks of grain put up in a field are resorted to by flocks of these birds, which frequently cover them so entirely, that they present to the eye the same effect as if a brilliantly coloured carpet had been thrown over them. They cling around the whole stack, pull out straws, and destroy twice as much grain as would suffice to satisfy their hunger." Audubon went on to describe how the birds took tiny unripe pears and apples to extract the seeds. The birds would pass from branch to branch picking the fruit in search of mature seeds but of course found none. They would strip entire trees in their futile search. The farmers, unsurprisingly, didn't approve.

The parakeets were shot in the millions and, like many other parrots, they didn't depart when fired on but instead stayed loyally to help their wounded and dying companions. They were easy prey. Farmers had the additional incentive of shooting them for the pot. It really was a question of killing two birds with one stone. On top of all that, they were killed for their fine green feathers, which were used to adorn ladies' hats.

As the native forests of the eastern U.S.A. were cleared, so was the birds' habitat. Settlers often felled hollow trees to get hold of honey and in so doing deprived the birds of their nest sites. With the retreat of the forests, the birds were forced into greater contact with people. The slaughter continued. By the second half of the nineteenth century, the Carolina Parakeet was in freefall decline, and by the end of that century it survived in only two states, Florida and Oklahoma. Following the death of Incas in Cincinnati, there were a few reports of wild birds still hanging on; the last was from Okeechobee County in Florida. Parakeets seen there in 1926 could have been of this species or perhaps of some other type escaped from captivity. A few unconfirmed reports followed, but by the 1930s the Carolina was certainly extinct and probably had been for some time. The U.S.A.'s only unique native parrot had been struck from the register of life.

Not so obvious are the millions of species disappearing with the parrots. Talkative, colorful birds in demand as pets are noticed, recorded, described, and cataloged. Not so for many inconspicuous species. Despite the widely held feeling that we know a lot about the living treasures of our planet, the opposite is in fact the case.

During the 1980s Brazilian scientists found a new species of monkey living in a fragment of surviving forest within an hour's drive of São Paulo, one of the world's largest cities. This is almost the equivalent to discovering a new species of badger on the outskirts of London or an entirely new raccoon in the suburbs of Los Angeles. And it was not an isolated event.

More worrying than our ignorance of what is still to be found is our reckless disregard of species we evidently prize very highly: Even big bright blue birds valued at thousands of dollars each could be pushed to, or even over, the brink of extinction with no one noticing. At the dawn of the twenty-first century, after more than three centuries of intensive effort, people have managed to describe and give names to about one and a half million different life forms; this includes plants, bugs, slugs, fish, birds, and the rest. But this is by no means a full inventory of life. While the headline writers salivate at the possibility of life on Mars, the living threads of this planet's web of unique organisms are slashed with barely a mention.

Estimates of the total number of different species that share the earth with humans extend to more than 100 million. In the rain forests, amid the coral reefs, in the depths of the oceans, and even in the soil beneath our feet, there are living systems about which we are still grossly ignorant. Whether you believe this incredible diversity is the result of evolution or creation, the fact is we don't know the half of it. On the contrary, if the top-end estimates of total species numbers are correct, it may be that we know much less than 2 percent of it.

Much of this incredible variety is located in quite specific places with many species of plant and animal restricted to very small areas. Many of these places are islands like Jamaica or the Mascarenes, where isolation has brought forth unique life forms through evolutionary processes working for millions of years to change the ancestral species that arrived there by chance.

What is less obvious are the many biological "islands" scattered across the continents too. Rift valleys, volcanoes, mountain ranges, huge rivers, and climatic differences have all conspired to isolate, in an evolutionary sense, different parts of the earth's surface from neighboring areas. The collective result is a mind-boggling assemblage of animals and plants, until recently perhaps the greatest single array of life seen during the whole of this planet's billions of years of biological history.

Birds—parrots included—are, generally speaking, the best-documented group of animals. More is known about them than any other comparable creatures. For that reason the International Council for Bird Preservation—now BirdLife International—decided in the late 1980s that a good way of working out where to focus their and others' efforts in the pressing struggle to hang on to as many wildlife species as possible was to map out where the birds confined to particular small areas actually lived.

Researchers set out some simple criteria and began their gargantuan task. The intention was to map the distribution of all birds confined to a total range of less than 50,000 square kilometers; that is about equivalent to the size of Costa Rica, a little larger than Denmark, or a bit smaller than West Virginia. After years of trawling through all the records and reports they could find, including manuscripts and reports from the early European explorations, they produced a new world map.[31]

Instead of countries and cities, this map showed with colored dots, stripes, and patches where the birds with restricted ranges lived. The logic was simple. Given that birds are the best-known life forms, mapping the places where the ones with restricted ranges dwelt should give clues as to where terrestrial evolutionary forces have been operating for millions of years in isolation. Since the unique biological conditions that had given rise to the birds (including many rare parrots) might have influenced the development of other species, too, mapping the birds could in turn identify where everything else is most different: mammals, freshwater fish, plants, insects, reptiles, and so on. If such centers of natural uniqueness were identified and protected, then perhaps it would be possible to save more of the earth's natural diversity than if national parks and nature reserves were sited less systematically, or with less comprehensive information.

The research found that fully a quarter of the world's bird species naturally occurred over areas of less than 50,000 square kilometers. Among them were 110 species of parrot, nearly a third of the whole family. The clusters of the restricted-range birds identified 218 places around the world where evolution had generated unique birds. And the locations of rare parrots, in common with the other birds, proved accurate signposts to rare plants and other life forms.

One such area was marked as a brown blob in the interior of northeast Brazil. It was labeled B46—the caatinga. In this quiet corner of the globe the bird researchers found eleven species confined to there and nowhere else: six with ranges below the 50,000-square-kilometer limit and five more found slightly more widely but still only in the northeastern drylands. Of the six that were strictly limited in their distribution to a total range of less than 50,000 square kilometers, one was only discovered while the mapping work was going on. This was the Caatinga Nighthawk (*Chordeiles vielliardi*), found in 1994 in just one locality on the banks of the São Francisco River. The others were the Pygmy Nightjar (*Caprimulgus hirundinaceus*), Tawny Piculet (*Picumnus fulvescens*), Red-shouldered Spinetail (*Gyalophylax hellmayri*), and two species of blue macaws, Spix's and Lear's. Four out of the six were on the cusp of extinction.

Until the 1990s the caatinga had from a biological point of view really been a forgotten corner of the world.[32] It had been a place of gradual biological impoverishment for four hundred years, but the process was slow and not very dramatic—certainly not the stuff of television news reports. The caatinga seemed to be a hot dry desert, not like the moist rain forests that teemed with colorful life. Predictably, few people gave it their attention. It was largely ignored. The outward appearance of a dry and unvarying wasteland was, however, misleading; the fact was that it had given rise to up to eleven of its own special birds. This suggested a long period of biological isolation and the prospect that other unique life forms might be found there too.

Eleven species may not sound like a lot given the millions of species that most likely exist today, but the birds were indicators. There are only about 10,000 species of bird and many of these are quite widespread. Indeed, the nearest place to Washington, D.C., approaching a similar level of avian uniqueness to the caatinga is more than 1,500 kilometers away in the Caribbean, while the nearest such place to London is in the Canary Islands, some 2,500 kilometers distant, off the coast of Africa. And in the Canary Islands, there are only four unique birds.

At the same time as ornithologists began to put the caatinga on the world conservation map, there was growing interest in the place from botanists too. One program was undertaken by the Royal Botanical Gardens at Kew in England working in collaboration with Brazilian scientists. Their initial findings revealed that the caatinga is a major evolutionary center for plants containing many unique species and genera. The botanists' preliminary investigations conducted during the middle of the 1990s showed that over 300 species and 18 genera of plants were confined to the caatinga and in danger of extinction. Many of those species were hardly known in terms of their potential to provide new drugs, industrial materials, or crops.

The São Francisco River valley, like the islands of the Caribbean, had been subject to the effects of European colonization for centuries. The occupation of the interior was at first not rapid. Indeed, in 1615, one hundred years after the Portuguese discovered Brazil, there were still only three thousand Europeans living in that vast new territory. But one hundred years after that, their numbers were rising fast, and the newcomers were already having a major impact on the land and the forests, including the dry northeast.

The river provided an incomparable route for colonial exploitation of the interior. Portuguese, Dutch, and other adventurers were at first drawn inland from the coast by legends of emerald mountains and vast silver mines. Later travelers more realistically came in search of natives to enslave. In due course the colonial activities along the river became more settled: At its headwaters in Minas Gerais in the south, the São Francisco became an important artery for the mining economy, while its lower course was the scene of missionary activity. In its middle reaches around Juàzeiro it became a land that would draw its character from the herdsmen who settled there.

Towns developed on the sites of the old Indian settlements infiltrated by Jesuit missionaries. Large ranching estates emerged. In the remoteness of the interior, isolated from the more economically and culturally dynamic coastal estates and cities, a feudal land-use system evolved. Cut off from the rest of the country and abandoned to its fate, the remote northeast later became known as "the backlands."

Separation from the civilization at the coast, intense droughts, and the unforgiving land bred determined survivors. Sinuous dark-skinned people with a rugged toughness came to characterize the hot dry interior. These mestizo people remained distinct from the men and women at the coast, where Africans pressed into service on the huge estates added to the blend of humankind that the colonial powers mixed there. The caatinga economy also spawned a unique kind of cowboy—the leather-clad *vaqueiro*. His special clothes, leather armor to protect against the vicious spines of the trees and cacti, are still worn there today.

The land gradually changed as people began to settle in the middle reaches of the São Francisco valley during the seventeenth century. The larger trees were felled to provide timber for buildings and boats, while cultivation was practiced where some of the better soils lay—around Curaçá, for example. The main focus, however, was on cattle, and by the start of the eighteenth century there was already extensive ranching. To open land for grazing, the colonists used fire. Vast blazes were set on land parceled out for the new estates, but of course the flames met no boundaries on the parched caatinga. The fragile forests were devastated.

The colonial administrators in northeast Brazil foresaw the threat to the long-term health of the caatinga, and in 1713 decrees were issued to limit the burning. In this tinder-dry land no new law could on its own control the vast conflagrations; any fire was liable to quickly get out of control. And the native woodland was never able to recover from the burning because of the number of animals turned out to graze there.

More than a hundred years of intensive burning, logging, and grazing had already preceded the early nineteenth-century passage by Spix and Martius. What had come to pass in the special creeks by then we can only guess at, but given the rare moisture they held, the presence of big timber trees, and the potential for cultivation on their fine soils, it must be that their degradation was already well advanced by the time that Spix found the macaw that bears his name. Paul Roth believed that the wooded creeks once extended for 50 kilometers into the caatinga either side of the São Francisco River and occurred along a significant stretch of its middle reaches. By the time the last wild Spix was found in 1990, only two little patches remained.

Not only did the ecological impoverishment of the caatinga threaten wildlife, it undermined the human economy too. Even from the early days of settlement the region suffered cycles of economic boom and bust, in part caused by the vagaries of international commodity price fluctuations, but mainly because of severe droughts made worse by the gross environmental degradation inflicted on the land from the earliest times of colonization.

During the twentieth century, efforts were made to stabilize and improve the lot of the region's destitute people through large-scale "development" projects. In the 1950s the World Bank joined in. By then the valley of the São Francisco had land-use patterns typical of much of Brazil: large estates and plantations owned by rich landlords with the majority of the population living in extreme poverty as tenants, laborers, and squatters. Rather than face these deep-seated social inequalities, the World Bank decided to target its main effort on harnessing the potential of what one of the country's historians had called the "great highway of Brazilian civilisation," the São Francisco River. The Bank would provide funding for energy and farming projects that had one thing in common—they depended on lots of water.

In 1974 the World Bank provided finance for the Sobradinho dam. The reservoir created above the barrage some 50 kilometers upstream from Juàzeiro and Petrolina flooded a large area of the São Francisco valley, including any potential habitat for Spix's Macaw. Seventy thousand people were displaced too. Some of these dam refugees sold the little plots of land granted to them as part of a poorly conceived resettlement program, thereby increasing the size of the already huge estates that dominated farming in the region. Others moved to a different part of the caatinga, or to the rain forests where they were forced to clear yet more land to feed themselves. Many of them finished up in the expanding favelas that had sprung up in Brazil's cities.

The downstream effects were also dramatic. Because of changes to the river's flow pattern, the World Bank was forced to make another $65 million emergency loan for the construction of dikes and polders to protect the farms on the floodplain at the mouth of the river. Another 25,000 hectares of floodplain were also appropriated to establish five huge irrigation projects that claimed more of the land adjacent to the river and displaced another ten thousand families. Some attempts were made to help resettle them, but in the face of expanding irrigated sugar-cane production, most left the area or remained in extreme poverty where they were. So disastrous was the impact of the World Bank's "development" activities on the people of the caatinga that it led to the adoption of the Bank's first official policy geared to the resettlement of people affected by its own projects.

The result of the transformations stimulated by the World Bank's investments as well as Brazil's own farm policies was the gradual replacement of small-scale subsistence farming with capital-

fig 1: Johann Baptist Ritter von Spix (1781-1826).The first scientist to collect a Spix's Macaw in the wild.

fig 2: The tree-lined Melância Creek. This last fragment of the Spix's Macaw natural habitat was where the species was last known in the wild.

fig 3: Sketch map of the main vegetation zones of Brazil.

fig 4: This image of a Spix's Macaw was included in the 1878 Proceedings of the Scientific Meeting of the Zoological Society of London. The tree the Macaw is perched in looks like a caraiba.

fig 5: The four blues. Top row from left to right: Hyacinth Macaw, Lear's Macaw, Glaucous Macaw. Bottom left: two Spix's Macaws perched (pale bare face and pale stripe on upper mandible of bird on right denotes a young bird). Bottom right: the four blues in flight.

fig 6: Hyacinth Macaws come to ground to feed on fallen palm nuts.

fig 7: A pair of Lear's Macaws rest outside their inaccessible sandstone cliff-face nesting site in the remote Raso da Catarina, Bahia, north-east Brazil.

fig 8: The last wild Spix's Macaw with its smaller green maracana partner. Despite being different species, the two birds formed a pair, nested and laid eggs.

fig 9: Juan Villalba Macias is nipped by one of the young Spix's Macaws he rescued from rare bird traffickers in Paraguay.

fig 10: The original pair of Spix's Macaws obtained by Loro Parque in 1985.

fig 11: The last wild Spix's Macaw perches in the bare branches of a tall old caraiba tree.

fig12: Facilities were built in the Melância Creek for maintaining captive Spix's Macaws so as to assist with their release back to the wild. Here the last wild female awaits release in early 1995.

fig13: A pair of Spix's Macaws at Loro Parque, Tenerife. These birds finally produced only infertile eggs.

VOCÊ VIU ESTA ARARINHA?

Cyanopsitta spixii

A Ararinha-azul é uma das espécies mais ameaçadas de extinção do mundo

Ajude-nos a encontrá-la e preservar este patrimônio do sertão

Para qualquer informação sobre esta ararinha avise-nos
Em Curaçá: (075) 831-1155
Ou em Brasília: Cemave — (061) 233-3251

COMITÊ PARA RECUPERAÇÃO DA ARARINHA-AZUL

CEMAVE
Centro de Estudos de Migrações de Aves
Caixa Postal 04/034
Brasília · DF, CEP 70 000
Brasil

Apoio: IBAMA/Conservation International/Criadouro Chaparral

fig 14: Have you seen this macaw? Following the discovery of the last wild Spix's Macaw at Curaçá, posters were prepared and distributed in the hope that local people would come forward with news of other populations of the elusive birds.

intensive irrigated agriculture directed to supplying export markets. Later on, the predations of oil and gas prospecting and mining would add to the impact of agriculture and hydropower.

These progressive steps toward the commercial exploitation of the caatinga would enrich a few, but by and large they did not relieve the misery of the ordinary people. Thus were the natural ecosystems of the river valley liquidated in the name of development with little regard for their uniqueness or worldwide biological importance, and with very few benefits passed on to the people who were supposed to enjoy being "developed."

On top of that, the World Bank loans used to pay for the dams were lumped into Brazil's massive and growing debts to foreign banks and governments. This burden undermined the country's economic stability for decades to come and led to policies that would in their turn further damage the environment as the country struggled to raise cash to pay off its creditors.[33] The caatinga was left like a bombed city, the ecological equivalent of Hiroshima: utter destruction with the survivors hanging on in isolated groups here and there—in the Melância Creek, for example, where a few Spix's Macaws sheltered.

By 1990 the creek was one of a few last fragments of caatinga that gave clues as to what the place had been like before the European colonists arrived. The indigenous people who spent ten thousand years of prehistory in the creeks had certainly made their mark, too, in burning the land, cutting trees, and hunting game, but they had nothing like the profound impact of the foreign colonists.

Similar patterns of farming, energy, and natural resources policy can be seen throughout the world. The main difference between what is taking place now and the damage caused during the European colonial era is the scale and speed of change. Few people get a bird's-eye view of such trends. One person who has is Mario Runco, an astronaut on space shuttle missions in 1991 and 1993. "Most people don't get to see how widespread some of the environmental destruction is. From up there, you look around and see that it's a worldwide rampage," he said. That rampage is driving extensive habitat loss and the extinction of species. It is certainly dramatic, but why should we be bothered? The process of extinction is, after all, a perfectly natural phenomenon.

It is estimated, for example, that only around 2 percent of all the species that have ever existed are alive today. What is different now, however, compared to what appears to have happened under "normal" circumstances in the past, is the rate at which species are disappearing. Edward Wilson, the author of The Diversity of Life, one of the most authoritative accounts of the earth's natural diversity, estimated in 1992 that in the tropical rain forests alone "the number of species doomed each year is 27,000. Each day it is 74, and each hour 3." Based on such projections and comparing them to the clues about natural extinctions that we have gleaned from the fossil record, Wilson concluded that human activities have accelerated the expected background rate of extinction by between a thousand and ten thousand times. The great majority of informed scientific opinion agrees with him.

Such a rapid and sudden loss of species is not unprecedented but should nonetheless be a cause of serious alarm to us. The clues available from fossilized plants and animals point to several large-scale extinctions that have taken place in the past. The vast expanse of geological time in which there has been life on earth is punctuated with the dramatic disappearance of entire groups of animals and plants. The last time this happened was about 65 or 66 million years ago. What precipitated this event is unknown, although one idea has gained more support than others.

The most popular theory is that a comet or meteorite collided with the earth. One set of calculations suggests a 10-kilometer-wide object came down in the present-day Gulf of Mexico. The impact created a cataclysmic explosion that hurled billions of tons of molten rock into the atmosphere; great tsunamis rammed the shores of the world's oceans and blasted over the continents; forest fires raged everywhere. The debris and smoke blotted out the sun's light for years. Poisonous rain fell from the clouds, temperatures plummeted, and plant growth ceased. Food chains collapsed and many animals starved or died of cold in the "nuclear winter" that followed. So catastrophic was this event that it wiped out many of the species of animals and plants alive at the time. The impact of the comet also brought an end to the age of the dinosaurs.

The geological record of the last half-billion years (more or less the period over which animals and plants have left abundant fossil remains in the rocks) is punctuated with several so-called mass extinctions like this one. The earliest occurred about 440 million years ago, the next at about 365 million, the next at 245, and the next at about 210 million years before present. The last one was by no means the worst. The crash in the Permian period 245 million years ago involved the disappearance of between 77 and 96 percent of all marine animal species. The cataclysm that brought about this level of species loss defies comprehension.

The richness of the natural diversity that surrounds us is mind-numbing, so vast is its variation and uniqueness. The disappearing birds, however, provide us with more manageable insights into the wider trends now unfolding. The feathered animals we take so much for granted today are the direct descendants of the dinosaurs; and like those long-lost reptiles, many are now poised to follow their forebears to remain only as faint impressions in the rocks. Most powerful of all, perhaps, is the signal from the parrots. These birds have survived and thrived for tens of millions of years and become our closest emotional and social partners among the world's birds. Their rapid disappearance is making a most dramatic point.

Since the world was alerted to the plight of the disappearing parrots in 1988, the situation has continued to deteriorate. The most recent doomsday book, *Threatened Birds of the World*, has more than ninety species of parrot listed as at risk of extinction.[34] Wilson, in common with many other experts, believes that our species has itself initiated a new mass extinction episode, the sixth in the earth's long history. Like the canaries once taken into coal mines to warn of dangerous gas, the parrots are shrieking the alarm.

Nigel Collar's work documenting the plight of endangered birds leads him to reach a similar conclusion.

> We spend billions of dollars in the quest for evidence of life on other planets when we have it here in superabundance and at levels of sophistication that we have barely even begun to comprehend, all of it haemorrhaging out into oblivion as we turn our faces to the dead night sky and our backs on the rainforests and the reefs, the deltas and the deep. In our lifetimes the natural world will have shrunk by a greater amount than any human before us has ever witnessed. Fairly soon, at this rate, in 100 years time perhaps, our teeming earth will end up as a sterile, sanitised gridwork of concrete and crop-fields.

This time the rapid disappearance of different life forms is being precipitated by the direct exploitation of wildlife, large-scale habitat loss, and rapid climate change brought about mainly by the combustion of fossil fuels. Humanity's blind hunger for ever greater quantities of still cheaper raw materials and farm produce drives the now supercharged engine of destruction.

In contrast to some other environmental challenges facing the world at the start of the twenty-first century, the loss of the earth's biological diversity is irreversible, certainly in terms of any timescales comprehensible to people. And once birds like the Spix's, Lear's, and Hyacinth Macaws are gone, they can never come back. They will be gone for good. How in years to come future generations of humans will react to their passing is a matter for conjecture. Perhaps they will lament human folly as we have done at the passing of the dodo; perhaps our children will invent fantasies about how they could bring them back—a kind of avian Jurassic Park; or maybe they will invent computer-generated reconstructions to show how beautiful, graceful, and intelligent such birds were.

In 1990 for the Spix's Macaw this last question was still premature; only just, but still premature. One still lived, a symbolic last wild bird alone in the remote northeast of Brazil—not yet lost to the world, but as close as it could get. Hanging on at its beleaguered post in the shattered caatinga, the blue parrot had not yet gained the notoriety of the dodo in becoming a modern-day icon of people's indifference to the irreplaceable diversity of our planet. On the contrary, there was good reason to believe that it could instead become a new symbol of hope—better still proof—that the black harvest of extinction was not inevitable. It could become a new image for a new age, a time when people's unthinking exploitation of nature would be replaced with careful husbandry and thoughtful coexistence—an era when the value of life's diversity was not measured only by money but seen as worth keeping for its own sake.

The Spix's Macaw, if it survived and recovered, could inspire the world to see what was possible through cooperation and determined efforts to save the earth's natural riches. In that respect the last-minute rescue of the blue caatinga parrot could be a flagship, a vessel of hope and encouragement. If the captive birds could be bred, released, and restored to the wild, Spix's Macaw could become a symbolic phoenix rising from the ashes of a ruined world.

CHAPTER 7

Private Arks

W here there's life there's hope—at least that is what
some conservationists think. One such person was
Juan Villalba-Macias. On March 25, 1987, armed
with a search warrant and accompanied by five patrol cars, twenty
police officers, and the Paraguay Director for National Parks and
Wildlife, he stormed the house of a wildlife dealer in the
Paraguayan capital Asunción. He hoped this drastic move would
contribute to saving the Spix's Macaw from extinction.

Villalba-Macias was a Uruguayan zoologist and director of
TRAFFIC South America. He had been following the illegal shipment of rare parrots with keen interest. TRAFFIC, an international
organization established in 1976 by the World Wildlife Fund and
the World Conservation Union, monitored the trade in endangered
species. Villalba-Macias was in the house in Asunción that day to
recover two Spix's Macaws, the two baby parrots who were the last

offspring of the lone bird from the Melância Creek. Nine months later on Christmas Eve, that last bird would lose his partner to the trappers, and their last three eggs would be smashed.

For several weeks before Villalba-Macias's raid, investigators had been following the movements of the two young Spix's Macaws. A dealer in Petrolina had transferred the precious creatures to a middleman in the south of Brazil for $10,000, a fortune in the northeast. The second trafficker, based in the city of Curitiba, in turn supplied the parrots to the wildlife trader in Paraguay for $20,000.

The birds had been traced to the house in Asunción. The dealer there planned to ship the birds overseas. His name was Koopmann, the man whose daughter was prosecuted in 1994 for her part in assisting Tony Silva in the illegal shipment of Hyacinth Macaws into the United States, and who had also been involved in the shipment of Spix's Macaws to Europe (see chapter 4). Paraguay borders Brazil and, although landlocked, had become a notorious exit route to world markets for illegally captured Brazilian wildlife. It was intended that the two macaws travel via Switzerland to a West German importer who had agreed to pay $40,000 for them. Once in Europe, the birds would be worth twice that.

Meanwhile, CITES officials in Switzerland had detected that the export papers from Paraguay were forgeries. The smugglers' flawed papers were obvious: There weren't any Spix's Macaws in Asunción Zoo, so none could have been bred there! Villalba-Macias was alerted and traveled straightaway by plane from Montevideo to Asunción. On the morning of the raid he met with the Paraguayan minister responsible for CITES enforcement in the country. He explained that the birds were illegal exports from Brazil and should not be traded internationally. On hearing the evidence, the minister immediately ordered the police search of the premises where the birds were said to be held captive. By 1 P.M. the house was surrounded.

To the surprise of the authorities there was no sign that the birds had been there. No cages, no bird food, no macaws. At first it seemed that there had been a tip-off, but then Villalba-Macias noticed a second-floor door close abruptly. He ran upstairs to investigate and found in the room a servant with a traveling case in her hand, preparing to flee across the rooftops. Before she could leave, Villalba-Macias took the bag and opened it. Huddled inside, ready for shipping, were the two baby parrots. Had the raid taken place an hour later, the macaws would never have been found.

The fluffy blue birds had hatched a couple of months earlier from eggs laid in the great hollow caraiba tree by Melância Creek. They were the offspring of the last wild pair. Tiny and vulnerable, they were miniature versions of their parents—only with shorter tails, pale rather than dark bare faces, and with a light stripe running the length of the hooked upper mandible. A few of their longer plumes were still partly sheathed in the hard plasticlike cases that would soon burst open to reveal their first full set of fresh blue flight and tail feathers.

Villalba-Macias had expected to find bird food suitable for the young macaws at the house but did not, and the furious dealer refused to advise on what the birds should eat. Fortunately, Villalba-Macias had taken the precaution of packing a box of Quaker Oats. He mixed the cereal with water and was delighted to find that the young parrots happily fed on it.

Koopmann was arrested, and following the seizure, the birds were immediately transferred to the Brazilian Embassy, where asylum was sought for them. Like important government dignitaries seeking diplomatic immunity from persecution by a hostile foreign power, the birds sheltered there while waiting to be sent home to their native country. That afternoon the Brazilian government applied for their repatriation and the necessary papers were duly granted. The following day the young macaws were in transit once more, not en route to a European bird dealer but on a plane to São Paulo with Villalba-Macias.

Villalba-Macias remembered how "On our arrival at São Paulo we noticed an incredible number of journalists, photographers and cameramen, so that we first thought they were waiting for a rock star or someone from the international jet set." But the press pack had gathered to meet the parrots. A chaotic press conference followed. "Their performance was impressive—they showed themselves to be true stars as they strolled across the desk—one of them pulled a rubber stamp from its stand with its beak while the other flew on to my shoulder and, perhaps annoyed because I was telling the journalists his family history, he bit my ear." This friendly nip was captured by the photographers and broadcast and printed worldwide.

The seizure of the birds was a symbolic turning point. Villalba-Macias said later that " . . . just as the Giant Panda symbolises all the species threatened with extinction, for us in South America this sky-blue parrot is an emblem . . . our aim of saving it from extinction started the moment we opened that case at Koopmann's and found those two cute chicks . . . we felt deep inside the commitment to rescue them from extinction just as we rescued them from the hands of an unscrupulous trafficker."

The baby birds were, however, too young to be released back into the wild. Instead they were taken to São Paulo Zoo to be housed in aviaries hidden from public display and set among the extensive forested gardens at the edge of the city's vast concrete sprawl. At the zoo they would join three adult Spix's Macaws already in residence. These had been seized as well, way back in 1976.

The seizure in Paraguay was, however, a rare victory. Apart from one or two isolated actions, including the detection of two Spix's

Macaws illegally imported to the U.K. in 1979, the bulk of the traffic had gone unchallenged for years. The ones that came to Britain were brought into London Heathrow via Madrid from Paraguay with documents falsely claiming that they were a blue mutation of a commoner South American species. The bird trader responsible was the first person prosecuted under Britain's new endangered species laws and the authorities made an example of him. Bird trader Gordon Cooke was sentenced to six months' imprisonment and all of his licenses to import and export wildlife were revoked, thereby putting him out of that business for good.

Cooke's Spixes had spent a few weeks in the U.K. before being dispatched along with a shipment of Hyacinth Macaws to a collector in Colorado in the United States. The British authorities only learned that the birds had been in the U.K. after they had already been exported, and despite the successful prosecution, they were never heard of again.

By the late 1980s the available evidence pointed to one dealer in Paraguay as the principal source of birds shipped to international markets. As far as the trapping was concerned, most Spix's Macaws making their way to bird collectors during the 1980s had been supplied by just two dealers. One was based in the town of Petrolina in the northeast Brazilian state of Pernambuco, the other in Floriano in neighboring Piauí. "Carlinhos," the Pernambuco dealer, had, between 1984 and 1987 traded eight Spixes: four adults taken in 1984 and 1985, two young in 1985 to 1986, and the two youngsters taken from the nest who were recovered in Paraguay in the 1987 raid. The trader gave no details about the birds he had moved in the years preceding 1984.[35]

The Floriano trader, "Nascimento," had caught fifteen Spixes between 1977 and 1985, thirteen of them adults. Both said that all the birds they had sold—between them a total of twenty-three—had come from near Curaçá. It also emerged that the two babies taken from the wild in each breeding season from 1984 to 1987 had come from the same nest—that of the last breeding pair. It was their last two chicks that had been picked up in Paraguay during the raid on the trafficker's house.

Paul Roth had been told that the first nesting attempt of the last breeding pair in the 1985–6 breeding season had met with failure when trappers had tried to raid the nest too early. The eggs had not yet hatched and were destroyed when the trappers poked glue-covered twigs into the nest hole in their attempt to take the young. The adults made another attempt to breed some four kilometers from the first nest. This time the trappers came back at night, when the parents were in the nest, and blocked the hole in an effort to take out the whole family. The wily adult birds escaped through a second entrance that the trappers had not seen, but again the eggs were broken. The adult pair were determined to breed, however, and successfully produced two chicks. But despite their resolve to ensure they produced young, the babies were trapped in infancy and taken away.

Roth had also discovered that the traders from Petrolina and Floriano were not the only ones to have been taking birds from the only place the Spix's Macaws were known to live. The bird trapper who'd originally directed him to Curaçá had taken some too. One estimate was that at least 150 of the macaws lived in the creeks during the 1960s, and Roth had worked out from interviews with locals that in the early 1970s the population at Curaçá had stood at about thirty pairs. The stories of the population's decline were unremittingly grim.

Roth learned how in 1984 the trapper from Floriano had taken ten Spixes in one go. Against the will of a local landowner who had been misled by the trapper, seven adults and three babies were captured and removed. During transportation to Floriano, two of the adult birds had become stuck together with lime and one of them died. Some of this group were sold in São Paulo to Brazilian bird collectors, where they fetched $2,000 each—a very considerable sum at the time, especially considering that the comparable price inside Brazil for a highly prized Hyacinth Macaw was then just $50. In addition to these details, Roth discovered how in 1985 one Spix had been killed by a local rancher. It had been shot in a failed attempt to wound it so that it could be caught and sold.

Under these circumstances it was perhaps not surprising that the $965 "watching service" arranged by Roth and paid for by his Munich sponsors was no match for well-organized and armed bird robbers. They had been motivated to break the law and threaten violence by the money. By then the birds were changing hands for $30,000 each. Even though local people had agreed to watch the one dirt track that took outsiders to the Melância Creek from the distant tarmac highway, they were not prepared to risk life and limb, no matter how rare the bird was. And no one could blame them. They just happened to be poor people living in the place where a little band of beautiful blue birds fought a last stand against greed.

Following the seizure of the birds in Asunción, the Brazilian authorities did at last act and raided Carlinhos's house in Petrolina. Although the commitment to protecting Brazil's rare wildlife was strong enough in national government circles, the priority attached to upholding wildlife laws at the state level was patchy. In remote "frontier" regions like the northeast, it was not easy to make sure that the law was respected. Violence, intimidation, and corruption were commonplace, and the area to be policed quite vast. Even if compelling evidence was brought against trappers and dealers, a conviction was not assured. In the end Carlinhos was acquitted by a local judge who saw it as his duty to protect citizens against what he saw as the country's "crazy environmental laws." He walked free to trap another day. And trap he did; among other rare species that he specialized in was Lear's Macaw. So by 1990 only one wild Spix's Macaw was left. The only hope for saving the world's rarest bird now lay with the few scattered around the world in captivity.

Almost all of them had been taken in the face of Brazil's wildlife export ban introduced in 1967. It seemed that most had been shipped against the international trade ban introduced through the CITES treaty in 1975.[36] Locating the present owners was urgent but not straightforward. The longer the start of a proper captive-breeding program was delayed, the more perilous the plight of the lone macaw in the Melância Creek and the more slender the chances of any recovery of a Spix population in the wild.

The secrecy was compounded by rumors and counterrumors about who had new birds for sale and reports of alleged sightings of birds in the wild.[37] These stories abounded. They were short on hard evidence but provided endless grist for the rumor mill and kept the conservationists running in circles. But among the uncertainties, the location of a few captive birds was known for sure. Two were in the possession of a German-born parrot collector called Wolfgang Kiessling.

Kiessling had arrived in Tenerife in the Canary Islands during the early 1970s; he was then thirty-three years old and in search of a business opportunity. He decided to open a wildlife park. At the edge of the green subtropical town of Puerto de la Cruz on the lush north coast of the island, Kiessling bought some land. At first he could only afford to buy a small plot planted with bananas. There was no room for large animals, so the young entrepreneur decided to start with parrots. He didn't have a particular interest in the birds to begin with but was advised by his father that they made good business sense: People adored them, they lived a long time, and they didn't eat very much. He soon fell in love with them and began to build up a collection.

Loro Parque (Spanish for "Parrot Park") opened in 1972. The business initially struggled, but there was a breakthrough when a parrot show was introduced. Today the performing birds are still a great public attraction. In front of captivated crowds, brightly colored macaws and cockatoos ride little bicycles and operate vending machines. Macaws fly low over the heads of the seated audience, brushing faces with their long flowing tail feathers. One Blue-and-gold Macaw takes wooden shapes of the six main Canary Islands and on command expertly fits them the right way around into their correct slots on a large blue board. The birds seem to enjoy themselves and the crowds are charmed.

The park began to succeed and its owner acquired more land. Over the years Loro Parque grew tenfold and was transformed into an impressive modern zoo. Dotted with lush lawns planted with palms, fig trees, and cacti, it was immaculately maintained. Dolphins were added in 1987 and then sea lions. The marine mammals were provided with spacious pools and were highly trained to perform extraordinary acrobatic feats. A large aquarium with sharks was installed to draw in still more of the island's millions of visitors. In 2000 the park opened one of the most remarkable zoo exhibits anywhere in the world.

Planet Penguin is a controlled environment where several species of penguin are maintained in Antarctic conditions amid the subtropical warmth of Tenerife. Snow machines producing 12 tons of icy particles each day create a constant fall from the roof of a dome that encloses this refrigerated world. The artificial illumination was carefully designed to mimic the daylight and wavelengths of the natural rhythms experienced by wild penguins at 60 degrees south. Clear cold seawater surrounds a rocky peninsula on which the penguins shuffle around in the snow. Belowground a vast modern water treatment plant powered by wind generators located on the blustery coast and maintained by specialist engineers hums quietly. Inside their Antarctic bubble Magellan Penguins charge through the water ducking and diving like porpoises. The exhibit cost $15 million to install. Its tenants are surely the most pampered captive penguins on earth.

Visitors are transported through Planet Penguin on moving walkways like the ones found in large airports. On one side the penguins swim at eye level behind glass panels that hold back the water; on the other are audiovisual displays in Spanish, German, and English. In somber tones dire and well-founded pronouncements on the plight of penguins in the wild are broadcast; overfishing, pollution, climate change, disturbance, and mining. It is not only the temperatures that are chilling. These birds' prospects in the outside world don't look too good; the high-tech Ark is in some respects Kiessling's premonition of the shape of things to come, and to an extent mirrors his attitude toward Loro Parque's vast collection of parrots.

The large-scale loss of habitat and rapid environmental change that has driven birds to extinction and many other species to the brink of it has left Kiessling believing that there is a valuable role for breeding rare species in captivity—at least until they might be returned to restored and protected habitats. In a controlled environment they can be properly looked after, cared for, bred, and sheltered from the seemingly unstoppable forces that are wiping them out in the wild.

Planet Penguin and its other impressive attractions have truly put Loro Parque on the Tenerife tourist map, but the park's parrot collection remains Kiessling's proudest achievement. It is fastidiously maintained by a specialist staff and impressively presented amid the dense foliage that grows in the moist warm climate found on the island's northern coastal strip. The irreplaceable assemblage of parrots is cared for and nurtured by a team of vets and bird-breeding specialists. By 2001 Loro Parque had accumulated a collection of over 3,000 parrots from more than 300 species or subspecies. It had become the largest collection of parrot species in the world. By then nearly 25 million visitors had passed through the park, and its profile on Tenerife was huge. Almost no corner of the island was without promotional literature or posters. Not surprisingly, perhaps, Kiessling's flagship parrot for marketing his park is the charismatic Hyacinth Macaw.

In 1998 the Loro Parque Foundation opened the La Vera Breeding Centre, a few kilometers from Kiessling's now famous zoo, on another old banana plantation. Behind a high wall topped with razor wire and beneath the gaze of guards stationed in a watchtower, aviaries were built to house some of the world's rarest birds. Hyacinth Macaws from Brazil, Moluccan Cockatoos from Indonesia, and Red-necked Amazons from the tiny Caribbean island of Dominica were housed together with hundreds more varieties in an unparalleled collection. Remote cameras monitor movements in and out of electronically controlled steel gates; guard dogs sniff the perimeter for signs of intrusion. Careful quarantine procedures, a strict routine of cleanliness, and daily showers provided by sprinklers ensure the birds stay in good health and reproduce. Fourteen staff make careful records and ensure the parrots are properly looked after. Thousands of stainless steel bowls are twice daily filled with various combinations of seeds, nectar, and fruit, and cleaned in an industrial-scale dishwashing machine. A ton and half of fruit and seed is consumed there each week.

Although most species remain on public display in Loro Parque, the majority of the parrots (2,500 out of 3,000) were moved to La Vera. All of them were placed under the control of the Loro Parque Foundation. Kiessling established the foundation in 1994 to help fund projects to save endangered species in the wild. He saw the establishment of the foundation as a way of harnessing the commercial success of Loro Parque to support conservation. The establishment of the foundation marked Kiessling's transition from entrepreneur and parrot expert to an advocate for environmental causes and sponsor of projects to save some of the world's rarest birds in their forest homes.

Between 800 and 850 young parrots were bred at the La Vera center each year between 1998 and 2000. In 2001 the number of captive-bred parrots leapt to 1,100. The top priority of the center is to maintain its captive population, and birds are put aside for that purpose. Not only does this ensure the long-term future of the foundation's parrots, but it provides a resource for researchers studying the birds in captivity. All of the young parrots are recorded and tagged by the local wildlife authorities. Some are designated to join official collaborative breeding programs and some are exchanged with other centers, all in closely controlled programs overseen by the Association of European Zoos and Aquaria. Other young parrots born at La Vera are offered for sale to generate money to fund the foundation's conservation programs. In 1999 the equivalent of about $140,000 was raised in this way.

The rare jewel in the midst of the Loro Parque Foundation's colorful menagerie had for years been some Spix's Macaws. Wolfgang Kiessling first added this species to his collection in 1985 with a purchase from an international bird dealer based in Switzerland. It was relatively easy to take delivery of rare parrots in Spanish-administered Tenerife during the mid-1980s, and the birds came with paperwork recognized as legal by the Swiss authorities. Although the export from Brazil had been against the laws of that country, the import of the parrots into territory controlled by Spain had violated no domestic legislation since it wasn't then a signatory nation of CITES.

Kiessling rationalized the purchase on the grounds that it was best that he take them into his well-run facility. So two Spixes were installed. He kept them out of public view, not wishing the birds to be exposed to any disturbance that might reduce their potential to breed.

Kiessling wasn't the only successful businessman to have bought these most sought-after parrots and to acknowledge the fact in public. The June 1983 edition of *Singapore Aviculture* had carried some pictures of Spix's Macaws. They showed a family group of four held in the country by Terrance Loh, one of Singapore's main bird traders. Singapore had become a major transit point for rare wildlife, and it was not surprising that the Spixes had turned up there. The article claimed, improbably, that the baby birds had been captive bred. When the birds had arrived in Singapore was not clear, but Loh had them for between six and nine months before selling them, apparently for $60,000.

From Singapore, Loh said, the birds were shipped to their new owner, Antonio de Dios, a Filipino businessman.[38] De Dios had a trucking and heavy machinery business, but had also built up a commercial bird-breeding operation. He had made millions, partly by importing heavy equipment for the Filipino government departments that had assisted in the near total clearance of the dense tropical rain forests that once clothed the Philippines. The Birds International, Inc., exotic bird farm is located off a highway on the outskirts of Quezon City, the sister sprawl of Manila. So systematic was his approach that the center had become known as the "parrot factory." Surrounded by high walls and patrolled by uniformed security guards, he, too, had a priceless collection of parrots. He had kept animals for most of his life and it had taken him decades to build up a collection that by 2000 included 6,000 parrots from 160 species. Unlike Wolfgang Kiessling, de Dios's collection had from the start been geared to commercial breeding rather than tourism and conservation.

De Dios specialized in parrot rearing but also bred a wide range of other species, including cranes, hornbills, and toucans. He was skilled and successful. The four Spix's Macaws were at least in a situation where they would be given every encouragement to reproduce.

Two more Spixes were in the possession of Wolf Brehm, the German owner of Vogelpark Walsrode, a large bird garden near Hamburg. Brehm also owned another bird center in the Dominican Republic in the Caribbean. One of the Walsrode macaws was on loan from George Smith, an English aviculturist and vet. Smith said that he had bought the bird in 1975 for £350. Before he got the macaw it had been crippled as a result of being tethered by the leg. He thought it was a male but had no partner for it. In 1980 he lent it to Brehm to see if it would pair up with his single bird. Another single Spix languished at the Naples Zoo in Italy. It had been there for years and was probably past or near the end of its reproductive life. It had reportedly arrived in Naples in 1954 and was still alive in the mid-1980s making it the longest-lived Spix's Macaw known in captivity. The date of its death is unknown to the author (but occurred before 1990). This may have been the bird supplied by Álvaro Carvalhães (see page 30).

In 1988, by the time it was thought the last wild ones had been caught, there were very few Spix's Macaws acknowledged in captivity. De Dios had achieved a breakthrough in managing to breed from his birds and there were seven in residence at his Birds International aviaries in the Philippines. There were two in Tenerife, two with Walsrode, and one in Naples. Thus the known captive population outside Brazil was twelve.

Besides these, rumors circulated about as many as nineteen others. Unconfirmed reports suggested there were two in Majorca, where the birds were rumored to be with a German living in Alcudia. Two more were said to be in Northern Ireland, where they resided in a private collection in County Antrim. Others were possibly in Germany, Gran Canaria, South Africa, Argentina, Paraguay, and Uruguay. One more was claimed to have been kept by a leading American country-and-Western music singer. Others were said to have been owned by Imelda Marcos, wife of the infamous Filipino president. Another pair were apparently exported to Yugoslavia, sent there during the 1970s as an official gift from the government of Brazil to President Tito. Tito, the wartime partisan leader who later became head of state, had a private zoo on the Adriatic island of Brioni, and that is where the two Spixes were claimed to have been sent. The fate of Tito's parrots, if they existed, was unknown: in any event, by 1987 they were presumed dead. On top of all these rumors, there were new whispers that some of these special macaws were being kept in Switzerland.

The situation was equally uncertain inside Brazil. Because of the official restrictions imposed on the keeping in captivity of native wildlife and the commercialization of rare species, only a few private bird keepers designated by the Brazilian government as "scientific breeders" were allowed to keep them and therefore openly declare the fact. One such breeder was Carlos Keller, a private bird keeper and the director of his own facility, the Tropicus Breeding Center. Although Keller did not have Spix's Macaws himself, his connections with aviculturalists and Brazilian bird-keeping circles enabled him in the late 1980s to put together an estimate of the birds held in captivity in the country.

In all, Keller estimated that there were up to fourteen, but more likely eleven, in captivity in Brazil. The five in the São Paulo Zoo were well known. All had been obtained through the confiscation of illegal wild-caught birds, including the two picked up from the raid in Paraguay. The remaining six to nine were with private owners, many of whom preferred not to be identified lest they risk confiscation of their irreplaceable charges.

Several single birds kept at secret locations were in the hands of anonymous keepers. One was kept by a man Keller believed to be a competent breeder who could not locate a mate for his bird. Another was kept by a collector in Piauí. This macaw had been procured directly from the dealer in Petrolina and was thought to be a female. She was not expertly looked after and was being fed rice and bean scraps from the table. Keller had tried to obtain the lone macaw from its wealthy owner so that it could be paired and bred. The man wouldn't part with it, however, and since he was not only wealthy but politically powerful, there was no prospect of an official confiscation. If this bird was going anywhere, Keller thought it likely that it would join the international trade via the bird dealers who knew of its existence and had repeatedly tried to obtain it. Keller felt that their persuasive powers were stronger than his.

Two more birds were in another private São Paulo collection. They were owned by a breeder called Cardoso. Cardoso had the largest collection of parrots in Brazil; his birds were well cared for and he had indicated to Keller that he was interested in joining a captive-breeding program to save the Spix's Macaw. The remaining two were with another successful parrot breeder, Nelson Kawall. He was quite famous among Brazilian bird keepers, not least because of his high-profile sponsorship of a leading brand of birdseed.

Keller had identified several other accomplished aviculturists who could breed Spix's Macaws if they had them. One was Mauricio dos Santos, who had a bird-breeding center in Recife in the northeast. Dos Santos was another self-made businessman with the financial means to purchase birds like Spix's Macaws. His personal wealth was accumulated from a successful haulage business. He was near to the smuggling routes, and Keller had predicted that he would before long acquire Spix's Macaws. In 1988 he did. It was the bird in the Polaroid photo, the last female from the last pair taken from Melância Creek during the Christmas holidays of 1987—the penultimate wild Spix.

During a visit to Brazil in 1983, George Smith claimed to have seen, over the course of what he described as "a leisurely two-day period," twelve Spix's Macaws. All were tame, and he believed they had been taken from wild nests for rearing in captivity. Three were in São Paulo Zoo and the remainder in private hands. The sex of none of them had been determined, and therefore they could not be paired for certain with partners of the opposite sex, and none, in Smith's opinion, was in a suitable breeding aviary. He concluded that "the main, often the sole, incentive for keeping the collection was that all the animals were difficult to obtain and expensive to buy. The marmosets, and the birds, were but objects for ostentatious display." Aside from the motives attributed to the bird keepers by Smith (who had kept one himself), the more significant information was about the numbers held in captivity at that time. Smith claimed twelve compared to Keller's eleven estimated four years later. The estimates made by these two insiders were remarkably close and highlighted just how desperately serious the situation had become.

Scattered across four continents, the remaining Spix's Macaws could not have been more far flung from the little creekside woodlands where they had been brought into being. Unnoticed by the world, they had been caught, transported, and sold to the very point of extinction. Now their future depended on people who had never met one another, who had no common plan to save the species, and who did not even speak the same language or share the same culture. From celebrities and millionaires to heads of state and private bird collectors, the one thing that bound them together was their privilege: All owned the rarest of the rare.

Thus by mid-1987 there were a maximum of twenty-four Spix's Macaws in the world that could possibly be scraped together to take part in a coordinated captive-breeding program. That figure was a top-of-the-range estimate. Scattered across the face of the earth, at least half, and probably the majority, of these were outside Brazil, and as far as the Brazilian government was concerned most were illegally held. Some of those inside Brazil were kept in secret and were also illegal. On top of that, conservationists in Brazil who had spoken out against the trade in Spix's Macaws had received death threats. In that country such intimidation was not taken lightly.

This was the shaky launchpad from which an emergency rescue plan for the world's rarest bird began to take shape.

CHAPTER 8

The Rarest Bird in the World

Even before the final confirmation in 1990 that Spix's Macaw had reached the precipice of extinction in the wild, proposals for a last-minute rescue plan were being frantically discussed by the world's leading conservation agencies. It had been widely recognized since 1986 that the most urgent priority was to set up a proper captive-breeding program. This would act as insurance against the dreadful possibility that this most exquisite of birds could become extinct in the wild.

Breeding wild animals in captivity is not a new idea and this job might have appeared fairly straightforward. People have, after all, bred animals in captivity for thousands of years to provide food, hunt game, companionship, and transport. Others had been bred for ornamental or decorative purposes. During the twentieth century, people had also developed expertise in breeding animals and birds to save them from extinction. By the 1980s there was a growing track record of success and lots of know-how on the best methods available.

The idea of conservation breeding is not to be selective in a genetic sense but inclusive. The retention of genetic diversity is vitally important. Careful plans must be laid to ensure that all of the genetic diversity in small captive populations of endangered creatures is passed through to future generations while simultaneously expanding numbers. To be avoided wherever possible is repeated reproduction between individuals related to one another. The results of such inbreeding can be manifest in a host of genetic disorders that may ultimately lead to extinction of the captive population.

A tool commonly employed to prevent inbreeding while maximizing the potential of the captive population is a studbook. Studbooks record details of who is related to whom, how old each member of the breeding program is, and what their reproductive history has been. The proper recording and use of this kind of information is the very foundation of scientifically conceived conservation breeding programs.

Studbooks were first used during the eighteenth century to render more systematic the selective breeding of domestic stock. There was at the time no understanding of the science of genetics as we know it today, but in order to pass favored traits between generations of animals, breeders realized, it was necessary for proper records to be kept. The first official studbook was the *General Studbook for Thoroughbred Horses* set up in England in 1791. The name is thus derived from the stud, a horse-breeding establishment. More than 130 years later, the first studbook for a wild animal kept in captivity was opened. It was established to save the European Bison.

In 1922 the last wild population of the northern (lowland) subspecies of European Bison (*Bison bonasus bonasus*) was exterminated in Poland. Seven years later, the Caucasus (highland) subspecies

(*Bison bonasus caucasicus*) went the same way. Fearing that the small captive population would disappear, too, a meeting was held at Berlin Zoo to establish a coordinated captive-breeding program. In 1932 a studbook was prepared. In some instances it charted the lineage, and therefore the relatedness between individual animals, back to 1880.

The breeding plan derived from this first studbook for an endangered species worked; the captive population did not die out, bison bred in zoos were released back into the wild, and thriving populations now live at liberty in Poland and the Caucasus. Today the studbook is maintained by Polish scientists based at the Bialowieza National Park in Poland, where the animals were released and once again breed in their natural habitat.

There was a steady increase in the number of conservation studbooks, with a sharp rise during the 1980s and 1990s as more and more species faced the specter of extinction in the wild. The captive populations of rhinos, tigers, bears, gazelles, great apes, and a host of other animals are today carefully monitored through computer programs comparable to latter-day Arks.

The majority of participants in modern conservation studbooks are official zoological associations. Their common purpose, through breeding loans and swaps, sharing of information, and collaboration in reintroduction efforts, is to achieve self-sustaining captive populations and to provide, where necessary, individuals for release back into the wild. This last aim was of vital importance to the Spix's Macaw.

When it came to the captive Spix's Macaws, however, "collaboration" and "sharing of information," let alone birds, were not going to be straightforward. Aside from the legal issues, the birds were expensive collector's items. Most of the known captive birds did not belong to reputable breeding zoos, they belonged to individuals with no institutional responsibilities. Most of them had been bought privately—and mostly illegally—for large sums of money, and were thus jealously guarded prizes, the centerpieces of private collections. There was uncertainty over, for example, who would own the offspring produced as a result of the pairing of birds from different collections. And although most people who had these rarest of parrots said that they wanted to join a breeding program, no one wished to lose sight of his own birds to another breeder, not least because of the intense jealousy, rivalry, and suspicion between them. The collectors were going to be even harder to pair than the parrots. Thus politics threatened to take precedence over genetics.

A debate arose as to whether birds should be seized from their "owners" by the authorities in different countries on the grounds that they had been traded illegally. Some conservationists believed that this would be the only way to gain effective control of any future breeding program. Others disagreed, including the Houston Zoo official Natasha Schischakin, who would later be given control of the Spix's Macaw studbook. She sided with the owners and argued that the seizure of birds would result in legal wrangling that could last for years, thereby wasting yet more precious time during which birds would languish with customs authorities, where they might not be properly cared for and would certainly not breed. In the end moves to seize Spix's Macaws kept or traded against the law were not pursued. Instead of using coercion, the conservation bodies sought cooperation. The decision to pursue a collaborative tone rather than press for the seizure of birds was a very significant watershed.

In 1987 the location of some of the captive birds was quite well known, and Wolfgang Kiessling offered to host a meeting of the owners at Loro Parque in Tenerife. Kiessling paid for fifteen people from all over the world to attend. But despite his efforts, the meeting that took place on August 17 and 18, 1987, lacked some key people. Antonio de Dios was too busy in the Philippines with his trucking business and sales of heavy road-building equipment. Officials from the São Paulo Zoo and Brazil's conservation agencies could not leave the country because of a government-imposed ban on foreign travel by public servants introduced for financial reasons. Walsrode declined the invitation because their curator was transferring an endangered Red-necked Parrot from their German center to the Caribbean. Even the chair of the World Conservation Union's Parrot Specialist Group was forced to cancel at the last moment.

But despite the failure of key people to show up, an agreement was drafted and circulated to the then confirmed owners, who between them had seventeen birds—seven in Brazil and ten outside. Some other birds that were earlier believed to have existed in captivity had not materialized, and still others had died. Any more Spixes, if there were any more Spixes, only existed in rumors.

The Tenerife agreement proposed a so-called Consortium for Propagation to be composed of expert agencies, a representative of the Brazilian government, and those with custody of the birds. The consortium would direct the breeding program to ensure the best pairings of birds. A husbandry guide would be produced, too, with the aim of setting out best practice for keeping and breeding the creatures in captivity. A vital aspect was to determine the sex of those birds where this basic but vital information was lacking. These details, along with what was known about age and genetic relationships between the different birds, would be used to compile a studbook and breeding plan.

Beyond these practical arrangements, there were some very sensitive political issues touched on by the agreement. One concerned the ownership of offspring produced by the breeding program. If, for example, Kiessling and de Dios provided an adult bird each for a pairing that produced three babies, who would own them? Since young birds had been changing hands among other collectors on the black market for upwards of $30,000 apiece, this was a very real issue. Another delicate matter concerned the supply of birds for reintroduction in the wild. Whose birds would be involved, how would they be selected, and how would their recovery program and release be funded?

Since the breeding program was to save an endangered species and was not a commercial arrangement, a clause to prohibit the sale of birds was included: There were to be no financial transactions for bird transfers. Perhaps the most sensitive issue was who ultimately owned the existing birds. An early draft of the agreement said that the birds were owned by Brazil; another said they belonged to their present owners. So polarized were views on this point that nothing was said at all in the final document from Tenerife. Ownership remained an unresolved issue. But since ownership is nine-tenths of the law, there was little the Brazilians could do but insist that the Spix's Macaws were the sovereign property of their country.

Both Kiessling and de Dios signed the agreement, but the Tenerife initiative was soon to lose impetus and stall. The loss of momentum happened mainly because Brazil was not involved—it had in the end turned into a private breeders' initiative only. Without the Brazilian government's authority, the agreement could not be implemented. It was time to change tack.

A second effort was launched in September of the following year, 1988. A new agreement was drafted between the São Paulo Zoo and a couple of the international conservation agencies, and put to the Brazilian government's official forestry department that would be expected to chair the new body. Like the mired Tenerife initiative, the main objective of the accord was to breed the birds in captivity with a view to future reintroduction to the wild.

Compared with the agreement negotiated in the Canary Islands, however, there were some important differences. For a start, this time the Brazilian government's forestry institute, which was responsible for conservation policy, had been involved from the outset. Also the CITES authorities, who would need to approve and support future transfers of birds between countries, were there too. Cooperation would be sought from the owners outside Brazil, but they would be bound by the decisions of the committee.

The agreement was then passed to the meeting of the Parrot Specialist Group[39] that took place the following month in Curitiba in the south of Brazil, and on October 18, 1988, the plan was endorsed by leading conservation experts. But even this was not without incident. A blazing public row broke out between an official from São Paulo Zoo and one of the private Brazilian owners. Each accused the other of poor bird-keeping standards and insisted that the other's birds would be better off with them. This was not the atmosphere of cooperation needed to pluck the Spix's Macaw from the teeth of extinction.

Nigel Collar from ICBP witnessed the outburst. "The argument at Curitiba showed how hard it was doing to be to get the holders to agree to exchange birds. These people had after all paid big money for the rarest parrots in the world. They did it either for personal prestige or because they genuinely believed in conservation or because they wanted to make money out of it. But whichever it was, their sense of collective responsibility was depressingly absent."

Nevertheless, exactly two months later, Brazil's forestry institute officially declared that it would participate in the new working group. This was a major breakthrough, but in the following months there was a radical restructuring of Brazil's environmental agencies.[40] Although this again substantially delayed the start of the recovery plan for the Spix's Macaw, on September 22, 1989, more than two years after the Tenerife meeting, a new law was passed in Brazil. This set out the arrangements for the new body officially established by the Brazilian government. Its legal mandate was simple: Save the Spix's Macaw from extinction.

Despite the initial frustrations and delays, there had been at least one concrete outcome of these early deliberations between Brazil's official bodies. The São Paulo police declared that they would assist in the recovery program as necessary. A directive was circulated to ninety-seven police offices detailing the enforcement actions necessary to help the Spix's Macaw. Although by then all of the known wild Spix's Macaws were assumed captured and the initiative was very much a case of shutting the stable door after the horse had bolted, it did demonstrate growing formal involvement of Brazilian government agencies in the birds' cause, and to that extent it was very welcome.

And the new Brazilian law set up a group of experts, including ornithologists and captive-breeding specialists, who would work alongside government officials and zoo representatives for a limited period to determine the structure and rules for a permanent committee. Under the new law they were given sixty days to complete that job. The temporary committee was also given the utterly unrealistic task of appraising the situation of the species in the wild, establishing an agreed-upon rescue plan for its recovery, and making sure that the birds in São Paulo were finally identified by sex. Paul Roth had spent three years on this first job and failed to reach a firm conclusion, while the question of getting the birds' sex identified had defeated even the most determined efforts. As for sorting out a rescue package without the full participation of the breeders outside Brazil, who were not yet members of the new Brazilian committee, the participants had no chance.

While the Tenerife accord had faltered because it did not include the Brazilian government, the new one was in danger of going nowhere because it had so far excluded the owners of the birds outside Brazil. And the need for a program that could involve everyone was now more urgent than ever. The bureaucratic and diplomatic cogs ground forward with agonizing slowness. Collar remembered that

it took ages, it was like watching rocks form or a glacier flow. There was no sense of urgency, I still can't understand it. We needed a brisk and businesslike approach but instead got a series of painfully long silences punctuated by abrupt invitations to meetings at short notice. The Brazilian authorities were clearly overstretched and underfunded whereas the owners could each in his turn attempt to dictate terms, and were in no hurry whatsoever to act on anyone else's behalf. It was crazy.

Even when things did move more quickly, they did not go according to plan. During the summer of 1989, Loro Parque was making moves to increase its complement of Spix's Macaws from two to four. The proposal was that the single bird held by Walsrode and one of the seven now kept by Antonio de Dios in the Philippines be brought together in Tenerife. This plan would create a new pair from two singles and would increase the chance of breeding. In the case of the Walsrode bird, no money was to change hands. Instead a swap was proposed with a rare Red-necked Parrot that Kiessling had in his collection. The Philippines bird was to go to Tenerife on breeding loan. However, both the World Conservation Union and the London Zoological Society, which were responsible for the approval of official international conservation studbooks, believed that such transfers should not occur in the absence of a proper breeding plan or without the agreement of the Brazilian government. Because there was still no accord that included all the key players and still no person or organization responsible for keeping a proper studbook, these organizations recommended that the transfer be blocked. It was.

While on the one hand the conservationists were, with some good reason, holding things up, on the other they were getting desperate about the lack of progress. Considering the demonstration of national pride from Brazil and its claims of sovereignty over the Spix's Macaw, the lack of effort to breed the birds at São Paulo Zoo was remarkable. American conservationist Don Bruning was the chairman of an international group of parrot experts. He went so far as to write in a letter in early 1989 to the head of São Paulo Zoo that "I believe that it is long past time for the São Paulo Zoo to get a [breeding] facility built, get the birds' sexes, and negotiate with the private owners to set up a cooperative breeding effort. If the São Paulo Zoo is unwilling to do this I believe they should arrange to send the last Spix somewhere else so that a real effort to breed them can be made." Bruning concluded his communication with a desperate plea: "Please help save the Spix Macaw. Time is running out."

Time really was against the Spix's Macaw. Some of the captive birds were getting old. For any of them to be kept alone without a partner was disastrous from the point of view of the species' vital long-term genetic future. Any single one of them dying could remove vital genes held by no others. Should the remaining birds gradually become inbred it might well be the end. There was no guarantee that there would be new wild birds to bolster the gene pool. Every opportunity had to be taken with whatever was available in the various collections.

With a growing sense of urgency now bordering on desperation, further meetings of the informal group established under the new Brazilian law took place. The first discussed again the outstanding matter of determining the sex of the birds in the São Paulo Zoo. Despite this job having been recognized as a priority more than two years earlier in the Tenerife agreement, the Spix's Macaws there were still not known to be males or females. And now, following the death of one in September 1988, only four were left. More depressing still was the fact that the postmortem had revealed that this macaw had died from a congenital heart defect, a possible sign of inbreeding. It was a wild macaw that had been taken from near Curaçá in 1976. It was a gloomy portent of genetic problems—evident when there was a far larger population of wild Spixes. Worse even than this, the four remaining Spix's Macaws at São Paulo Zoo were not reproducing.

Although the science of genetics was developing fast in the late 1980s, it was still usual to determine the sex of captive birds that outwardly showed no difference between males and females through use of a laparoscope. A laparoscope enables trained personnel to look at the internal organs of birds and in so doing to establish whether they have ovaries or testes. Although such a device had been loaned to São Paulo Zoo from the Bronx Zoo in New York, it had been returned to the owners unused. Concerns that the birds might be injured in surgery had led the staff at São Paulo to regard sexing by laparoscope as too risky a procedure to use on such irreplaceable creatures. Instead they wanted the sex of the birds to be determined from genetic material collected from the shafts of plucked feathers.

Following more frustrating delays, it was finally decided that feathers would be collected from the São Paulo Zoo birds and flown to the U.S.A. for analysis. Following the granting of the necessary quarantine and other permits, feathers were collected. Tissue samples had to be delivered to the lab within twenty-four hours for the analysis to work. The feathers made it to the lab in Memphis in under sixteen. The examination of the samples revealed that the two birds seized in Paraguay in 1987 were males, while the other two, which had been confiscated by the authorities in 1976, were a male and a female.

The second informal gathering of the temporary committee took place in October 1989. The idea was to build the vital but still missing bridges between the Brazilian government, international conservation bodies, and the owners of the Spix's Macaws. A meeting was convened in the Swiss city of Lausanne. Located on the shores of Lac Léman, Lausanne is a neat and affluent French-speaking city. Built on the steep bluffs that fringe the long glacial lake, the city affords views over the deep cold body of water to the opposite shore and France. In the distance is the western end of the arc of the high Alps. It was in this opulent setting that the world's governments had gathered to debate and decide on one of the most controversial issues in CITES history. This was not, however, the future of Spix's Macaw, but whether African Elephants (*Loxodonta africana*), mainly because of intensive poaching for their tusks, should be subject to a total trade ban.

Unnoticed by the droves of media who had turned out to cover the fate of the elephants, a select, and in some respects more vital, private gathering had been arranged in a quiet room. It had been convened to discuss the future of an even more endangered species. Representatives of the Brazilian government, senior CITES officials, and leading scientists were present. All of the known foreign owners of Spix's Macaws had been invited too. Wolfgang Kiessling and his new curator at Loro Parque, the American aviculturalist Tony Silva, had turned up. Silva had made several attempts to get bird breeders to rally behind the cause of the Spix's Macaw, not least to improve the reputation of aviculture. Among the ranks of wildlife campaigners milling round the conference center, he in particular looked a little nervous.

Unknown to the others at the meeting, Silva had that month banked checks received in payment for Hyacinth Macaws he'd smuggled into the U.S.A. from South America (see chapter 4, p. 77). Despite these hidden activities, he sat around the table negotiating the recovery of one of the world's rarest birds. Silva's coconspirator, Antonio de Dios, who supplied Red-vented Cockatoos to U.S. buyers, was there as well.

It was a very important moment. In this quiet meeting a deal was struck that would later be the basis of the whole recovery effort. Kiessling, owner of the Tenerife collection, remembered the key to the new agreement: "They promised us that the Brazilian Government would be giving an amnesty if we would collaborate with no movement of birds, no selling, no nothing. We would be allowed to keep our birds and to breed our birds."

Kiessling and de Dios agreed. A deal had been done between the Brazilian government and some of the key foreign owners of Spix's Macaws. A plan to save one of the world's most beautiful birds could now get into full swing.

On July 12 and 13, 1990, in Brasília, just a few days after the ICBP team had found the last wild bird, the inaugural meeting of the Permanent Committee for the Recovery of Spix's Macaw took place. Owners, government officials, scientists, and conservation bodies were at last, and for the first time, around the table together[41] and in a position to thrash out a plan to save the world's rarest bird from impending extinction. But there was a big problem. Although there had earlier been an indication that some twenty-four birds might be available in the global captive population, this first meeting could muster only fifteen. Others had died or simply not materialized.

Of the fifteen, six were inside Brazil. One was in São Paulo with the private breeder Nelson Kawall (he had previously owned two, but one had died). Another was in Recife in the northeast, in the aviaries of Mauricio dos Santos. Four more were in São Paulo Zoo. The rest were scattered around outside: Two were in Tenerife, six in the Philippines, and one in Germany.[42]

With this desperately small number of macaws, the participants resolved to breed the parrots with the ultimate aim of releasing the species back into the wild. A recovery plan would be produced and a studbook established. There was to be research to find out the best way of breeding Spix's Macaws in captivity and details gathered on the best health and nutritional care. Criteria were to be agreed upon for the movement of birds between breeders, and the sex of those still not known was to be determined as soon as possible.

The recovery program received a boost in February 1991 when the Brazilians publicly declared an unprecedented amnesty for owners who had so far not come forward. The announcement was basically an official repeat of what Kiessling and de Dios had been told in the Lausanne meeting more than a year before. The deal was that in return for cooperation with the recovery program, owners would be allowed to retain their birds without fear that Brazil would insist on official confiscation. (The amnesty was open for a limited period and expired in 1996.) Like owners who were already members of the committee, any new participants would need to sign the agreement that set out basic ground rules, including the commitment not to sell birds and to cooperate with the new rescue effort. The amnesty encouraged a potentially crucial new contact from Switzerland.

Dr. Joseph Hämmerli, a medical doctor who lived in the town of Affeltrangen in the east of the country, had been in negotiation with Swiss CITES officials for some months so that he could carefully come into the open confident that he had made all the necessary arrangements to ensure that he could retain possession of his parrots. He claimed to have first obtained Spix's Macaws in 1978 from another Swiss bird collector called Leumann, who had in turn obtained them from the wild the year before. But this was not the whole story.

In September 1986 Hämmerli had taken possession of a couple of baby Spix's Macaws exported illegally from Paraguay. Like those intercepted the following year by Juan Villalba-Macias in Asunción, the birds had been caught in Brazil and taken to the trafficker Koopmann's house. It seems that these two were also taken from the last nest in the Melância Creek and shipped to Koopmann's daughter ready for export to Europe. The same cover had been adopted: It was falsely claimed on the export papers that the birds had been bred in captivity in Asunción Zoo. The papers stated that the parrots were destined for Hämmerli's "zoo," in reality his own private aviaries. By the time Hämmerli declared his ownership of Spix's Macaws after the amnesty offer, he had three of them.

Even though at least some of his birds had been procured illegally, the presence of the additional captive macaws was good; the news of the single Spix's Macaw still found to be living in the wild was a bombshell.

Many of the efforts undertaken since early 1988 had assumed that the species was extinct in the wild. The discovery of the lone bird in the Melância Creek overturned the notion that it had completely disappeared and provided exciting new information about its habitat. Until this point it had been assumed that the Spix's Macaw had a vast range in the interior of Brazil embracing several different habitat types, including buriti palm swamps, cerrado, and dry caatinga. But the evidence collected in the Melância Creek strongly suggested the Spix's Macaw was a specialist inhabitant of the dying gallery woodlands. Any serious reintroduction effort would therefore necessitate actions to save its habitat as well. There was every reason to carry out conservation activities in the gallery forests of the caatinga as well as through the various bird collections.

But what should be done with the last wild Spix? Should it be captured, as suggested by Tony Silva, so that its precious genes might be represented in the captive population, or should the lone bird be left outside to act as a tutor for birds that would be released? On the one hand, trappers might take it, a hawk might finally catch the macaw, or one of the wild cats in the creek might make a meal of it, as might one of the ranch hands. If any of those things happened, the entire species would be placed closer to final extinction—lost completely in the wild and further reduced in numbers. On the other hand, if the wild bird was removed, then what would be the argument for saving the last remnants of its rare woodland habitat? Moreover, what would be the effect on local support for the recovery plan? And what would be the prospects for novice captive-bred birds let out into an alien world where there would be none of their kind to learn from? Captive breeding could take years before there were birds available for release. How long could the last Spix be expected to last?

Experience with other species had already showed how releasing captive-bred mammals and birds was not a straightforward matter. For species like parrots, which learn a lot of their behavior and gain crucial knowledge from their parents and other flock members, the situation would be especially difficult. The last wild Spix knew where to find water in the dry season, it knew which seeds and fruits were good to eat, and it knew where to get them. The macaw knew where the cats and owls hid and from where the hawks were most likely to attack. That last parrot was a vital cultural lifeline, a link between the captive birds and realizing the dream that one day there might be a successful release of macaws to repopulate regenerated and protected gallery woodlands.

This argument finally won the day. In late 1992, more than two years after the discovery of the wild bird, the Recovery Committee decided that it would be best to leave the last macaw out there. In addition, it was agreed to select a bird from the tiny captive population to be released to be his partner. If a wild pair bred successfully, then released captive-raised macaws, learning from a small wild flock, would have a much better chance of contributing to the successful recovery of the Spix's Macaw in its native woodlands. But before one of the irreplaceable captive birds was released, it was absolutely vital to determine for certain the sex of the wild bird.

Female and male Spix's Macaws are identical, but the expedition members who located the lonely blue parrot in the Melância Creek were convinced that it was a male, not least because of the way it had been observed attempting to mate with the *maracana*. But if we were mistaken and the wild bird somehow turned out to be female and another female was released, that would be a disaster. Female macaws of breeding age were precious and rare; risking one of those in a premature and failed pairing attempt with the wild bird would be a catastrophe.

It was decided that one of the captive birds would only be made available if the wild Spix's Macaw's sex was confidently determined. Any attempt to catch it for a surgical examination was ruled out because of the high risk of injury or death. Instead it was decided that DNA would be extracted from a fallen feather. In October 1993, molted plumes were collected by the fieldworkers now permanently stationed in the caatinga from beneath one of the bird's favorite perches in the Melância Creek. The samples were rushed off to the Zoology Department at Oxford University in England, where two molecular biologists had agreed to analyze DNA fragments to determine the bird's sex.

Since the samples were not freshly plucked from a living bird, like those sent to Memphis from São Paulo Zoo a few years earlier, a new technique had to be developed. The groundbreaking preparatory work behind the new test took the researchers eight months to complete. The procedure was based on a method called polymerase chain reaction. This works by multiplying DNA fragments and was thought to be the only viable approach, considering the tiny quantities of genetic material that would be available from a molted feather. The researchers used genetic data from Hyacinth Macaws that had already been compiled by scientists in Cambridge, England, in order to identify likely genetic markers that would work for the Spix's.

A control test was run using feathers from captive birds of known sex. Once this had established that the test worked and was reliable, the molted feathers from the wild bird were examined. Three feathers were available at first, but none of them yielded enough DNA for the scientists to arrive at a confident verdict. The initial results in fact suggested that the bird was female. More feathers were requested so that the test could be repeated. This time the scientists reached a conclusive verdict: The last Spix was indeed male.

The results from the new DNA test had produced a certain result but taken up yet more precious time. It was January 1995 when the final result was sent to Brazil. By then the male bird had been alone for about seven years; it was an astonishing survival story that he had lasted that long. Any day he could be killed, and with his departure would disappear possibly the best chance that remained to save the species. It was vital to release a female into the wild without delay. The right bird would of course need to be female, of the right age, in excellent health, and ideally with the experience of living as an adult in the wild.

Only one bird fit the bill. It was the female held in Recife at the aviaries of Mauricio dos Santos. She had been captured in 1987—she was the last wild male's original partner.

No one knew if it would be possible to reunite a separated pair of parrots in the wild. Would they recognize each other? Could the released bird count on the support and protection of the wild male again? Or would she be perceived as a threat? She would have to be prepared to live on her own and had to be given the chance to relearn and hone her survival skills.

Life in the wild was very different from a caged existence. The released bird would need to fly dozens of kilometers each day in search of food and water. She would need to have the agility and speed to avoid predators and the skills necessary to identify and open wild food items. She had been there before, seven years earlier, but she would need careful preparation and conditioning. The leap in fitness she needed to achieve was equivalent to taking a human couch potato and training her to swim the English Channel or run a marathon.

The Recovery Committee, with funding from the Loro Parque Foundation, had already decided to develop release facilities, and buildings and aviaries had been built at the Melância Creek near to the Concordia farm. Scientists monitoring the last wild bird worked from this base and everything necessary to keep the rare birds on site had been provided for. Living conditions were difficult in this remote place; so were the logistics of keeping captive birds in good condition. Veterinary supplies and food for the macaws had to be kept refrigerated on site—not an easy task in such a hot and remote spot.

Despite these logistical difficulties, two Spix's Macaws were transferred there from dos Santos's aviaries in Recife. One was the female who was to be released; the other her male partner, who had been sent to dos Santos's facilities from São Paulo Zoo in June 1991. He was one of the young males picked up in Asunción and had been moved to pair up with the single female. No breeding had yet taken place, which may have been just as well from a long-term genetic point of view, because he was probably one of her babies, removed from the last nest site in February 1987. In August 1994 these two birds had arrived at the large new release aviary.

Housed in the 20-meter-long concrete, steel, and mesh enclosure fringed with razor wire, the two macaws could feel the heat and dryness of the caatinga. They could hear the sounds of the gallery forest, including the intermittent calls of the wild bird. Large wild fruit trees grew inside the aviary, and it was located so that its inmates could get a good view of the bush and the nearby trees. The captive male was kept in the aviary so that the female wouldn't wander too far while she got used to the idea of being outside. Another potential value of having the male there was that if the wild bird had turned out to be a female, then an acclimatized male would instantly have been available. The DNA test had clearly indicated, however, that he was to remain caged while his companion was released.

The months leading up to the planned release had been spent in assessing the female's readiness for liberty. The researchers who had been monitoring the bird had been delighted at how she had right away taken to wild food, expertly opening the seeds and fruits collected from local trees. After a time she showed a distinct preference for this food over her captive diet. They had also been impressed by her ability to recognize predatory birds that had flown over her enclosure. At the sight of a hawk's silhouette, she would dive for cover. That was exactly the correct response. She had also interacted with the wild male. When the highly strung wild bird had called from the nearby trees, she had replied. By February 1995, with final proof that the wild macaw was a male and the researchers satisfied that the female was fit and ready for release, the last pair of Spix's Macaws was ready to be reunited.

About to take place was one of the most remarkable events in the history of human efforts to conserve the natural world. More than seven years after her capture and seven years of his total isolation, they were about to meet again. Against the odds, the diplomatic, political, and legal intrigue, and the scientific uncertainty, they were about to be back together.

At 7:22 A.M. on March 17, 1995, the door of the release aviary at the Concordia farm was opened.

The female bird took some time to emerge. She had been used to being fed and had come to associate the presence of humans with the provision of a high quality and varied diet. Things would now be very different. After twenty-five minutes she made her first flight back to freedom. She flew a short distance and landed in a tall caraiba tree next to the Melância Creek. She spent some time there before flying back to join her caged companion. Although they had not bred, the two birds evidently had a close relationship and frequently called to one another.

The released bird fed on the fruits of wild trees and soon adapted. The initial signs were good. But what about the wild bird—what would be his reaction? One factor that had haunted the researchers planning the release of the female bird was the possible indifference of the wild male.

In the years since his partner was removed he had developed a relationship with a *maracana*, or possibly several *maracanas* from different flocks that he came across during his long flights over the caatinga. Pair bonds between parrots are very strong and it might be that he would now ignore a Spix's Macaw in favor of the other species. With this in mind, there had been an agonizing debate over whether it would be wise to capture, or even shoot, the *maracana* most closely paired to the male Spix's Macaw lest their relationship unduly interfere with the attempted re-pairing with his old mate. In the end it was thought that if the *maracana* was removed by force, the experience might traumatize or disorient the wild Spix's Macaw and delay or prevent him teaming up with his old partner. Instead nature was allowed to take its course.

The female bird at first flew on a north–south axis through the gallery woodlands, while the male tended to trace an east–west route on his daily foraging trips. But the birds did meet and showed signs that their relationship was being rebuilt. The female soon attained the fitness she needed to keep up with the male and they were seen flying together and interacting. Sometimes the green *maracana* flew with them in a trio. It seemed that a truly remarkable feat had occurred. A wild pair of Spix's Macaws had been established. There was, after all, a chance to cheat the Grim Reaper of extinction. The media went so far as to compare the reunited pair with Adam and Eve.

Not only was there cause for encouragement from the birds in the creek, but moves to generate local support for the program had gathered an effective pace too. The decision taken by the 1990 expedition members—with official Brazilian endorsement—to publish the location of the last wild bird had met with fierce criticism because of the potential to alert trappers to the existence of the last Spix. We knew we were taking that risk but figured that since the species faced such a desperate situation anyway, public attention might make a difference. In any event, the opposite to what the critics feared actually occurred.

The caatinga people strongly identified with their lone blue parrot. Like them he had suffered the tragic loss of family members; he lived on his wits and depended on no one, he was a survivor—the harsh caatinga and greedy trappers had not got the better of him. For all of that he became a local hero.

A year after the discovery of the last bird the mayor of Curaçá had adopted the Spix's Macaw as the symbol for his reelection campaign. At the same time, local church sermons included the struggle of the beleaguered blue bird of the caatinga. The blue parrot was even displayed on a float in the Independence Day parade, where it was a source of national pride and Brazilian identity. The media, politicians, and even the church took up the cause of the last Spix Macaw. In this atmosphere the trappers didn't dare to go near him.

Stickers and posters of the macaw were passed out among local cafés and to truck drivers. A phone number was printed for people to call with information about the bird. The poster slogan read: HAVE YOU SEEN THIS BIRD? Old-fashioned transistor radios scattered through the little houses and television sets in bars had broadcast news of the last bird's plight to even the farthest-flung of the illiterate natives of the caatinga. It was very rarely that the world's gaze alighted here, and the people loved the Spix for bringing attention to their forgotten corner as much as they loved him for what he stood for—resistance, defiance, and determination.

The Recovery Committee and the Brazilian government realized early on that it was vital to build on this local goodwill. The appointment of a Brazilian biologist, Marcos Da-Ré, had in this respect given the bird's prospects a big boost. Da-Ré worked locally and spent his time communicating with the communities living in the area where the last bird was found. Da-Ré initially had the help of Francisco Pontual, one of the Brazilian members of the 1990 ICBP expedition that had found the last bird. The two men used market days when people from isolated farms were gathered together to distribute posters and stickers. They gave talks and visited schools and gradually developed a strong body of local support for the macaw's cause.

Da-Ré and other field staff based at the Concordia facilities also sought to involve the local caatinga people in the recovery work and to support work of benefit to the local community. In addition to educational materials being passed out, a schoolhouse for twenty-two local children was opened with support from the recovery program in February 1995. The little school was located next to the Melância Creek and was involved with the restoration of the bird's habitat by establishing goat- and sheep-proof fences nearby to allow the regeneration of the caraiba trees. It was called the Escola da Ararinha—the school of the little macaw.

In Curaçá the recovery program continued to make its mark. A road sign welcomed visitors to Curaçá, "the town of the Spix's Macaw." In town, in addition to the opening of the Blue Macaw restaurant was the staging of a play about the macaws at the town's dilapidated old theater. With words, music, and colorful (mainly blue) costumes, the play told the story of the Spix's Macaw. Despite the dreadful plight of many local people, the storyline was optimistic. It told of the terrible loneliness of the last macaw, the loss of his loved ones to poachers, and of his choice to pair up with a different species. The players portrayed the return of his long-lost mate and ended with the birth of blue baby Spix's Macaws in the birds' favorite hollow tree in the Melância Creek.

The play was performed at the same time as a meeting in nearby Petrolina involving Wolfgang Kiessling and other members of the Recovery Committee. They saw it during a visit to Curaçá. As a result, the restoration of the little theater became one of the projects supported by the recovery plan. The Loro Parque Foundation provided $50,000 that was matched by the local community with work and materials. In 1996 the restored theater opened in time for its hundredth anniversary. It was given a full refit and a new coat of paint—blue, of course.

More serious than these acts of local cooperation, the Spix's Macaw recovery program had during the early 1990s become involved in relieving a famine caused by one of the most terrible droughts in living memory. Government employees used the name of the Spix's Macaw rescue plan to raise donations of seven tons of basic foodstuffs to be distributed to rural households in the project area. Food was passed out via schools to households in need. This was an important part of the desperate campaign to conserve the world's rarest bird. Trying to save a parrot, no matter how unique or beautiful it was, while people died of hunger was not going to work. Either both causes were linked and pursued together or at least one of them would fail.

The plight of the macaw was not missed nationally in Brazil either; it was, for example, given recognition as the subject of a postage stamp. Outside Brazil, too, the single wild bird became a high-profile figure; so did the cause he stood for. So widespread had his fame become that his struggle even was featured as the subject of an English-language comprehension examination set for schoolchildren in the United Kingdom.

The local educational, cultural, and support work paid off. The Spix's Macaw recovery project had gained strong local backing. It had nurtured exactly the kind of cooperation that would be vital later on, when more birds were released. When that happened, local people would be essential allies in protecting the birds' habitat from goats and their nests from trappers.

The captive-breeding program had made progress during the early 1990s too. In addition to the transfer of the bird from São Paulo Zoo to pair up with the lone (later to be released) female in dos Santos's aviaries in Recife, some other important new pairings had taken place through the new committee. One was to unite the single male bird at Walsrode with the female bird owned by Nelson

Kawall in São Paulo. Both of these birds had been caught from the wild—the male in 1975 and the female in 1982—and were vital for the long-term genetic health of the breeding effort.

Both Hämmerli and de Dios had become desperate for new blood to invigorate their breeding efforts, and they were pressing hard for permission to swap birds with one another. In March 1992 an exchange took place in an attempt to establish new pairs. A captive-bred female was transferred from de Dios's Birds International aviaries to Hämmerli in Switzerland, and in return a captive-bred male was sent to de Dios.

Even though some transfers had not been agreed upon by the Recovery Committee, the movement of birds was now taking place in the open with proper permits and the full knowledge of wildlife and customs authorities. Even the SwissAir magazine included a feature in its March 1992 issue that pictured the beaming Joseph Hämmerli sitting in the business class of a SwissAir 747. He was photographed on the plane in Manila ready to depart with a young female Spix's Macaw sitting on his arm. She was to be paired with one of his wild-caught birds. She and her partner were about to become very important macaws.

Partly as a result of this and other exchanges and the successful breeding methods employed by some of the owners, the population of captive macaws began to gradually rise.

There was now some cause for optimism. A pair had been established in the wild, new pairs were breeding in captivity, and a rescue program was more or less functioning. But the situation was extremely precarious. The Spix's Macaw had only just managed to cling to existence. Its fate was now entirely in the hands of a group of men who happened to own these most unique and precious creatures. The fate of the world's rarest bird was now up to them.

CHAPTER 9

Uncharted Territory

In Fort Lauderdale, Florida, during November 1994 the hurricane season was in full swing. The flat sprawl of Lauderdale's watery cityscape, beset with luxury yachts and visiting ocean liners, had been battered by high winds and squalls, and tornadoes were forecast. In a gleaming metal-and-glass conference center a fierce political storm raged as well. Another CITES conference was in progress, with governments once more locked in bitter dispute. This time their argument was about whether there should be trade controls on mahogany plundered from the Amazon rain forests by logging companies. In the shadows cast by this bitter debate, a separate meeting had once again been arranged in a quiet corner of the conference center. It was convened to discuss progress with the captive-breeding plan of the Spix's Macaw.

Some four years had elapsed since the Recovery Committee was first formed, and remarkably this was the first meeting of a working group set up to make decisions on captive breeding. Until this point the swaps and transfers had been done without overall coordination. The idea had been to organize a get-together of the owners of the birds to evaluate the captive breeding to date and make recommendations for new pairings. A studbook had by now finally been collated. Although Houston Zoo in Texas didn't have any Spix's Macaws, one of its bird specialists, Natasha Schischakin, had put herself forward to do the job of pulling the studbook together and maintaining it.

Schischakin spoke Portuguese, had many contacts in Brazil, held strong views about parrot conservation, and was determined to make an impact on the Spix's Macaw's fortunes. Saving the world's rarest bird guaranteed a place in history—it was certainly one of the most exciting endangered species recovery programs going on anywhere. The information she presented showed that, despite the lack of regular scientific meetings, some transfers had already taken place, and there were some encouraging breeding successes to report, even though progress was soured somewhat by the fact that unauthorized transfers had taken place. Alongside the good news were some serious setbacks.

The captive population had risen to thirty-one, but only eleven were females; this 2:1 male ratio could be yet another sign of inbreeding setting in. On top of that, the previous year had seen the catastrophic deaths of two females. One was a wild-caught bird kept at Loro Parque since 1985; the other belonged to private breeder Nelson Kawall in São Paulo. The second was a particularly serious loss. She was a bird taken from the wild in the early 1980s, but although she had laid eggs, she had never reproduced in captivity. Her genes were now lost to the flock for good. At least the one that died in Tenerife had left one offspring. The loss of these birds had also left two males of breeding age unpaired.

The pair set up at dos Santos's collection in Recife had not bred, and neither had the birds in São Paulo Zoo. At least one pair of Spix's Macaws had been in residence there since 1969, but still no breeding had ever taken place. Other new pairings had been arranged following a buildup of numbers in de Dios's and Hämmerli's aviaries. The Filipino breeder now had eighteen birds—well over half of the world population at that time, including two reproductive pairs—while the Swiss Spix's Macaw population stood at five, with one proven breeding pair among them.

Against this background of only three reproductively active couples (one of which, in the Philippines, was an incestuous liaison comprised of siblings), new matches were recommended by the meeting's participants. The overriding aim was to get more of the macaws producing, especially those that had not yet passed any of their genetic uniqueness on to a new generation. At the same time the new pairings were intended to establish different lineages at the different breeding centers so that one pair of macaws would not in the future swamp the entire population with its genes.

The most urgent proposed transfer was to shift the lone male macaw from Nelson Kawall to a facility where it could be paired with a female bird. This macaw was well traveled, having been caught in the wild and then transferred to Germany. From there it had gone to the Dominican Republic and then back to Brazil. It was now proposed that it be sent to the Philippines.

The pair from São Paulo Zoo were to go to Kiessling's facilities in Tenerife. São Paulo Zoo was in some respects more like a refugee camp than a Noah's Ark. The Brazilian police had seized many of the animals and birds kept there from their owners and smugglers. With cramped facilities and a steady stream of new arrivals, the last thing zoo staff wanted the animals to do was reproduce. As a result there was limited expertise there on breeding techniques, and certainly not the history of conservation breeding of certain North American and European zoos. Some also questioned the quality of the birds' accommodations and general care in São Paulo. It was these considerations that had lain behind Don Bruning's impassioned plea in 1989 that the zoo think seriously of sending its macaws to other facilities.

The São Paulo macaws were the single old female kept there since the mid-1970s and the other male taken in Paraguay in 1987. It was decided to create two new pairs out of these four birds since it was quite possible that they would prove more compatible in a new combination. With these four birds, Kiessling and Tony Silva would redouble their efforts to see if they could do better. The remaining single male from the São Paulo Zoo would go to Switzerland, and a female from the Philippines to dos Santos's facilities in Recife.

The Fort Lauderdale meeting also tried to restart previously failed efforts to map the DNA of the captive birds. This would shed light on which birds in the breeding program were closely related to one another and therefore give clear signals on the best genetic pairings. Such information was crucial to the recovery effort, and an attempt to gather it had first been made in 1991. Consultants were hired in London and tissue samples had been collected. But there had been problems.

Some of the DNA was successfully analyzed and this was helpful, but the results were incomplete and some data was technically deficient. This meant that some transfers of birds had taken place without details on the possible genetic implications of the new pairings. This was potentially very problematic. Not only was there already breeding between relatives in the captive population, but there might have been inbreeding in the wild too. All of the wild-caught birds appeared to have come from two or possibly even only one small population near to Curaçá, and it was quite likely that parrots kept in different parts of the world were in fact close relatives. The gaps and problems with the DNA mapping had to be corrected, and it was resolved that further analysis would have to take place.

O ut in the caatinga six months after the Fort Lauderdale meeting, the newly reestablished wild pair of Spix's Macaws were being closely monitored by research staff based at the field station. These two birds were among the most closely scrutinized living things on earth. Marcos Da-Ré, the Brazilian biologist leading efforts in the creek, had by now spent over three years there. He had carefully noted what the last bird ate, where he went, and what he did. The close observation of first the single wild bird, and now the pair, had shed valuable light on the behavior of the species.

It had been found that the macaws fed from other trees than just the caraibas. These included the fruits of the faveleira tree (*Cnidoscolus phyllacanthus*), pinhão (*Jatropha mollissima*), joazeiro (*Ziziphus joazeiro*), pau-de-colher (*Maytenus rigida*), and braúna (*Melanoxylon* species). These and other food plants are widespread in the region where the last bird lived, thereby suggesting that food availability was probably not a limiting factor for Spix's Macaws, at least in the recent past. The lone macaw varied its diet depending on what was available at different times of the year. There had also been further investigations of other creeks in the region. The researchers had found that the Melância Creek was not just the last place where the macaw still persisted, it was also the only place where such a variety and abundance of trees could be found. It was a truly special place.

Despite the frustrations and drawbacks with the captive breeding, the field researchers were able to report encouraging news from the wild pair. They had been seen courting. The female bird was, after several weeks at liberty, well habituated to her new surroundings and getting along promisingly with the male, even though the little green *maracana* was still in tow most of the time.

The newly released bird had stopped going back to visit her captive companion, who was still kept at the release aviary. She had gone native. It had taken a nail-biting seven weeks for the reunited pair to settle down together, but it looked as though the big gamble had paid off. It was May 1995.

Da-Ré and his colleagues could rely on the locals for help in keeping watch over the birds. Throughout the local creekside woods where the birds flew, the researchers were familiar to the cowboys and farmers and their families. Da-Ré had worked hard to build up good relations with the local people and his efforts had paid off in inspiring support for the project. Over a hundred local families had been recruited. They had become known as Spix's Cowboys. The result was a constant flow of reports of sightings and details on the birds' behavior provided by people only too happy to help with the conservation of their own uniquely special celebrity parrots.

Some of the locals were also employed by the recovery project. One was a local cattle rancher called Jorge de Sousa. Then in his forties, he remembered seeing flocks of ten or more of the blue parrots as a boy. He recalled the bird traffickers coming to catch them but had no idea how rare or valuable they were. When it was explained to him, like many other local people, he wanted to help.

No amount of local goodwill could, however, guarantee success. And when things started to go wrong, they did so spectacularly. First of all, the male began to show more interest in his little green partner. Worse still, the female Spix's Macaw increasingly detached herself from them; and then she disappeared.

A search party of thirty people, including the scientists and many locals, scoured the bush but could find no trace. Her fate was a complete mystery. One theory was that despite her fitness and guile she had been taken by a hawk. Her tail had been slightly shortened by painlessly clipping its tip before release so that she could be easily distinguished from her partner. Some thought that this might have affected her maneuverability. It was also possible that she had made some seasonal movement and would come back. But she didn't. Only years later did her true fate come to light.

A cowboy came forward in 1999 with a story that in June 1995 he had found the dead body of the female macaw beneath some nearby electricity transmission lines. The pylons had been driven through the region quite recently to bring electricity from the huge hydropower works on the river to the poor rural communities. The new lines had been fitted with bright-colored balls to alert flying birds of danger, but there were none in the section where she fell. It was a spot where dead birds were regularly found.

The cowboy decided to keep quiet about what he had witnessed. The attempt to save the Spix's Macaw in the wild had been a symbol of hope and a source of outside interest in one of the world's remotest, poorest, and harshest places. He feared that if he broke the news about the dead bird it would mean the end of the project and yet another blow for the hard-pressed people around Curaçá.

The death of the female not only dented local hopes that outside interest in their forgotten land would continue, but it killed dreams of the establishment of a family of the macaws in the Melância Creek. This was the third adult female lost in a year. There would be no more releases until numbers had been significantly built up in captivity. The male Spix would find himself alone once more, except for his little green *maracana* companion.

The unlikely pair of parrots—the little green one and the bigger

blue one—continued their liaison. The female half of this partnership still dwelt with her own kind for some of the time, and would
be dropped off by her partner at the place where the local *maracana*
flock roosted before he himself retired to spend the night alone on
top of a prickly cactus. He would pick her up again at dawn and
they would fly together during the day to forage for fruits and
seeds. This behavior demonstrated how divided the *maracana* was
in her loyalties.

This was not new. As far back as November 1990, it had been noticed that the last bird was left alone when his *maracana* mate returned to flock with her own kind for the breeding season. At that
time the lone Spix's Macaw was seen defending its old nest hole in
the large caraiba tree that had been a traditional breeding site for
the blue parrots for decades. The *maracanas* tried to breed there but
the Spix's blocked the entrance with its body and cried loudly.
Poignantly, the bird defended the nest site even though he had no
prospect of breeding. His urge to defend the traditional Spix's
Macaw nest site in the old tree had overridden any sense of futility.

But in December 1996 the two birds' relationship took a new
turn. The researchers had noted the parrots' greater activity around
the old Spix's Macaw nest hole, and when the female stayed in, they
suspected eggs had been laid. They found three. With the backing
of the Recovery Committee, the field team decided to remove the
clutch and to replace the eggs with those removed from a nearby
maracana's nest.

It was assumed that the eggs removed from the hybrid nest
would be sterile. But amazingly a close examination by scientists in
São Paulo revealed that one had indeed developed an embryo. This
was the first time that there had ever been a recorded hybridization
between these two species, either in captivity or the wild.

The embryo was 24 millimeters long, a third of which was accounted for by its head. The beak was clearly visible and the wings were well developed with the main dorsal feather tracks present. It was estimated to have been ten or eleven days old. The embryo was later confirmed to contain DNA from a Spix's Macaw—it was indeed a hybrid. But it was a dead hybrid. Perhaps killed off by some fatal genetic defect resulting from the biologically unique union of its parents, it stopped growing in the artificial incubator where it had been placed by the researchers.

This embryo, carrying the genetic inheritance of the Spix's Macaw, was another desperate but doomed attempt at survival. Perhaps comparable to a last human seeking to perpetuate *Homo sapiens* by breeding with a gorilla or chimp, the last wild bird had been forced into a liaison that nature would normally guard against. The stimuli that would lead him to breed with his own kind had now gone—but his will to leave offspring carrying his genes was undiminished. Nature never gives up: No matter what the odds, surrender is not in her vocabulary.

This remarkable turn of events at least demonstrated one thing—that the birds had successfully mated. Even if these eggs had hatched and the babies matured to adults, it would be unlikely that they would reproduce. Most offspring from interspecies breeding are sterile. More important still in the short term was the possibility that hybrid young, if they did hatch and live, would divert the male's attention even more from his own kind. In spite of the dangers, the hybrid nest was still a new opportunity. The recovery effort for the Spix's Macaw really was now in uncharted territory.

If this unique pair of birds could not produce viable or fertile offspring, or in the judgment of the scientists be allowed to risk raising hybrid young, perhaps they could still act as foster parents for pure Spix's Macaw eggs taken from a captive pair. It might even be that they could rear captive-hatched babies placed in their nest.

There was little else that could now be done to reintroduce more birds back into the creekside woods. Using the hybrid pair as foster parents really was a completely untried approach, but the scientists believed it was worth a go.

Marcos Da-Ré had now been replaced at the field station by another Brazilian biologist, Yara de Melo Barros. She would now work closely with the Recovery Committee to try some daring last-chance tactics with the hybrid pair. Having already replaced the hybrid clutch with *maracana* eggs, Barros's first job was to determine whether the two parrots could actually hatch fertile pure-bred eggs and then raise infant parrots. Spix's Macaws' eggs were considered too valuable to risk in the experiment. But if they could hatch other eggs and rear the babies, it would show that they were capable of rearing young Spixes.

It was now almost six years since the last bird had been located and almost nine that he had been alone. Every day that passed was closer to the inevitable moment when he would die and leave the species extinct in the wild. It was vital that this bird bequeath his local knowledge to future generations of the blue parrots. It was seen as essential that he leave some cultural lifeline behind him so that young macaws released later could be integrate into a wild existence. The experiment would show if successive generations of the last wild Spix could be reared in the hybrid couple's nest.

The birds did take to the replacement *maracana* eggs and successfully hatched them out. But once again disaster struck when the young were eaten by predators. The creeks were home to all kinds of hungry animals to whom a couple of succulent young parrots would make a nutritious meal: snakes, hawks, and various predatory mammals. The researchers believed the most likely culprits were either opossums (*Didelphys albiventris*) or little marmoset monkeys (*Callithrix jacchus*). These clever omnivorous creatures inquisitively search every nook and cranny in search of food and make no distinction between the nest of the rarest bird in the world and that of the most common. With the young parrots eaten up by predators, it was all over for that breeding season. The researchers had to wait another year before they could renew their attempts.

The months crept by until it was possible to make another cross-fostering attempt with pure *maracana* eggs in the 1997–8 breeding season. This attempt also met with failure when the eggs were eaten. Whether either member of the hybrid pair would be alive to try again by the next breeding season was anybody's guess. It was difficult to imagine a more precarious lifeline than that which tethered the Spix's Macaw to existence in the Melância Creek.

They did survive, and in the next breeding season the birds made two nesting attempts. The first failed yet again, in December 1998. However, the unique pair of parrots laid another clutch of eggs and a fourth effort was started to get the birds to raise young. The researchers were determined to do all they could to assist. The nesting tree was made predator-proof by fitting a smooth metal collar at the base of the trunk. This would stop the troublesome monkeys and opossums climbing up to the birds' nest hole. Traps were set so that any prospective thieves would be caught even before they got to the tree. And when the hybrid pair's eggs were laid, an additional safeguard was applied. Instead of replacing them as before with *maracana* eggs, they were exchanged for artificial wooden ones. Wooden "eggs" couldn't be eaten but would still stimulate the birds to demonstrate their breeding behavior and maintain their urge to incubate and to be biologically prepared to feed babies at the right time.

In January 1999, after observing a twenty-three-day "incubation" period, the researchers removed the wooden eggs and replaced them with two tiny, newly hatched *maracana* chicks. The pair fed

and nurtured the fragile young macaws, and turned out to be great
parents. They foraged for food in the creek and ground it into paste
for the young birds to eat. They provided water and warmed the
chicks in the chill before dawn. They were clearly capable of bringing up young together. In March a family emerged from the nest
and the foster parents proudly flew in the creek with the two
youngsters in tow. The babies had strongly imprinted on their father and called with a typical Spix's Macaw voice. This was a good
sign, in that it demonstrated how his influence might affect young
Spix's placed in a nest mothered by a *maracana*. Plans were now
made for the ultimate test—the replacement of hybrid eggs with
young Spix's Macaws. But that would have to wait. The next breeding season was a whole year away.

In the meantime, Barros and her colleagues were holding their
breath to see if another daring experiment had worked.

In early 1997 the Loro Parque Foundation donated twenty
young *maracanas* to the Spix's Macaw recovery program. This band
of young parrots had been reared at the breeding center on Tenerife.
The plan put forward by Wolfgang Kiessling and David Waugh, the
new scientific director of the Loro Parque Foundation, was to release the birds bred in aviaries into the wild at the Melância Creek.
It was to be a dry run for the future release of captive-raised Spix's
Macaws. The assumption was that the challenges would be quite
similar in the release of both species but that this bold move should
be tried with the less endangered species first.

But unlike the female Spixes in 1995, the *maracanas* had never
known life in the wild. Some of the twenty birds had not even been
raised by their own parents, but instead by human hand. The hand-
raised *maracanas* had been quite deliberately selected for release, and
the results of such an experiment would be indispensable in planning the coming phases of the recovery plan for the Spix's Macaw,

which would inevitably involve hand-raised—and very probably *only* hand-raised—Spix's Macaws too.

The proposed release of the *maracanas* was initially resisted by the Brazilian researchers, who didn't see this work as a priority. But by early 1997 they had been persuaded, and the parrots were shipped with the necessary CITES permits and other permissions to the aviaries of Mauricio dos Santos in Recife, where he had built a new quarantine block for this purpose. The Loro Parque team and the Recovery Committee believed that dos Santos's center was a suitable quarantine facility. It appeared to be a well-run private collection and employed a veterinarian. It was also believed that the dry warm climate there with daylight hours the same as in the caatinga would help to more quickly acclimatize the birds than if they were sent to the south of Brazil—to São Paulo, for example.

The *maracanas* arrived and were placed in small wire cages so that the initial veterinary checks could be undertaken prior to a planned transfer after thirty days to a larger aviary where the birds could fly and socialize. But things went wrong. Although it had been arranged that a large flight enclosure would be built to house the new arrivals, it was not ready. In the cramped conditions, one of the birds died. Quarantine dragged on for months, during which time the birds' condition deteriorated.

Loro Parque heard what was happening and Kiessling dispatched his vet to investigate. Eight of the birds were found to be in terrible shape. Confined in small cages without stimulation, they had plucked themselves and were suffering from terrible self-inflicted wounds. They were still in the same original wire cages and had been there for months. It was decided to bring the eight birds in worst shape back to Loro Parque for rehabilitation. That these birds had been allowed to deteriorate to this condition was tragic, but at least they weren't Spix's Macaws.

Of the original twenty captive-bred *maracanas* that had arrived in Brazil, one had died and eight had been evacuated; this left eleven. In November 1997 these remaining birds were recuperating in the large adaptation aviary in the Melância Creek, originally built for the female Spix's Macaw released back in 1995. When the birds eventually arrived in the creek, the project scientists were aghast at the severity of the feather plucking and self-mutilation the birds had inflicted on themselves.

Work began on the parrots' recovery from the trauma they had suffered in Recife. The birds gradually settled down and began to adapt to their new circumstances. A release would go ahead as soon as possible. In order to maximize the information that could be gathered from the birds to be set free, they were to be fitted with radio collars so that their daily movements could be followed and their behavior more closely studied.

The intention had been to test the radio collars on the birds prior to release. A particular design was selected following a review of other studies, but the electronic transmitters were shipped to Brazil without having been subject to trials with live parrots, as had been agreed. In June the birds in the release aviary were fitted with the new tracking collars. It was a complete disaster. The *maracanas'* behavior became pathological. Some of the pairs broke up, dominances in the group changed, two of the birds were killed in fights, one by its own partner, and a couple of homosexual pairs formed. On top of it all, they destroyed the expensive collars. It was a failure in every respect.

More delays followed this demoralizing experience while different arrangements were made. A dummy run with alternative tracking equipment in the form of lighter undertail transmitters was carried out in Loro Parque in September 1998. Students working at Kiessling's breeding center tagged six captive birds and found almost no impact on their behavior. The tagged parrots were monitored constantly and found not even to be looking at the new unnatural baggage fitted on their tail plumes. Even though the tail transmitters would very likely only last a maximum of six months compared to the two years of a collar, it was decided to use the lighter, less obtrusive devices. The field researchers would get less information, but it would be more meaningful.

The Loro Parque Foundation bought a supply of the new transmitters and flew them to Brazil. At the release aviary the researchers fitted them to the nine *maracanas* that were left. Once the birds had settled down after being handled, one was set free. A second was released the next day and three more two days after that. It was the first week of December 1998.

The other four were kept in the aviary. Although they had the transmitters mounted, they were to stay there for another month. The idea was to release only one partner from each of the firm pairs that had formed so that the birds already at liberty would stay in the local area. Food, water, and nest boxes had been placed outside to ease the hardships of a wild existence on the newly released birds. The macaws were closely monitored by Barros and her team and, as hoped, they stayed around the aviary. The strategy worked and the other half of the pairs were released in January.

Four weeks later one disappeared. The researchers had no idea where it had gone. A second bird was then lost. This one was found dead, probably killed by a hawk. The transmitter took the field team to where its body lay. The other seven lived.

Yves de Soye, a young German conservationist, had by now replaced David Waugh at Loro Parque. He worked closely with the Brazilian team on the release and follow-up research, and monitored closely how the birds responded to their new lives. Despite some difficulties being weaned to a diet of wild food, the birds eventually adapted to their new lives. Each month the birds moved farther and farther away from the release aviary and started to stay away at night from the release point. So successful was the experiment that immediately after release they made a breeding attempt. In Loro Parque the birds would breed from February or March until July. At Curaçá it was around December to January—the normal nesting season. This demonstrated how they had adapted to local conditions.

Despite being reared in the Canary Islands, some by hand, the captive-bred *maracanas* adapted completely to life in the wild in their native Brazil. The seven survivors lived, thrived, and went native. A successful reintroduction had taken place. This was a breakthrough for the field team. The results from the release and the fostering experiments could now be used to support several possible recovery strategies involving the release of juvenile Spix's Macaws through the hybrid nest or from the aviary.

But time was passing. By October 2000, the last wild male had been out in the creek on his own for about thirteen years. This link in the wild could obviously not be relied on to last forever; each day that he flew safely up the creek the research staff breathed a sigh of relief. Now was the time to try a release of Spix's Macaws from captivity.

Antonio de Dios had agreed at a meeting of the Recovery Committee that took place at Houston Zoo in late 1999 to provide five young Spix's Macaws for release into the galleried woodlands of the Melância Creek. The birds would be carefully selected so as not to jeopardize the genetic base of the captive population. There would be three females and two males. With the wild male, there was the prospect of three pairs at liberty in their natural habitat.

This was more like the size of population needed to begin a recovery in the wild. Meanwhile, the 1990s concluded on a positive note in relation to the captive population also: There were now over sixty captive birds and numbers were steadily increasing. Yves de Soye from the Loro Parque Foundation remembered a feeling of optimism: "The situation we had in September 1999 was good. We had finished the reintroduction pilot experiment, we had established that the hybrid pair had reproductive value, and for the first time ever we had a captive population that was large enough to think about reintroduction."

It was time to change gear. A draft timetable was set out that foresaw the reintroduction taking place at the end of 2000 or in early 2001. This would allow for the necessary permits to be granted, the birds to be quarantined, and preparations to be made for the planned release of a small population of Spix's Macaws back home. It would be the first definite demonstration that a real step back from the precipice of extinction in the wild was achievable.

CHAPTER 10

Betrayal

The fifth of October marks an important anniversary in the history of the caatinga. That was the day in 1897 when government troops of the new Brazilian Republic finally put down the two-year-long rebellion led by the religious leader Antonio Conselheiro.

Conselheiro's movement that rose in the parched and forgotten lands of the northeast was a loose coalition of disaffected bandits, landless peasants, and rebels. They prepared to wage war against the government and the urban civilization of the coast. To the backland peasants, the government was a reason for their poverty and misery and the rebellion was in defense of their right to self-determination and equality. The uprising made its headquarters in Canudos, a remote settlement by the banks of the river Vasa Barris about 150 kilometers southeast of Curaçá. As more and more of the caatinga's people moved there to join the campaign of resistance against the government and the hegemony of the cities, a huge shantytown of more than five thousand houses grew up on the slopes of Mount Favella.[43]

Certainly the inhabitants of this makeshift town would have seen Lear's Macaws. These spectacular parrots still live there today. But perhaps they would have spotted Spix's Macaws too. In those days the Spix's population might have extended along the course of the river Caraiba, a seasonal tributary of the Vasa Barris named after the tall trees that fringed its course.[44]

For two years the rebels ranged over the caatinga from their stronghold, fighting guerrilla actions against the police and army detachments. They plundered ranches and looted and attacked towns. On one occasion many of the inhabitants of Juàzeiro evacuated the town thinking their homes were about to be ransacked by the insurgents.

In early October 1897, after two years of struggle, war, and misery, six thousand federal troops made their final assault on Canudos. The army had laid siege to the fortified town for three months. Despite their advantage of imported Krupp machine guns, in that time they advanced only 100 meters. Weeks of bitter hand-to-hand fighting had taken place among the wood and mud huts in a battle later compared to the monumental struggle for Stalingrad.

But the generals were determined this would be their last advance; there would be no more military humiliation, and there would be no mercy. This time the troops would finish the job.

At the end only two able-bodied men, a boy, and an old man remained. These four souls resisted to the last but, on October 5, federal government bayonets finally silenced them. Canudos never surrendered; it fell. The heroic resistance of the caatinga natives was over.

•   •   •

On October 5 103 years later, in the first year of the new millennium, another symbol of resistance in the caatinga finally succumbed to the overwhelming odds it had contested for so long.

The field team working at the Melância Creek had noticed that during the dry season the single Spix's Macaw would make longer flights in search of food and water, sometimes ranging up to 60 kilometers from his favorite haunt in the creek to find scattered fruit trees. On these longer trips the macaw would vanish from his usual creekside domain for up to two weeks. There had been tense moments in the past when he had disappeared for extended periods. In 1996 it was briefly feared that he was dead, but he had turned up again. In October 2000 it was different.

Despite the local people's continuing vigilance and keen interest in the parrot, no one had seen him since October 5. As time went by, the possibility that he had finally fallen grew and grew. Local people were organized into search parties, and a dragnet operation was launched across the caatinga. Remote farms and houses were visited and everyone encountered by the search parties was interviewed and shown pictures of the precious blue parrot. Posters were displayed that had phone numbers people could call to report any sightings. Days and then weeks went by, but there was no trace, no report of the blue parrot. The research team refused to give up hope.

Although his little green partner was still to be found near their nest hole, it was suggested that he might have paired up with a different *maracana* and taken up residence in another part of the creek. Perhaps he had made some long-distance migration and would return later on. Or maybe he had lost his way on one of his long flights and would reappear when he recovered his bearings. These were desperate hopes.

His disappearance coincided with prospecting activities by a mining company. The ironically named Caraiba Minerals had begun searching in the area for viable ore lodes. The company was cutting trails, drilling boreholes, and digging trenches in the caatinga in search of lead, copper, chrome, cobalt, and diamonds. The resulting disturbance might have made the Spix leave. It might have been a quite different reason. Perhaps the trappers had come back and taken him. Whatever the cause, the fact was that he had gone.

As the weeks without news added up, so did pressure for an official comment on the situation. On December 1, 2000, the Brazilian government agency leading the Spix's Macaw Recovery Committee issued a statement. "World's rarest parrot disappears from the wild," said its headline. The press release was, inevitably by now, downbeat and pessimistic, but it refused to abandon all hope that the bird might even at this late stage resurface somewhere. It didn't. By early 2001, the widely held view was that he was dead.

One unsubstantiated claim was that he had been caught to supply an order placed by a very rich Middle Eastern bird collector. Officials, however, believed that because of the strong local support for the recovery plan, "if the last wild bird disappeared, it is due to natural biological causes and not to trappers." No corpse was ever found.

The last Spix's Macaw had been alone for thirteen years; he had become globally famous as the world's loneliest bird. Grimly clinging to existence through droughts, he had miraculously found enough to eat and drink for every one of the five thousand or so days of his solitude. He had outwitted cunning predators and second-guessed the determined poachers who had repeatedly sought to claim the huge price on his head. There was no more wily a bird than that last macaw. He had become a regional symbol of resistance, surviving in that harsh place against the interfering and uncaring outside world, against those who would take him away, and against the rigors of the testing physical environment.

He had inspired even the tough and independent people of the caatinga, a feat managed by few human leaders. Despite his valiant solitary resistance, like the last rebel at Canudos he had given way to the inevitable. And with this last blue-feathered fighter had gone the world's total knowledge and experience of the Spix's Macaw in the caatinga. He was probably eighteen or nineteen years old. Now the blue parrots had crossed a threshold from which there might well be no return. Spix's Macaw was now destined to be officially categorized as "Extinct in the Wild."

Before our eyes, the most closely observed extinction of a wild species ever to take place had just occurred. But while news bulletins broadcast images of the Afghani Taliban blasting with anti-tank artillery unique thousand-year-old Buddha statues carved into an ancient mountainside, the world heard hardly a murmur about the loss of Spix's fabulous blue macaw. It was one more reminder of the human propensity to regard the destruction of its own creations as tragic and immoral while the annihilation of one of Creation's raises hardly an eyebrow.

Yara Barros, the Brazilian scientist leading the efforts in the Melância Creek at the time, described the bird's loss as "a terrible situation." She was guilty of understatement: it was a disaster. For the first time in hundreds of thousands, and perhaps millions, of years, there were none of the special blue parrots in the hot dry bush.

The implications for the whole recovery effort were calamitous. Only two weeks before the last Spix disappeared, the Brazilian media had reported the news from the Houston meeting that five of the macaws would be shipped from the Philippines to be released to join the single bird in the Melância Creek. Those plans were now torn up. And with the death of the wild parrot, plans to place young Spix's Macaws hatched from a captive pair were irrelevant too. There could be no reintroduction attempt through the hybrid nest either.

More than ever before, any recovery effort for the Spix's Macaw rested with the captive birds. But serious problems were now brewing.

C ompared with the number of captive Spix's Macaws at the time of the Fort Lauderdale meeting in 1994, the population had by 2000 doubled to over sixty. Captive-breeding successes at Hämmerli's aviaries in Switzerland and Antonio de Dios's facilities in the Philippines in particular had lifted the roll call to the point where it had been decided that five birds could be spared for the release attempt agreed to in Houston in September 1999. But although numbers had continued to expand, all was not well among the captive birds.

The population was becoming swamped with offspring from the same few parents. Of the twenty birds held in Hämmerli's aviaries in 1999, at least eleven (and perhaps sixteen) had the same parents. These were an older male bird caught from the wild in 1974 and the young captive-bred female transferred from de Dios on the SwissAir jet from Manila. The uncertainty about the parentage of the other five birds arises from the loss of records available to the author (and indeed the Recovery Committee itself) following the transfer of five birds outside the control of the agreed-upon decision-making structures.

At de Dios's facilities, where there had been a buildup of numbers to twenty-six birds, nineteen were from two pairs. One couple was the original adult birds he had obtained via Singapore. They had hatched twelve young; one of these was the female half of Hämmerli's successful partnership. The second pair (which had produced seven babies) were not only brother and sister but also offspring from de Dios's first pair. Nearly half of the captive population was therefore descended from just six parents, who were in turn mainly related to one another.

Because no one person or institution had been able to gain effective control over most of the birds, some pairings had been negotiated rather than determined by the best genetic information.[45] The fact that the parrots had not been kept in a flock but widely dispersed as single birds or nonbreeding pairs meant that the parrots could not choose their own partners. Thus even when transfers had the best genetic intentions, the birds had sometimes proved incompatible and had not bred. How many more breeding pairs there might have been if they had been kept at a central facility where they could have chosen their own partners (or been paired on the basis of least relatedness between partners) was a matter for speculation. But as time went by, the question of ownership and control of the world's most valuable parrots had become more and more sensitive.

The original deal had stipulated that while owners cooperated with the survival strategy for the species, they could keep their macaws. The moral responsibility (which later became direct pressure) to hand them back to Brazil had always been there but could not, under the agreement signed between the owners and Brazil, be insisted upon. The private owners couldn't lose. They were able to keep their birds (including those procured illegally) and were encouraged to exchange them to avoid inbreeding. Owners were forbidden to sell their macaws, but they didn't mind because they would much rather keep them anyway—at least initially, while they bred them and built up their flocks. In any event, if they really did want to sell their birds, who was going to stop them?

By early 2001, only one owner had formally returned the ownership of his birds to Brazil. This was Wolfgang Kiessling. Although he kept his macaws at Tenerife, formal control of them had been transferred to the government of Brazil in 1997. Despite this act of goodwill on the part of one owner, relationships between the Recovery Committee members began to deteriorate. And it was not just because of the ownership question.

There had always been tension in the committee arising from successful self-made men having to work in a group, which by definition needed to be collaborative and consensual. "These men got to where they are because of the way they operate," said David Waugh of the Loro Parque Foundation, who sat through many meetings and saw just how crucial it was. "They are driven men. For this kind of person compromise and consensus does not always sit comfortably. Some people round the table react badly to these robust types, some others react robustly in response."

The personality clashes were made worse by intense jealousy and personal pride. The owners were openly critical of one another's methods and disliked the sight of success where they had failed, whether in relation to parrot breeding or wider business activities. This further poisoned an already venomous atmosphere.

Another crack had opened in the committee because of Brazilian sensitivity to being dictated to by outside organizations who happened to have both the technical experts and money that they lacked. "We put forward lots of suggestions and technical advice to the Brazilian scientists on how best to handle the field experiments," said Waugh. "But it mostly wasn't done. We got the feeling that there was a distinct element of piqued Brazilian national pride. It got a bit awkward."

Another problem emerged from what was seen by some as Loro Parque's disproportionate influence over the committee. This impression arose from the fact that it had funded nearly all of the fieldwork throughout the 1990s. By 2001, the Loro Parque Foundation had granted over $600,000 in support of the work in the creeks and had devoted considerable efforts to breeding the birds in captivity. Although other funding agencies had contributed too, including the government of Brazil, the Loro Parque Foundation had been by far the most important organization bankrolling the field and community activities. This made the Brazilian government uneasy. They wanted to have control of the funding so that they could determine their own priorities and to avoid any impression that they were subject to influence arising from a financial relationship with one of the owners. But Brazil had not found another benefactor to pay for the program and had thus been forced to rely on Kiessling's Tenerife foundation. This funding support also made some of the other owners uneasy since they felt, correctly or not, that Kiessling was in a strong position to gain special favor.

Because of the money and expertise it had put into the program, Loro Parque and its foundation had, not surprisingly, developed a high public profile in the Spix's Macaw recovery campaign. Among the dozen or so field programs supported by Kiessling's foundation, the Spix's Macaw rescue work was the flagship. The macaw was adopted as the foundation logo and its bulletin was titled *Cyanopsitta*. Intentionally or not, the impression was reinforced in some quarters that Loro Parque was in the driver's seat. This in turn had created tensions, not least between Kiessling and Hämmerli and de Dios, who felt that their sustained efforts in successfully breeding the birds had by comparison gone unrecognized. Worse was to come.

Hämmerli, like the other members of the Recovery Committee who owned Spix's Macaws, had signed a statement promising that he would not sell his birds or transfer them without prior agreement. In 1991 he had gone further and committed himself in a letter to never going outside the requirements of the committee. This promise was in relation to a request he made to a Brazilian official for support in a proposed swap of birds with Antonio de Dios. Hämmerli wrote that "As I will never trade or sell my *Cyanopsittae*, I would exchange with Mr de Dios only under the guidelines of the Committee for the Recovery of the Spix's Macaw." He wrote in another letter to a Brazilian official that "I promise you that I am ready to comply with the Committee for the Recovery of the Spix's Macaw, accepting the Management Plan."

Inbreeding is not only a potential problem in endangered species recovery programs; it can also be a serious handicap for commercial breeders producing birds from a limited breeding stock for sale. Whether Hämmerli's request to make the transfers was at the time for selfish reasons or genuinely intended to help save the species from extinction cannot be known. But whatever his motivation, in 1999 Hämmerli decided to leave the committee, renege on the agreement and his earlier promises, and sell most of his birds to the Swiss businessman Roland Messer.

Messer, a tough and sturdy figure, slightly balding with spectacles, had a long-standing interest in parrots dating from his time as a young man working in Central America. He bought some birds while he was abroad and took them back home with him. He found the trade quite lucrative. From his initial interest, he became a professional exotic wildlife importer. He developed other business interests, too, and by the time he reached his early forties he was a self-made millionaire, having amassed a fortune from property development.

His interest in parrots had not gone away. He yearned to join the club of successful and influential men who owned Spix's Macaws. He had wanted to own the birds for years and had in the past falsely claimed to have them. But now he had a renewed enthusiasm to get hold of some of the exotic blue parrots. Two near-fatal illnesses had made Messer think about his future, and he said that he wanted to make a bigger contribution to the world. Saving Spix's Macaw would be his new life mission.

Messer gained membership of the exclusive Spix's Macaw owners' club in August 1999. He obtained most of Hämmerli's Spix's
Macaws and in so doing appointed himself as one of the people
who would help to keep the species on the right side of survival.
He would do it through breeding the birds at his own aviaries
under his own control. Although on the face of it legal with respect to Swiss law, there was no logic to the transfer of birds from
Hämmerli to Messer in terms of either the future development of
the studbook or Messer's breeding record with macaws. He had little experience in breeding birds, let alone rare ones, was not a
trained nature conservationist or ecologist, and had no experience
in designing or implementing endangered species recovery work.
But he did have the money. He also had a rather unusual track
record with rare parrots.

In November 1993 Messer had been found guilty of ordering the
theft of endangered parrots from another Swiss bird collector. He
paid three Germans a total of 24,000 deutsche marks to make two
separate robbery attempts from the same collection. The initial theft
was of twenty-three parrots, including Hyacinth Macaws and spectacular Palm Cockatoos. The valuable parrots were taken from their
cages and removed in cloth bags. The thieves went back ten days
later to steal the rest. By this time, however, the owner had set up
alarms. The police were called and the Germans were hunted down
with dogs in a nearby wood. The bird burglars were arrested and
right away described to the police the man who had paid them to do
the job. Messer's premises were immediately raided and the stolen
parrots were found and recovered. A Swiss newspaper ran the story
under the headline "Parrot-Gang Caught: Now They Sing." Messer
confessed and was sentenced to nine months in prison and fined.

Hämmerli claimed that he had given the birds to Messer on the
condition that he cooperate fully with the Recovery Committee. But

in reality Hämmerli knew full well that he could no more insist that
Messer cooperate with survival efforts for the species than the
Brazilian government could have required Hämmerli himself to
abide by his earlier promises not to sell his birds. In the end, the
agreement entered into between the owners and the Brazilian state
was really only a "gentlemen's agreement," not hard law, and to that
extent it was unenforceable by Brazil. It was moral leverage only, and
morals were hard to identify in the Hämmerli–Messer transaction.

Certainly Hämmerli didn't give his birds away; he sold them.
Messer paid a total of 340,000 Swiss francs (about $160,000) for fif-
teen Spix's Macaws and a handful of Blue-headed Macaws (Ara
couloni) that Hämmerli insisted were part of the package. Messer
took delivery first of five Spix's Macaws and then of ten more with
the Blue-headed Macaws thrown in. This price was quite low given
world black-market prices for these birds. However, since Hämmerli would have found it extremely difficult to secure the CITES
paperwork necessary for an international sale, he was forced to sell
inside Switzerland.

Hämmerli claimed that he had become frustrated at repeated
offers from bird collectors who wanted to buy Spix's Macaws from
him. He said that a sheikh had offered him $200,000 for a pair of
birds and that when he had declined the offer an additional
$100,000 was put on the table. But according to Messer, Häm-
merli had become depressed by attacks against him in the Swiss
media criticizing him for not doing more to save the species from
extinction.

Neither man mentioned another possible reason for Hämmerli's
wish to dispose of his birds. Shortly before the transfer to Messer,
Hämmerli was investigated by the Swiss customs authorities, who
were interested in the source of Hämmerli's birds so as to establish
whether his original breeding stock had been illegally imported.

No conclusion was reached on that question at the time because details of the birds' history had been lost in the many years since they arrived in Switzerland. According to the Swiss authorities, the difficulties of tracing evidence on the birds' real origin was compounded by the fact that Leumann, the breeder who Hämmerli claimed had supplied him his original birds, died of cancer just as the investigation began.

However, forged export papers prepared in Paraguay and now in my possession confirm that Joseph Hämmerli was the end recipient of birds exported from that country in September 1986. The same wildlife exporter's house in Asunción was the one raided the following March by Villalba-Macias, when two young Spix's Macaws were seized. Whether Swiss customs officers had access to these documents during their investigation is not known. And whether or not all this was the real reason for the sale, Hämmerli put to Messer a take-it-or-leave-it offer to buy the parrots. Messer took it, and handed over the cash necessary for him to buy the privilege of owning and controlling animals that were among the rarest and most precious creatures on earth.

Nor was this the full extent of Hämmerli's betrayal of the Recovery Committee's trust. Simultaneously, he transferred the other five of his twenty birds to another unknown destination. The birds changed hands for undisclosed sums and promptly went underground.

One person who was widely believed to have taken at least some of Hämmerli's five other birds was a Swiss parrot collector called Adolf Indermauer. He was already known to some of the Recovery Committee members. He had turned up at a meeting held in Brazil in 1996. Loro Parque's David Waugh was there too. Waugh remembered how "Hämmerli had suggested that Indermauer should come along and represent both him and de Dios at the meeting. The

Brazilians knew about this curious request, but they hadn't told anyone else."

Indermauer did not make a good impression. "How he behaved caused problems," said Waugh. "He showed pictures of young blue macaws that he had back home in Switzerland, including Lear's Macaws. There were real questions as to whether he had any understanding at all as to what the Committee was about. He seemed to think it was a trading operation and to have seriously misjudged what he should be doing there. He was probably there to help soften up the Committee to the idea that Hämmerli was going to sell some of his birds to other keepers."

Indermauer never attended another committee meeting and later denied that he had received any Spix's Macaws.

Later on, there were different rumors about the fate of these five lost macaws. It was said that birds had turned up in the U.S.A. via Canada. Some thought that these might have been all or some of the five birds that had disappeared from Hämmerli's collection in Switzerland and were rumored to have been smuggled out of Europe on an executive jet. If they were, then they were still outside the control of any coordinated recovery plan and underlined just how very far Spix's Macaw remained from salvation.

Wherever those five unaccounted-for birds went, Roland Messer was very angry that some of the birds he had obtained from Hämmerli turned out not to be the individuals he expected to buy. At the first Recovery Committee meeting he attended in Houston in 1999, he requested that a series of changes to the sexes and birth dates of birds previously held by Hämmerli be made in the official records held on the specimens in captivity. He also wrote to Hämmerli after the sale to say that "two of the fifteen bought Spix Macaws are not the ones mentioned in the certificates." One of the genetically most important birds had gone somewhere else, and therefore outside the reach of the committee. Messer declared in a letter to Hämmerli, "I request an immediate exchange of the wrong birds since this is of great significance for the continued existence of the species and I insist on it!"

Hämmerli replied by suggesting that he and Messer should in future conduct their communications via lawyers. Messer retorted with a reminder to Hämmerli of his past dealings in the birds. Messer wrote, "I would like to draw your attention to the fact that I am the only Swiss National who can prove where and how you bought the two first Spix Macaws." Messer said they were not, as Hämmerli had claimed, from Leumann, but from Paraguay.

Messer at least professed a strong personal conviction to playing his part in saving the species and had been to Recovery Committee meetings. He said, "I know what I have to do in my heart for the Spix's Macaw. I am for these birds one hundred percent. I will never fail these birds." Messer said that he would never sell his birds and that his interest was only in the conservation of Spix's Macaw.

Nevertheless, Messer had his own very strong views about what was the best way forward and had decided early on that he would "go his own way not looking right or left" with the birds that he bought. He believed he had no need to be bound by the demands of committees, governments, or wider recovery efforts. His plan was to breed the birds, cooperating with other owners as necessary, especially Antonio de Dios. The Filipino breeder had male macaws that it was vital for him to put with unpaired females in his group. To this end Messer met with Antonio de Dios and the studbook keeper, Natasha Schischakin, in Switzerland in April 2001. They also met with Swiss CITES officials.

Messer's view was that there should be no reintroduction attempt until there were at least 250 in captivity. Even if there was a proper studbook and effective survival strategy, that would take a long time, if it happened at all. His skepticism about releases was matched by a criticism of the community work at Curaçá. He thought it had been a waste of time and money.

In any event, in April 2001, in a small village on the western plain of Switzerland some 30 kilometers from the capital city of Bern, the world's second largest concentration of Spix's Macaws was housed. Behind the fences and hedges of a typical rural Swiss house was a rank of eight aviaries belonging to Roland Messer. In addition to a couple of pairs of threatened St. Vincent Parrots, these structures contained a quarter of the entire world population of the blue caatinga macaws. Under the gray spring sky in a chill lingering from winter, the exotic parrots looked dramatically out of place. It was hard to imagine a situation more alien or inappropriate for the blue birds of the hot wild thornbush. Their calls battered against the misty stillness. There was no reply.

If these creatures had been pterodactyls or tyrannosaurs or some other prehistoric animal believed to be extinct that had been rediscovered still alive somewhere, such an inappropriate setting would never have been tolerated. They would rightly have been treated as an irreplaceable treasure and the heritage of the world. They would have been guarded and cherished. There would be an international debate about what to do with them. Conservation agencies would send their best experts to look after them and plan their future; governments would invoke international law to ensure they were secure. Detailed plans would be laid and money provided.

But here was a priceless piece in the jigsaw of life on earth, beyond the calculation of any financial value in terms of their replaceability, dropped into the middle of the Swiss countryside with no sense of urgency, no sense of global responsibility or purpose. Seeing such rare birds in these circumstances felt rather like struggling to appreciate the glory of a Van Gogh painting that had been left out in the rain.

Although Messer pledged never to sell his Spix's Macaws, he regarded these rare parrots as his own personal property rather than the sovereign territory of Brazil, the heritage of humankind, or a wild species that must be returned to nature as a matter of moral imperative. He had unilaterally decided that, through the purchase of Hämmerli's macaws, his own back garden would be the front line against the irreversible loss of one of the world's most beautiful and unique creatures. I had the spine-chilling sensation in the still mist that these macaws would never return to their home in the caatinga.

Some of the birds were well and fit. Others appeared listless. One cage had a couple of old birds that looked out of condition with feathers missing. One had a bald head. In 2000, one of Messer's pairs laid three eggs and one young bird was raised. It was different from the adults with the characteristic signs of a young Spix's Macaw: a pale stripe along the length of the upper mandible and white rather than dark blackish gray bare facial skin. It was housed with a single male bird that sat rather forlornly on a shelf. He couldn't perch because his traumatized parents had bitten off his feet while he was a baby in a nest box at Hämmerli's aviaries. The source of such pathological behavior can only be guessed at—but its simplest interpretation must indicate the unnatural conditions faced by such birds in captivity. At least the most recent hatchling had survived. Including the new arrival, by early 2001 Roland Messer had sixteen Spix's Macaws. He hoped that more pairs would soon lay eggs.

The Swiss government took no action that would cause the birds to be returned to Brazilian ownership. Nor did it take steps to require that the people who owned them should join the international efforts to save an endangered species. Following the failure of the Swiss customs' investigation into Hämmerli's birds to reveal any wrongdoing, the official view was that birds born on Swiss territory were legal and aboveboard. Indeed, any legal action from outside would be met with stiff protection of Swiss nationals by the Swiss authorities. The only pressure that could be applied to Messer to save this endangered species was moral. The situation was rather similar to the official Swiss stance adopted toward gold and other treasure deposited in the country by the German Nazis during World War II. There was no political will to do anything: The birds stayed where they were, in the cold damp garden of the property developer.

The Swiss experience demonstrated how individual owners could determine their own "conservation" priorities. If those aims happened to be out of step with those of other key players, even the government of the country to which the birds belonged, then too bad. In this situation the only negotiating currency that counted was birds, especially breeding pairs. Possession really was nine-tenths of the law. Antonio de Dios was about to underline the point.

A few months after the Recovery Committee had met in Houston in 1999 to approve the release of the five Spix's Macaws bred by de Dios in the Philippines, another unauthorized transfer of captive birds took place. Although de Dios had previously pledged himself to be "religiously in compliance with the Spix Committee's program," he now did something that would suggest to an innocent observer that his word had lost out to his wallet. Without the consent of the committee—indeed, without even informing the committee— Antonio de Dios shipped four birds to the aviaries of His Excellency Sheikh Saud bin Mohamed bin Ali Al-Thani at his Al-Wabra Wildlife Centre in Doha, Qatar.

A highly educated member of the royal family of Qatar, the sheikh had completed a degree in international law at Cambridge

University in England and later came to represent his country on matters relating to art, culture, and national heritage. He was also a rare wildlife enthusiast in his own right and had entertained plans of setting up a huge collection of rare animals in Qatar. His brother kept an outstanding collection of gazelles, and the sheikh himself had traveled the world to see endangered species; but his real interest was in birds, especially rare ones. Parrots had become a passion, and as his knowledge grew he became more and more interested in the very rarest.

His attention became focused on blue macaws, and in the late 1990s he took delivery of nine Lear's Macaws. These birds, originally smuggled into Eastern Europe and then dispatched via the Middle East to Singapore, were smuggled into Qatar via Pakistan and Dubai—according to the sheikh—without his knowledge. Along with other rare species seized by the Qatar authorities, they were transferred to the sheikh's private collection, the only place in the country that he regarded as having facilities suitable for housing such creatures. Since no Lear's Macaws had been bred in captivity, it didn't require a lot of imagination to work out from where they ultimately had originated. But he had no intentions to breed Lear's Macaws either, because "they were in good shape in the wild."

Critically endangered Lear's Macaws were one thing, a species believed extinct quite another. In 2000 the sheikh hired a leading parrot expert to make a search for Glaucous Macaws. He said he didn't plan to publish the findings of the work but evidently had his reasons for funding an expedition to check out continuing and persistent rumors that such birds still lived. And his passion didn't stop there; he was also interested in Spix's Macaws. On January 25, 2000 he struck a deal that would ensure he got some of these rarest and most valuable parrots. A transfer agreement was signed that day between the sheikh and de Dios.

Four birds were sent to the sheikh's aviaries in Doha. All were second-generation captive-bred birds: two males hatched in 1993 and two females from 1998. The agreement was heavily slanted toward the conservation of the species and said that the unauthorized transfer was "for the purpose of cooperative captive propagation for the benefit of the species' survival in captivity." Significantly, however, it made no mention of saving the macaws in the wild or of any future attempt to reintroduce the birds to their native woodlands.

The deal was couched in terms of a breeding loan, but there was also a clause that said the sheikh would make a donation to de Dios "in order to shoulder part of the costs connected with the captive propagation of the Spix's Macaw." It was de Dios's view that since he was not allowed to sell his Spix's Macaws (unlike the other rare parrots he bred with great success), the committee was indebted to him for the expenditure he incurred in propagating and keeping the birds at his commercial facilities. The "donation," although not specified in the memorandum, was rumored to be $80,000 per bird.

The sheikh had ample funds to expend on his hobby. At a New York auction a few years earlier he had bought John James Audubon's 1850s *Birds of America* for $5 million. He also had an extensive collection of extinct birds. In addition to the skins of long-vanished parrots, he had bought a stuffed Great Auk and bones of now extinct moa birds that once lived in New Zealand.[46]

On the wall of his luxury central London apartment hangs a picture of the sheikh. The enormous color photograph shows him seated in his sumptuous library of unique leather-bound natural history and bird books. Open on his lap is a rare volume on the birds of Brazil, "the only copy I have ever seen." Flying past his leather chair is a bright blue Spix's Macaw, its flowing plumes conjuring an unsurpassable image of grace. The photo was taken about a year after he took delivery of the birds.

Sheikh Al-Thani's motives for owning these parrots are clearly mixed. In addition to the obvious pleasure he takes from having the very rarest and most exclusive ornithological treasures, he says his "dream is that one day these birds will go back"; but he also quickly adds that this will be "extremely difficult." He sees the problems as not least linked to the Brazilian government's lack of interest and lack of reliability. Declaring that "Brazilian bird protection is a joke," he casually reveals a recent offer made to him of fifty Hyacinth Macaw chicks taken from the wild. Although he laments that Hyacinth Macaws are "well on their way to being extinct," he evidently sees no contradiction between that thought and his personal ownership of the rarest blue macaws. He also showed no sense of irony when he suggested that those smuggling rare parrots should face "the stiffest penalties."

The sheikh's purchase of the four Spixes was different from that made by Roland Messer. Unlike the transfer between owners inside Switzerland, the movement of the birds from the Philippines to Qatar was subject to international wildlife trade controls and required a CITES permit for it to be legal. Staff at the CITES headquarters in Geneva were shown the proposed export permit by the Philippines authorities. The wildlife trade law experts were not happy about it, and they told the Philippines officials why.

Jim Armstrong is a robust Australian who had been involved with CITES for years and knew the treaty inside out. Since 1996 he had worked at the organization's international headquarters in Geneva. He recalled, "We were given a copy of the export permit from the Philippines. Four birds were on the permit. We have not seen the studbook since 1994 so didn't know what the situation was in captivity." One reason why Armstrong and other interested parties had not seen the Spix's Macaw studbook was because it had not been published.[47] This was a breach of international standards for studbooks and created a serious impediment to Armstrong and his team's efforts to uphold international wildlife trade laws. Under CITES rules, captive breeding can't be claimed unless it is clear that the origin of the parental breeding stock was legal. The studbook was vital for understanding which birds were involved and what their legal status was. "Our concern was that the Philippine Government was responding to information provided by the exporter, de Dios," said Armstrong. He asked the Philippines CITES authorities to clarify why they regarded the birds as captive-bred on the export permit given the origin of the parents. "We never received an answer to that," he said.

Another issue concerned the purpose of the transfer. Endangered species protected under CITES rules should not be traded for primarily commercial purposes. Armstrong argued that if de Dios was getting compensated for his troubles by receiving a large sum of money, then the transfer was a commercial transaction. Armstrong took the view that the transfer did not comply with CITES requirements, but the Philippines government issued the permit anyway.

(This transfer was not the only controversial sale that de Dios clinched. By 2000 he had agents working for him to sell his rare Philippines-bred parrots to collectors worldwide. One such sale involved six Hyacinth Macaws transferred to the U.K. in 1998, supposedly for breeding purposes. The British authorities, who understood that the parrots would be put into a captive-breeding program, granted an import licence. They weren't; instead they were split up and sold by a company called Bobs British Bred Birds to individual collectors. When their true fate came to light, they were seized under the U.K.'s Control of Endangered Species Regulations.)

Although there was no legal remedy, not least because Qatar had not signed CITES and was not therefore bound by its provisions, the correspondence between CITES headquarters and the Philippines authorities on the transfer to the sheikh were copied to the Brazilian government. They received all the relevant details in advance of the next meeting of the Recovery Committee that would be held February 19 and 20, 2001, in the capital Brasília. At this meeting the shipment of the macaws to Qatar was to prove a turning point. With the loss of the last Spix and the recent sales, unauthorized by the committee, the atmosphere was very different from the optimistic tone in Houston in September 1999.

The twenty-odd members of the committee and their advisers gathered in a small room at the upscale National Hotel in downtown Brasília, a venue often used for government functions. Seated around a long U-shaped table beneath the harsh glare of striplights, an acrimonious meeting began.

Yves de Soye from the Loro Parque Foundation was there. "Everyone knew it was going to be a crucial meeting. We knew from the start that Antonio de Dios was not participating. He sent a man called Friedrich Janeczek as his representative." Janeczek was a Czech vet living in Germany. He had been acting as Antonio de Dios's representative and had recently offered Philippine-bred Spix's Macaws for sale in the United States and in Europe on de Dios's behalf, a disclosure that further damaged the Filipino breeder's credibility as an honest and committed participant in the recovery effort.

Janeczek put two proposals on the table. The first was that the sheikh, as a new owner, should be invited to join the committee without any conditions. The other was that a new approach be taken toward the captive breeding of Spix's Macaws. This would involve setting up independent breeding centers around the world where competent aviculturists would have full charge of the birds. The idea was that such breeders would cooperate with one another but not be bound by any committee.

The Brazilians exploded. They had not been consulted about the transfer of birds to the sheikh and further relocations would certainly reduce even the limited control they now had. They and most other members believed that the transport of birds to Qatar had violated the agreement de Dios had signed with the Brazilian government. Kiessling argued that if such a proposal were adopted it would allow holders to sell birds to breeding centers of their choice, thereby generating huge financial incentives. His view was that if the committee really was about saving an endangered species rather than operating as a rare parrot laundering service, then surely the studbook would be better run on the basis of central genetic control rather than as a business.

Janeczek persisted. He set out the vision of Antonio de Dios whereby in ten years' time there would be a proposed ten breeding centers around the world with at least four pairs of Spix's Macaws each. Ten times four pairs is eighty birds bred in captivity. The macaws would be supplied to independent owners, who would be granted the right to own the parrots on the strength of criteria set out by the breeders. Janeczek confirmed that de Dios had used his own criteria in selecting the sheikh because he knew the committee wouldn't accept a proposed transfer. Since the value of Spix's Macaws was at least $25,000 to $50,000 per head (possibly more, depending on the buyer's purse), Janeczek's proposal would involve the transfer of at least $2 million worth of parrots—in other words, big business.

De Dios's vision was also said to include the establishment of ten birds in the wild in ten years' time. But all-important matters about what the legal implications of this would be—how the birds would be selected, paid for, released, and monitored—were left unspecified. And it must be stressed that at this stage there was still no agreed-upon plan for the release of the five birds that had been earmarked for return to Brazil back at the Houston meeting in 1999. Certainly, if there was to be a prospect of success from this attempt, then clear plans would be needed for the release methods as well as clear and approved plans for follow-up releases of additional captive-bred birds in future years. (Antonio de Dios was repeatedly contacted by the author and invited to contribute his views and reactions to these points, but did not respond.)

To the dismay of many committee members, the studbook holder, Natasha Schischakin, supported Janeczek and spoke up in favor of the sheikh, agreeing that he should be invited to join the committee without conditions. Schischakin had already been to visit his aviaries in Qatar and showed a video of the royal bird-keeping facilities.

One motive for her efforts on the sheikh's behalf was quite transparent. He was extremely rich and had previously registered an interest in helping the recovery effort. He had, for example, considered buying the land that included the Melância Creek so that it could be properly conserved. There was clearly the possibility that he might bankroll the Recovery Committee and its future projects. This would diminish the Brazilians' reliance on Loro Parque's funding and help secure the alternative sources of financial backing that Schischakin saw as "critical to the independence of the program." Her view was that the "control" over the committee sought by Kiessling had become "an incredibly serious problem" to the extent that the "holders are at a point where they refuse to be in the same room with him." As she saw it, a different source of money could solve that problem. These comments of hers were included in a letter to the head of Houston Zoo in June 2001 in which she responded to other views of the recovery program. (She, too, was repeatedly contacted by the author but would not directly discuss her role in the transfer of birds to Qatar.)

She had all the studbook data and was in a strong position to recommend which birds would make the best genetic choices to ship to the sheikh. The four birds selected were indeed taken on the basis of a detailed kinship evaluation made possible only with the studbook. Schischakin was thus a pivotal figure, with unusually close control of the vital data necessary to run the breeding program. That she was now working behind the scenes to arrange an unauthorized transfer was a big problem. She was also now in direct conflict with Kiessling and his Loro Parque colleagues.

Loro Parque claimed that the role Schischakin had adopted was quite inappropriate. "Her function was meant to be as mediator and coordinator of the captive-breeding working group," said Yves de Soye. "She should be gathering data and presenting it to the Committee so that it can take good decisions. Her job is to provide technical contributions and expertise where needed and leave the political work to the Committee and the Brazilian Government. That is unfortunately not how she has played it."

She in turn implied that the Loro Parque position on the transfer to the sheikh was based on sour grapes because de Dios had refused in 1999 to transfer two of his birds to Loro Parque for public display and educational purposes in exchange for a donation of $50,000. This deal was proposed through official channels in the committee after de Dios had told its members that he expected compensation for his costs in keeping so many Spix's Macaws at his facilities.

Kiessling then pointed out his frustrations at unfulfilled commitments made by the studbook keeper at previous meetings. There was still no published studbook that complied with internationally approved standards. The husbandry guide, seen as essential as long ago as the first Tenerife agreement in 1988—and for which she had accepted responsibility—had not been compiled either. It was thus still the case that none of the experience about breeding the birds in captivity and how to look after them had been collated or published. There was still no vital DNA testing to assess the actual relatedness between the captive birds as the Fort Lauderdale meeting had agreed seven years ago would be done by the studbook holder.

The authorities in London responsible for the approval and coordination of international studbooks say that the lack of information available about the Spix's Macaw is an almost unique situation. Repeated commitments were made by the studbook keeper to supply relevant data but nothing ever materialized over seven years. The Status Survey and Conservation Action Plan for the world's parrots published by leading conservation agencies in 2000 makes the understatement that "coordination among parties has not been entirely transparent."

Other clashes broke out in the Brasília meeting. Messer, for example, argued with Brazilian scientists over the timing and desirability of providing birds for release into the Melância Creek. With raised voices, bad tempers, accusations, and counteraccusations, the meeting deteriorated. The detached scientific discussions that were desperately needed to wrest a critically endangered species from the jaws of extinction did not take place. Instead there was an enormous row.

The day before the meeting started, the Brazilian government had decided that there were two choices: Either come up with some new agreement that addressed the ownership question or dissolve the committee. With Schischakin's endorsement of the transfer of birds from de Dios to Sheikh Al-Thani, the Brazilian government representatives grew furious, and they went for the second option. On February 20, 2001—the second day of the special meeting—the group established with so much pain and effort twelve years before met for the last time. There was no formal revocation of the Brazilian law that established the Recovery Committee, but it was suspended with a view to dissolving or restructuring it later. This body blow, perhaps the death blow, for Spix's Macaw was the result of the disastrous clash of human styles, egos, pride, and vested interests.

For more than a decade the owners of Spix's Macaws had been allowed to keep their parrots on the condition that they collaborate with the Brazilian-led recovery attempt. During that time, their participation had enabled the owners to exchange birds to ensure the genetic strength of their stock. But in the end, the sales of the birds showed that some of the owners were unable to put their own interests and ideas to one side and collaborate as part of a wider rescue team.

The collapse of the committee came at a critical moment. For the first time in ten years, the captive population had declined. With the disappearance of five Swiss-held birds to an unknown location and four more to the sheikh, whose willingness or unwillingness to fully collaborate was still unpredictable, nine had been removed from the sixty-three "controlled" by the committee at the start of 2001. And most of the remaining fifty-four were related to one another. On top of that, only four of these birds were ones taken from the wild. Just four individuals who had felt the heat of the caatinga, tasted wild food, or faced the fear of predation. And at least two—if not all four of these—had departed from their natural home in the creeks as infants.

One of the four was with Messer, an old macaw that could not be expected to live much longer. Another was in Mauricio dos Santos's aviaries in Recife, Brazil. This was one of the two young males seized by the authorities in Paraguay in 1987. The other two were in Tenerife with Kiessling. One was the old original female at São

Paulo caught in 1976; her reproductive abilities would now be in decline. Her partner was the brother of the other male bird taken from the last nest in the Melância Creek in 1987, another offspring of the last pair, who were both now dead. All the others had been bred in captivity.

Juan Villalba-Macias, the TRAFFIC official who seized the baby Spixes in Paraguay back in 1987 and who was one of the people behind early efforts to get the committee going, witnessed the last days of the committee. "All that has happened has been really frustrating," he said. "On top of the extinction of the Spix in the wild is the fact that the majority of the birds in captivity are in the hands of traffickers, for example Messer, people who give priority to money, like de Dios, or 'rare stamp collectors' like Sheikh Al-Thani." He added that it was "A sombre outlook . . . the situation of the species is the chronicle of an extinction foretold."

CHAPTER 11

An Extinction Foretold?

The closed-circuit TV monitor at the Loro Parque Foundation's La Vera breeding facility showed live coverage of a pair of contented Spix's Macaws in their nest box. Pictures were transmitted via a tiny camera in the birds' nest to the screen in the neat little offices next door, where the staff maintained a constant watch. The keepers' dream in the spring of 2001 was that someday soon they would arrive at work to find an egg.

On screen the blue parrots rolled on their backs in the clean straw placed in the nest box. They playfully tussled with one another, hooking their black bills together for a tug of war, pulling each other's long tails, or grappling with their feet while lying there on their sides. The two parrots looked to be in peak condition: They had glossy bright plumage and an alert and sharp disposition. They were evidently happy in one another's company.

The male bird was one of the two baby macaws seized during

the sting operation in Paraguay fourteen years before. His partner had come with him from São Paulo Zoo. She was another wild-caught bird and thus the pair comprised half the wild-caught birds that remained. Despite her age, the couple showed signs that they might procreate.

The aviary was spacious and planted with trees and shrubs, and offered a choice of six different nest boxes in a variety of shapes, sizes, and positions. The parrots were fed a carefully controlled diet and subject to constant scrutiny to ensure that they were in good health. Other macaws, including playful young Hyacinths, croaked and squawked nearby.

The Hyacinths were housed in a mixed flock so as to develop their social skills. One mischievous young individual—perhaps the emotional equivalent of a human teenager—hung by his beak from the tip of the tail of a beautiful big Green-winged Macaw. The angry Green-winged hung from the aviary roof by one foot. He lunged at the young parrot that taunted him, but could not reach him. The Hyacinth croaked in delight as the red and green bird struggled, and failed, to dislodge him.

Another Spix's Macaw sat alone in a separate aviary. If this bird had any inkling of the predicament of her species, there was nothing she could do about it. A few months earlier, in December 2000, one of the four Spix's Macaws then at Loro Parque had died. It was the old male bird from the original pair bought by Wolfgang Kiessling in 1985. A postmortem found that he was infertile, probably because of old age. His younger female partner, however, was a prolific egg layer and had produced seven clutches. None had hatched. Now she had no mate at all. With the simple, natural death of an elderly parrot another bird was left abandoned, the genetic diversity of Spix's Macaw further reduced, and the entire genus of unique birds brought one step closer to complete annihilation. It might have been a quiet death, but the consequences were momentous.

Because of the collapse of the Recovery Committee in February 2001, there would be, for the foreseeable future, no male joining this lone bird. The Loro Parque Foundation requested that the studbook keeper make a recommendation for a new pairing. The relationship between Natasha Schischakin and Loro Parque was, however, now very poor and she did not reply. Since she had failed to arrange crucial pairings of single birds and had contributed to the deep divisions and difficulties that now dogged the Recovery Committee, in September Houston Zoo terminated her role as studbook keeper. But this did not immediately help the Spix's Macaw: the female sat all alone; so did a male bird in Recife, two others in São Paulo, and more in Switzerland with Roland Messer. It would not be until March 2002 that a new studbook keeper was appointed. Brazilian Carlos Bianchi got the job.

Despite Schischakin's departure, the Brazilian authorities tried to press ahead with new pairings of various scattered captive birds. With new transfers being considered by the Brazilians, Roland Messer made a trip to Brasília in October 2001 to meet government officials. The meeting, however, made it clear how setting up new pairings between the different owners was still a highly problematic process. Far from making an unconditional commitment to cooperate, the Swiss collector offered two Spixes to Brazil in return for a pair of critically endangered Lear's Macaws. He also asked what price the Brazilians would be willing to pay to purchase Spixes from the owners.[48] Although on both counts the Brazilians refused to negotiate with what they saw as quite unacceptable proposals, the incident again highlighted the difficulties arising from private owners controlling such rare creatures—even when the owner in question had previously said he would never sell his Spix's Macaws!

Under these circumstances, not only was a proper captive-breeding program further stalled, but the unraveling of the recovery effort by now had led the Loro Parque Foundation to suspend its funding of the work in the creeks. With the last wild bird gone and only very limited Brazilian funding to continue community work in the bird's natural range, contacts between the macaw's wild home and attempts to save the species in captivity were severed. The lowest point in the history of Spix's Macaw had been reached.

The final collapse of the Spix's Macaw recovery program was accompanied by a trade prohibition notice issued by the Brazilian government that restricted any movement of Spix's Macaws except with their permission.[49] Brazil had direct control over only eight birds[50] and the notice put out to other CITES countries would at least stop the parrots moving from where they were. The Brazilians' firmer approach applied not only to Spix's Macaw, but also to another of the country's critically endangered parrots, the Lear's Macaw. From 2000 onward, if any of these birds turned up in international trade without proper paperwork, a swift challenge from Brazil would soon follow, accompanied by a demand that the birds be returned to their native land.[51]

In April and again in May, 2000, the British Customs and Excise authorities raided Harry Sissen, widely known in British avicultural circles for his self-proclaimed success in breeding macaws. An extensive collection of 140 rare parrots that he kept in aviaries on his farm at Northallerton in Yorkshire in the north of England was confiscated. The raids had taken place because the authorities believed that Sissen had bought and illegally imported some Lear's Macaws.

During the 1980s Sissen was the only British parrot keeper believed to have Lear's Macaws. He had obtained them from zoos that had failed to breed them and who had decided to transfer them to private owners. The parrots were old and probably beyond their reproductive time, but because they came from reputable zoos they at least had proper CITES permits and were therefore aboveboard. Sissen kept them openly at his aviaries. It was one of these birds that had been wrongly announced in 1991 to have been a Glaucous Macaw.

However, Sissen's story began to take a darker turn when he woke up one day to find his precious Lear's had been stolen. Not only that, but the thief who took them had apparently tried to blackmail Sissen by selling the birds back to him. Where they went was a mystery. Gutted by the loss of his unique parrots, Sissen set out to replace them.

When he was offered more of the endangered parrots, he jumped at the chance. In 1997 Sissen packed up his car and drove to Yugoslavia to collect two Lear's Macaws. He then drove on to Slovakia, where he purchased six Blue-headed Macaws from a second dealer. He crossed back into the European Union at the Austrian border and from there drove back to the French port of Calais via Germany and Belgium. Sissen made a second trip in 1998, following a similar smuggling route, to obtain a third Lear's Macaw.

To conceal the true origin of the macaws he craved, Sissen created a trail of false documentation to cover his tracks. But his attempt to disguise his activities prompted a lengthy investigation called Operation Palate. This led to the raid in May 2000—one of the most important rare wildlife enforcement efforts ever seen in the U.K.

Sissen's farm was the end point of a smuggling operation that began in the remote northeast of Brazil and took its main route via Eastern Europe. The birds were gram for gram more valuable than heroin, with a pair of them fetching a staggering £50,000. The prosecution lawyer at the trial said that Sissen had a "particular obsession with owning Lear's Macaws."

Macaw expert Carlos Yamashita was flown in from Brazil to testify for the prosecution on the rarity of the macaws and to speak about the threat they faced from trapping. Nigel Collar was called on to outline the rarity of the birds and their status under international law. A third prosecution witness was William Hague, then leader of the Conservative Opposition in Parliament. It happened that Hague was Sissen's local Member of Parliament and that he had been lobbied by the disgruntled parrot breeder following the raid on his premises by Customs and Excise.

In court, the Conservative leader said that he wouldn't make any parrot jokes and asked that the trial be taken seriously. In response the *Sun* newspaper, one of the U.K.'s mass-circulation tabloids, ran a front-page photo montage showing Hague's head on the body of a parrot. The paper compared his political fortunes to the dead parrot in the Monty Python sketch.

Hague contributed to a surreal scene in court where the leader of Her Majesty's Opposition peered over the heads of a pair of stuffed Lear's Macaws removed from Sissen's home by customs officers. Hague said in court that Sissen had admitted to him that he had smuggled three Lear's Macaws into the U.K. from Yugoslavia. His testimony helped to convict Sissen. It was a modest gesture, but still one of the more important contributions to environmental protection that Hague would make in his four years as Opposition leader.

Sissen was found guilty of illegally importing Lear's and Blue-headed Macaws. The trial judge pointed out that Sissen had previous convictions for bird smuggling and described him as "A devious and scheming man who as a result of the verdicts is both a liar and a hypocrite"; he was sentenced to two and a half years in prison and ordered to pay £5,000 costs. Sissen appealed but the case against his conviction was dismissed.

According to the Brazilian authorities, the macaws were sovereign property of their nation. They argued that the birds had been taken from the wild against Brazilian and international law and should go back. At the time of the trial there were very few Lear's Macaws in captivity and very few had been bred in confinement. This meant that Sissen's birds had almost certainly been caught from the wild. The only Lear's Macaws held legally outside Brazil were two at Busch Gardens in Florida. A similar stance successfully secured the return of two other Lear's Macaws seized in Singapore. These were transferred to São Paulo Zoo after a bird smuggler, Kuah Kil Choon, was jailed for trafficking the species in November 2000. This policy of insisting on repatriation was new.[52] The different approach highlighted the extent of Brazilian frustration at negotiating with the "owners" of rare wildlife illegally procured from their country. Also, it once again demonstrated the centrality of the ownership issue in attempts to save the Spix's Macaw.

Moreoever, the question of who owned the birds was not only of great importance for the last Spix's Macaws. It was an example of a new and growing phenomenon—"biopiracy."[53] Modern-day buccaneers seek booty in the form of valuable species stolen from the countries where they evolved. These are replicated and then sold on with no benefit to the nation of origin. The macaws trapped in Brazil, bred overseas, and then traded for large sums were an example of the modern-day biological plunder.[54] Like the captains of pirate vessels marauding the Spanish Main in the seventeenth and eighteenth centuries, the practitioners of this new pillage know that there are fortunes to be made from scarce natural resources. Centuries ago, it was gold; today rare birds are included in the priceless loot.

The fact that the Brazilians could do so little to prevent Spix's Macaws being sold confirmed that they had lost control. It was now too late to implement a policy similar to that now being pursued in respect to Lear's Macaws, and there could be no reliable coordination of the breeding stock. The birds sitting alone in Tenerife, Switzerland, and Brazil demonstrated the defeated position of Spix's Macaw—no one could agree to save the species.

But if control could somehow be achieved, then not only would the prospects for the isolated birds be transformed, so too would the future for an entire species and unique genus. Experience from other parts of the world demonstrated how, even on the edge of extinction, the possibilities were considerable. One unlikely source of inspiration came from the island where the dodo once lived.

By the late twentieth century only a few of the original bird species that were unique to the Indian Ocean island of Mauritius survived: the Mauritius Pink Pigeon (*Nesoenas mayeri*), the Mauritius Kestrel (*Falco punctatus*) and the Echo Parakeet. In common with the Spix's Macaw, these rare birds had been driven by farming and human settlement into a small patch of remaining natural habitat where very low numbers clung on.

Last-ditch efforts to save them were initiated during the 1970s, at the last imaginable moment: By 1974 the kestrel had been reduced to six birds and the pigeon wasn't doing much better. With the support of Gerald Durrell's Jersey Wildlife Preservation Trust, captive-breeding programs were started. The birds were raised in cages where intensive methods of hand-raising were employed. When numbers were built up, releases took place. It worked; both species recovered and reestablished growing wild populations.

Partly because of the intensive effort employed to save the pigeon and kestrel, there was at first little attempt made on behalf of the Echo Parakeet; its numbers continued to fall. By 1988 the total population in the wild was estimated at eight individuals (five of which were males). In captivity there was just a single pair and their two offspring, and the history of captive-breeding attempts that went back to the 1970s had not been impressive. In the early 1990s the World Parrot Trust joined the Jersey team in bolstering assistance to the Mauritian government.

All of the remaining birds lived in Mauritius and belonged to the country. There were no private owners to negotiate with and no far-flung collections to coordinate. Under these circumstances the team trying to save the species could freely use different methods to breed the parrots and get them established in the wild. One of the most important techniques they used was downbrooding. The parakeets generally have two chicks, sometimes even three, but they can rarely raise more than one, especially if the food supply is bad. So the idea was either to take them into captivity to assist with the breeding program or to move a spare chick to another wild nest that was not successful and let the unsuccessful parents raise a chick from another bird.

The team went to straight hand-raising: taking birds from nests, hand-feeding them, and putting them back out again. Reintroduction of captive birds back to the wild began in the late 1990s and involved training young birds to cope with life at liberty. The young parrots were taken up to a big release cage in the forest and kept as tame free-flying parrots. They were trained to recognize nest boxes as home and to take parrot pellets out of hoppers. In this way they would be released with close support for their most important needs—enough food and safe places to lay their eggs and raise young. The birds slowly worked their way back into their natural habitat.

There was also intensive control of the predators introduced centuries before from passing ships. Rats, cats, monkeys, and mongooses that plundered nests and killed the adults were trapped, and the nest boxes and nesting trees fitted with protection measures.

Not only did the rats take eggs from nests but they also stole the birds' food. Black rats lived in the trees and ate a lot of the forest fruit, as did the monkeys. By providing nest sites and sufficient food, controlling disease, predators, and competitors, and releasing birds raised in captivity, by early 2001 the wild population of Echo Parakeets had reached about 120 with twenty more in captivity. The interventions had been a resounding success.

This was not the whole story, however. The forests found by the first Europeans who arrived on the island had nearly gone. As in the Spix's Macaw's creekside woods, there was very little native flora left, and what did remain was in bad shape. This vital natural home of the native birds had been cleared away for farming or damaged and degraded by introduced plants that, like the rats and cats, had aggressively spread over the island. If the birds were to have a long-term future, something had to be done about that as well.

Although captive breeding could not repair habitat destruction and general ecological impoverishment, the buildup of numbers of birds in cages did help. In direct response to the successful breeding and release efforts for the island's endangered birds, the Mauritian government created a national park in the Black River Gorges. The island's authorities also paid for out-of-season sugar cane workers to fence off and weed large blocks of the remaining native forest. The introduced deer and pigs were also kept out so all of the native tree seedlings could regenerate.

The trees that grew in these improved and "renaturalized" patches of forest proved much better for the birds than those in the degraded areas. The wild birds found more fruit. The forest improvement work has been on a trial basis, but having established the principle, it is clear that larger areas of habitat can be restored. In this respect the parrot had given protection to an entire ecosystem and within it a whole host of other endangered species. If this could be achieved on the island of the Dodo, the place where the very symbol of extinction originated, what could be done elsewhere? Could similar treatment be achieved for the endangered gallery forests of the caatinga by putting the Spix's Macaw back there?

It is attractive to think that it could and should be a quite straightforward matter. But ten years of failure suggest otherwise. Despite vast resources and effort devoted to research in the Melância Creek, no details have been published in scientific papers on, for example, the habits of the last bird. Yet such findings will be vital for future reintroduction attempts. Even in 2001 the only map available of the remaining caraiba gallery woodlands was the sketch produced in a few days in 1990 by the ICBP team. And there was still no official protection for the woodlands and no long-term plan to combat the ecological damage caused by excessive grazing. IBAMA (Instituto Brasileiro do Meio Ambiente e dos Recursos Naturais Renováveis) initially signed an agreement with the local landowner (the owner of the Concordia farm), but this expired after five years. A proposal to purchase the most important areas was drafted in that period but had not been acted upon as of 2001. Some fencing of important areas of woodland took place, but there is still no long-term plan to combat grazing pressure and its effects on the Spix's Macaw's unique habitat.

If the macaw's habitat were restored, and it is certainly straightforward to do that, other challenges would exist. Reintroduction is one thing with parrots like the surviving species on Mauritius, where there were at least a few wild individuals to help captive-bred individuals back to a natural existence. What happens when, like the Spix's Macaw, the species has become extinct in the wild? Many feared in the case of the Spix that once the precious last bird was finally lost, all hope of reintroducing the species would be lost with him. But again, experience from other parts of the world shows that such a terminal outcome is not inevitable.

The California Condor (*Gymnogyps californianus*) was lost from the wild for a time but has now been successfully reintroduced following a carefully planned captive-breeding program undertaken by the San Diego Zoo. Baby birds were famously raised by keepers using glove puppets in the shape of an adult condor's head. In this way it was hoped that more of their natural wild instincts would be preserved.

Another remarkable example of an animal coming back to the wild from captivity is Przewalski's Horse (*Equus przewalski*). This diminutive ancestor of the domestic horse with its pale brown coat and stiff brushlike brown mane was once widespread. Cave paintings from France, for example, show that animals similar to these lived in Western Europe around 10,000 years ago. The last known population of wild horses was finally finished off in Central Asia during the 1960s. The last ones were sighted at the end of that decade in southwest Mongolia. Their end came from habitat loss, crossbreeding with domestic horses and persecution from herdsmen who saw them as competition for the grass and water that their animals needed. Fortunately, before their total demise, a few had been taken into captivity.

From a founding population of thirteen animals plucked from the wild at the start of the twentieth century, zoos and private collections built up by 1977 a population of some 300. In that year the Foundation Reserves for the Przewalski Horse was founded in the Netherlands with the sole aim of returning the species to the wild. But the steppe habitat once favored by the horses was severely degraded by grazing and cultivation and, like the caatinga, was in a very poor condition. Researchers did, however, find a small area of steppe in a more natural state at Hustain Nuruu in Mongolia. The area was designated as a national park and herdsmen were gradually encouraged to use alternative areas.

During the 1990s, several shipments of the horses were made back to Mongolia. The public greeted the return of their long-lost animals with the kind of celebration normally reserved for a football team coming home with the World Cup. The animals were transported to acclimatization pens at the release area where they could learn to cope with the harsh climate and form the new social units they would need to survive in the wild. Following a blessing from a Buddhist monk and ceremonial offerings from herdsmen, the gates were opened. The first unfettered steps, after more than sixty years of a wholly captive existence, were taken. Following thirteen generations in captivity, none of the horses had experienced anything resembling a wild existence. None of them had even been to Asia before. What would be their reaction to an attack by wolves?

Rangers following the released animals were amazed when on being approached by a small pack of the calculating predators the horses adopted a collective behavior pattern not seen in their species for decades. The mares formed a tight circle inside which the pregnant animals, yearlings, and foals gathered. The stallion went out to approach the wolves as if to attack them. The wolves, themselves recognizing an ancient defensive maneuver, withdrew. The horses' natural instincts had survived intact.

They bred in the wild and their numbers increased. And as was the case with the rare birds on Mauritius, the victory was not only for the charismatic rare animals that had been raised in captivity. The new national park protected a rare fragment of ancient steppe that was home to other plants and animals whose fortunes were lifted by the return of the horses.

Not only do cases like that of the wild Asian horse give grounds for optimism for Spix's Macaw, the research work carried out during the late 1990s with the last wild bird and his *maracana* mate showed how there might be other effective approaches to getting birds back into the wild. Future recovery work could involve the release of eggs or baby Spix's Macaws via wild *maracana* nests. Perhaps better than this would be the release of juvenile birds directly back into the wild, as was in the end successfully achieved with the radio-tagged *maracanas* set free during 1999 in the Melância Creek. This might be more difficult in terms of getting birds used to a wild diet and so on, but would avoid the danger that their unique Spix's Macaw identity would be lost through being raised by the "wrong" parents.

Assuming the captive-breeding and release challenges are not insurmountable, what about the problems of inbreeding? Several experts say that even in the face of this very real danger there is room for hope. The world's leading authority on endangered birds is one of them.

Nigel Collar points out that even though the number in captivity is not large and that all of the existing Spix's Macaws could all be members of one family, "there is still a good chance that it can be pulled through." He fully recognizes the threat posed by inbreeding, but he qualifies it. "Then again, all the golden hamsters in the world come from one single family. Every single golden hamster that you can lay your hands on has ultimately come from three siblings taken from a wild nest; two brothers and a sister."

The Golden Hamster (*Mesocricetus auratus*) has multiplied from the tiny original nucleus taken from the wild in Syria in 1930 to build a world population today of many millions. It demonstrates how some species can become highly inbred and remain totally healthy. For some animals it seems that low genetic diversity does not matter. "Spix's Macaw might be one such species, or it might not. But there is nothing to be gained by assuming the worst," says

Collar. Instead, Collar argues, what is urgently needed is a detailed genetic analysis of every captive bird in order to determine the best possible combinations to minimize unnecessary inbreeding. That job was seen as a priority for the studbook keeper back in 1994.

If the inbreeding proves not to be fatal and successful releases can be achieved, it will be vital that the local people who live in the area where the Spix's Macaw once lived continue to support attempts to save the species. Westerners sometimes gain the mistaken impression that people in poor countries don't care about the environment. They often do, and if their support can be gained, then the prospects of endangered species recovery plans can be quite transformed.

One man who knows all about that is Paul Butler. He arrived on St. Lucia in the Windward Islands in 1978. He had read that the spectacular Amazon parrot that lived there was doomed and had gone there to help save it. He soon gained firsthand experience of just how serious the bird's plight had become. He conducted a survey and found that there were only about 100 left. Much of the parrot's habitat had been cleared away and the birds were being shot for food. On top of that, a few were being taken into captivity.

He discovered that apart from seeing it as a source of food, almost no one on the island knew anything about the parrot, and certainly not that it was unique to their country. His idea was to engage people and inspire them to support the protection of the island's special endangered bird. He used music, religion, puppet shows, and other popular cultural events. He also linked saving the parrot to people's daily lives. He showed them that protecting the forest was of benefit to them as well as the parrot.

It worked. The St. Lucia Amazon Parrot (*Amazona versicolor*) was adopted as the national bird. New legislation to protect the birds followed. Hunting was outlawed, land was protected, and the maximum penalty for taking one of the parrots rose from a fine of 48 East Caribbean dollars (about U.S. $15) to one year of hard labor. A forest trail later opened in the new park set aside for the parrot raised more than a million dollars (U.S.) from tourists in less than four years. Saving the parrot made sense; more important, the people could see that it did. The combination of national pride and self-interest did the trick. Numbers recovered, and by 2000 there were more than 500 of the birds in the forest. Flocks of up to twenty were regularly seen—an unthinkable sight twenty years before.

In 1988 Butler went to St. Vincent to help the rare parrot that lived there. His public awareness campaign quickly paid off; it led to new protected areas and legislation. Butler then island-hopped once more, this time to Dominica, where the two rare parrots there were rapidly disappearing. Among other remarkable feats, Butler got 80 percent of Dominica's schoolchildren to sign a petition calling for the birds to be saved. Many of them also gave the small token sum of 10 cents to aid the bird. In a very poor country even this tiny amount was important. People literally bought into saving their very own special rare parrots. And the people who had bought in were very important people—they were the next generation who twenty and thirty years hence would be farmers, government ministers, and hotel operators. If they cared, then the bird would live.

Again it worked. The parrots on St. Vincent and Dominica bottomed out after hundreds of years of decline and began to recover. Today their numbers continue to rise as they head out of immediate danger. For these little island nations, the great gorgeous parrots of the rain forests are among their most precious national treasures. And anyone interfering with them can expect to feel the full force of the law.

Training local people in conservation skills was a crucial component of both Butler's work and the campaign to save the Echo Parakeet. Getting local people to the point where they can do the work themselves is a key long-term investment. Certainly this should be an important part of any future plan to bring the Spix's Macaw back to the creeks. And if the macaws can come back, then the prospects for other disappearing species in the caatinga will brighten too. So will the lives of the poor and marginalized people who live there. Indeed, if their lot doesn't improve, then the long-term diagnosis for the macaw will not either.

In some respects, though, the practical challenges posed by the remoteness of the Spix's Macaw's natural habitat and that it is extinct in the wild is the least problematic set of issues. Conserving the bird's unique gallery forest, overcoming the fact that there are none left to tutor captive birds back into the wild, and dealing with the genetic dangers are nothing compared to the lethal cocktail of egos, jealousy, law-breaking, suspicion, politicking, and greed that has all but wiped them out.

While no one person is properly entrusted to direct a scientifically sound recovery effort, and while political difficulties dominate the survival strategy, the chances for the bird's return are slim indeed. The law has proved insufficient to regain effective control of foreign-held Spix's Macaws. In this situation the only other means is persuasion.

Nigel Collar is among several who have tried that approach:

> In 1988 I stood up at the international parrot meeting in Brazil and said that if the holders of the Spix's Macaws do not cooperate in order to save the species then they will go down in history as the people who brought about its extinction. What I said then still applies. If this fabulous bird becomes extinct, their names will be written forever in conservation's book of shame.

If you have something as beautiful as a Spix's Macaw, the

thing itself deserves to be conserved and to be looked after. It's the same as taking a van Gogh and burning it—however many van Goghs you have left, everyone would be outraged at the very idea. They would see that act as part of a diminution of the world's riches.

But whether moral concerns about extinctions or pleas for selfless cooperation will be sufficient incentive for the owners of the world's rarest bird to collaborate is an open question.

Collar has devoted his working life to stemming the tide that is sweeping hundreds of endangered bird species toward the final abyss of extinction. He says that the main lesson to be learned from the desperate straits now faced by the Spix's Macaw is that in the future critically endangered birds should never be allowed to get into this situation in the first place. "There should have been zero tolerance shown to those trapping and trading the birds and every effort made to protect the last remnant population in the wild."

Leading conservationists almost speak as one on what now needs to be done. The best way forward would be to establish a top-quality breeding station in Brazil—preferably in the Spix's Macaw's natural range in the northeast. From such a center attempts could be made to reintroduce birds back into the wild using the same "soft release" techniques that have been used elsewhere. Such a program should be under Brazilian control but with the support of the best experts, no matter where they come from. Arrangements should be made to train Brazilians so that the whole effort might ultimately be handed back to the country. The rescue attempt would, of course, need to be supplied with birds passed back to Brazil from the present owners. With the correct approach Spix's Macaw can still be saved. The fact that several other endangered parrot species have come back from the brink proves it.

Even now—even after the extinction of Spix's Macaw in the wild—it could still work. It would need the best scientists who have succeeded elsewhere. It would need the best parrot breeders the world has to offer. It would need some money, courage, and above all, someone to lead the effort who can inspire trust from the many interests involved and who is able to chart a course through the politics and bureaucracy that go with most conservation projects. Such people do exist and would be willing to go to the caatinga to help save this most charismatic of endangered species.

It will also depend on the people who are obsessed with owning blue macaws. The men who have so consistently and ruthlessly sought to cage and control these creatures have between them ultimately destroyed the object of their desires. Although it appears this was not their intention, it has nonetheless been the result.

To blame all of the ills of Spix's Macaw on the few people who happen to own the last ones would, however, be too easy. Returning Spix's Macaws to the wild will depend on the wild still being there. It is now quite clear that if there is to be a long-term resolution between the needs of endangered species and those of the world's fast-growing human population, then the rest of us must appreciate our own contribution to the final ravaging of this planet's natural riches that is now taking place. Cheap gasoline, meat, metals, paper, wood, sugar, coffee, and the rest of the seemingly endless flow of commodities that those of us lucky enough to live in developed countries use and waste with such abandon come at an ecological cost rarely reflected in the prices we pay. Footing the bill for our growing demands are the earth's last remote ecosystems and most beautiful species. There can be a different way, but we are very far from embarking on it.

Looking several decades ahead, many possible futures for this spectacular bird can be foreseen. In one there's a thriving creek with young trees regenerating in the shade of the majestic old caraibas; a growing wild population of Spix's Macaws flies among them. The local people are enthusiastic collaborators in bringing the birds back to the creeks, they are helping the conservationists in regenerating the woodlands and making sure trappers do not return. Another future shows a single aging bird sitting alone in a cage in the collection of a rich bird collector, many thousands of miles from the creeks—the last of his kind—like Incas, the last Carolina Parakeet, soon to die of grief.

On July 7, 2001, the pair of macaws in the nest box at Loro Parque laid an egg. Another followed on the tenth. It was a triumph for the dedicated staff in the breeding facility whose patience and persistent husbandry had finally paid off, but was also a bitter disappointment. It transpired that the male bird, one of the youngsters seized in Paraguay in 1987, was infertile and the eggs contained no embryos.

Even this blow does not, however, mark the end of the story. That remains to be written. Will this exquisite blue bird yet rise as a phoenix of inspiration in the wider struggle to save the world's beautiful and endangered species and ecosystems or will it disappear as another tragic casualty of human indifference and greed? That remains to be seen. The means to save Spix's blue macaw are still available. Whether they will be deployed in time to avert the imminent extinction of this superb blue parrot will, like the extinction of the Dodo, be an important and historic landmark in people's relationship with the living world around us.

Spix and Martius did not know that their trek through the hot caatinga in 1819 would produce the dried blue corpse that would for decades be the world's only clue that this beautiful blue creature existed. Today we are on the verge of returning to a time when the only physical evidence that the fabulous blue caatinga parrots ever lived will once more be dried blue corpses. The fate of the blue parrots still hangs in the balance, as does the future of other countless species whose survival depends on human cooperation, foresight, and generosity.

Epilogue

In September 2002 I was in the luxurious surroundings of a casino in Tenerife to present the story of Spix's Macaw to an audience of 850 parrot specialists and enthusiasts from all over the world. There were parrot owners and collectors, leading avian vets, field scientists, and suppliers of parrot merchandise ranging from paintings to seed and from books to incubators. It was like a trade fair for parrots. This curious cross section of global society had gathered at the casino for the V International Parrot Convention organized by Loro Parque.

The participants had come to hear expert speakers, to learn of each other's parrot experiences, and to generally share their passion for these most wonderful and sought-after birds.

On the morning of my speech, coffee was being served on the lush green lawns that lay around the casino grounds. The great high peak of El Tiede, the island's volcano, was beautifully bathed in late summer sunshine and the vast blue Atlantic Ocean sparkled peacefully. Spix and Martius had passed by Tenerife en route to Brazil. I wondered if from this vantage point it would have been possible to spot their two ships; I idly imagined what the early nineteenth-century explorers would have made of the convention.

The participants wandered inside for the meeting to reconvene. My contribution to the convention was essentially a summary of the story you have just read, and the occasion marked the official launch of Spix's Macaw. On taking the podium, and before beginning my forty-five-minute canter through the saga of this rarest of rare parrots, I warned the participants that at the end of my presentation I would ask them a question. I would ask them to vote on a simple proposition: Should the sixty to seventy Spix's Macaws now scattered across the globe in various private collections be returned to the custody of the government of Brazil?

There would be three voting options: yes, no, or abstain. I had hatched the idea of the vote only a few moments before delivering my speech. My thinking was that it would be a very helpful barometer of opinion about the future fate of Spix's Macaw from a key constituency of people—helpful, that is, if it went the right way. I was far from certain as to what the outcome of this poll might be, but the casino seemed an ideal place for such a gamble.

Natasha Schischakin was there, as were Wolfgang Kiessling and his Loro Parque colleagues Yves de Soye and David Waugh, the latter having just moved there from Scotland where he was the Director of Edinburgh Zoo. Harry Sissen had turned up, so had Tony Pittman. Nigel Collar was present, so was Rosemary Low. Iolita Bampi, the Brazilian official who had for years coordinated the Brazilian-led committee on behalf of IBAMA, was there as well. She had arrived not only to join the conference but to take personal charge of the unpaired female Spix's Macaw that was at Loro Parque. This bird would finally be going home with Iolita to be paired with a lone male at the facilities of Mauricio dos Santos in the northeast of Brazil. The cast of characters was most fitting for the occasion.

I was especially pleased that Iolita was there. I hoped to find out more about the momentous decision made by the Brazilian government in July 2002, just as *Spix's Macaw* was first going to press. This decision was to permanently terminate the official recovery committee. Following the meltdown at the meeting in Brasília in February 2000 (because of the unauthorized sale of birds by Antonio de Dios to Sheikh Al-Thani), the Brazilians had considered various options for restructuring the recovery effort. They had circulated proposals to the various owners on possible ways forward. With the exception of Loro Parque, the owners did not even reply (such is their contempt for Brazilian claims over birds stolen from that country and now in their custody).

The lack of cooperation from the various keepers of the last Spix's Macaws in Switzerland, the Philippines, and Qatar had finally convinced the Brazilians that a different and harder line was needed. This decisive point in the fortunes of Spix's Macaw had been accompanied by a call from Brazil that the birds in private hands be returned to them. At least one government had responded: Switzerland, essentially to say that birds in that country were legal and that Brazil had no right to insist on their return. That morning in the casino appeared to be the ideal moment to see if Brazil's new and controversial proposal was supported by a major cross section of the world's parrot-keeping elite, if not by key governments or the nominal "owners" of the macaws.

Many people at the parrot convention in Tenerife quite correctly asked if there was the capacity inside Brazil to properly care for such rare birds, breed them, and manage a successful reintroduction attempt. After all, São Paulo Zoo had never bred them and official monies available for conservation in Brazil were always insufficient. It was clear that any program undertaken by the Brazilians would need considerable external assistance. Whether this would be forthcoming remained to be seen. In the absence of an answer to that question, and as I drew my presentation in the casino to a close, I prepared to conduct the vote from the podium.

I asked the convention participants first of all how many of them believed that the Brazilian policy of taking control of the birds themselves was the correct way forward. About six hundred hands were raised. I then asked who believed the birds should stay where they were, in the various private collections. A handful of hard-core parrot collectors and dealers signaled their support. A few more said they didn't know or abstained.

It was an overwhelming endorsement from the parrot world for Brazil's new approach. But whether signals like this would sufficiently isolate or exert pressure on those with birds in their custody to hand them back was a quite different matter. One unrepentant figure was Harry Sissen.

As the meeting closed and the participants dispersed, he followed me into the grounds of the casino and berated me for what he saw as my incomplete understanding of the issues and harangued me for what he had evidently received from my lecture as an attack on private parrot keepers. He told me how he believed the Brazilians could never pull off a proper conservation program and how birds like Lear's Macaws were better off with breeders like him. If they were left out in the wild, they would be shot or trapped and their forests were being destroyed anyway, he said.

Harry had recently been released from prison, where he had served time for illegally importing critically endangered Lear's Macaws to the U.K. As we heatedly exchanged views, he set out some large sheets of paper on a low wall for me to look at. I found myself contemplating the most exquisite drawings of Lear's Macaws I had ever seen. Harry had used his time in captivity to create images of his beloved macaws for posterity. In pencil, beautifully detailed, expressive of the bird's unique character and in gorgeous proportion. As he talked me through the pictures, tears welled up in his eyes. He quivered with rage and sadness at the fact that his most precious macaws were now kept by the British authorities in conditions that he felt were quite inappropriate. They had been there for years, ever since they were seized from his Yorkshire farm in 2000 and were still the victims of complex international legal wrangles between Brazil and Britain.

I made my departure and strolled away down the hill toward the town center wondering why it was that people's love of wild creatures could sometimes prove so destructive. People's tendency to possess, own, and control, it seems, is often stronger than their ability to let go of their own immediate and personal desires to collaborate for the greater good. Although this kind of love is essentially selfish and for the benefit of the adorer, people can still somehow convince themselves that it is noble and good. Listening to Sissen reminded me how humans have an incredible propensity to convince themselves that they are right and just, no matter how strong the evidence to the contrary. And he was convinced that he was right.

As I navigated the narrow streets of Puerto de la Cruz, my thoughts drifted away from the events of the morning and back to those of the previous evening. I had found it fascinating to share stories over poolside drinks with the gathered parrot clans. As usual there was a good deal of gossip and rumor. And as usual in such company, the gossip involved the Spix's Macaw. I had heard again rumors about birds held in the U.S.A. Although none had ever come out into the open there, it was a consistently strong story. The claims sounded convincing, but without hard evidence not much could be done about it.

A couple of weeks later I was in the city where the Spix's Macaw's ultimate demise had been sealed: Asunción, Paraguay. I had arrived for a meeting with my colleagues from Friends of the Earth International, hosted by our excellent local people. While I was there I thought a great deal about what had happened in the 1970s and 1980s, about how one of the world's rarest birds had been trafficked unnoticed through the city from Brazil and exported to destinations worldwide via the little international airport.

My Paraguayan colleagues told me stories about their environmental campaigns. They gave me a full briefing on what it was like to press for the protection of the dwindling forests in a country with a military government and what it was like to work with corrupt officials and rigged elections. Their stories made me think that Friends of the Earth's environmental campaigns back home in England were, by comparison, rather straightforward.

We spent an evening walking on a hill in the city overlooking the Rio Paraguay. Downstream from where we stood was once the home of the now extinct Glaucous Macaw. On the opposite shore of the river was the great open vastness of the inland basin of the Chaco. A huge expanse of grasslands, swamps, forest, and palm savanna—one the world's great empty wildernesses; an area the size of Germany with a human population of only about 100,000 souls, many of them indigenous people. Upstream was the huge Pantanal, another largely unspoilt ecosystem that comprised the world's largest freshwater wetlands.

The weather had been intensely hot, reaching 46 degrees centigrade during the day and there had been a prolonged drought—more signs of the rapidly changing climate, we speculated. A bluish haze hung across the vast horizon. My Paraguayan colleagues casually explained that the haze was smoke and that the Pantanal and Chaco were on fire—being burned to open up more land for cattle and to improve the existing grazing lands. It seemed that not much had changed since our search for the Spix's Macaw back in 1990.

The last frontier wildernesses were still being cleared, destroyed, and degraded in a never-ending search for wealth and prosperity. And it still wasn't working. Most people in Paraguay remained poor, and they would be poorer still once their natural treasures were stolen by international banks, transnational corporations, and the country's corrupt political elite.

We retired to town for dinner and then I returned to my hotel and prepared to leave for London. During my journey home I called Sue, my wife, from São Paulo airport, the place where Juan Villalba-Macias had triumphantly arrived at the famous press conference in 1987 with the two baby Spixes he had wrested back from the traffickers in Asunción. She told me that only hours before a message had been left at home concerning the seizure of a single male Spix's Macaw in the United States. I was astounded. Rumors were one thing, a real bird quite another. This was in early October 2002.

I sat in the airport lounge awaiting my connection to London. I wondered where this surprise player might have come from. It could have arrived in the U.S.A. via several different routes. It might have been the last wild male that lived in Melância Creek—not dead at all, but like the other last Spix's Macaws spirited away by trappers and dealers. After all, no corpse had ever been found. It might alternatively have been one of the Spix's Macaws that crossed the Atlantic from the U.K., having briefly been in the custody of British bird trafficker Gordon Cooke. These birds were sent there back in the late 1970s, so if it was one of those, it would have been old. It could conceivably be one of their offspring, I thought.

More likely, I mused, it was one of the birds allegedly imported by Tony Silva in the late 1980s. These would have been among the last wild members of the species and had come to the U.S. (if they were indeed trafficked by Silva and his accomplices) via Asunción. It also quite plausibly might have been one the five birds that

Joseph Hämmerli had owned and passed on to unknown keepers. It might have come from somewhere else altogether. But wherever it came from, there was the exciting prospect that this precious live bird might carry genetic uniqueness crucial for the rescue of the entire species.

The Brazilians were notified and they responded immediately; insisting that the bird went back to Brazil. It was a sign that the policy really had changed. The diplomatic niceties of the committee did indeed seem to be in the past. The mood was now more determined and more concerned with recovery and custody than with the often fruitless negotiations with rare bird collectors. Happily, and unlike previous cases where birds had surfaced outside Brazil, this one was soon on its way home.

The person who first raised the alarm about the bird was Mischelle Muck. She was the one in the vet's office who had answered a call from a woman claiming to have a Spix's Macaw in the living room of her house in a Denver suburb. Muck thought the woman was mistaken and that her story was most unlikely to be true, but she made a visit anyway. She was stunned and delighted to find that the blue parrot there was a Spix's Macaw, but was appalled at the conditions it was being kept in. Its cage was too small, it could not perch comfortably because of the cage furniture and was surviving on an unsuitable diet of commercially produced bird pellets.

Muck alerted the U.S. authorities, they in turn spoke to their Brazilian counterparts, while she took the macaw away and cared for it herself. The blue parrot was kept in virtual isolation to avoid any risk of infection. Due to its poor treatment, the bird needed care and attention to help it recover and build its strength for the journey home. San Diego Zoo paid a visit to collect blood and feather samples with which they confirmed it was a male.

From Denver, the bird flew with Muck to Miami. The pair sat

in economy class with the macaw safely stowed inside Muck's shirt. At Miami Airport, Iolita Bampi from IBAMA was waiting to return the precious macaw to Brazil. The macaw first went to São Paulo Zoo, and then on the hot dry northeast to join the breeding program.

The World Parrot Trust, which had helped bring the bird into the open, soon released information about the macaw and where he had come from. Apparently, this macaw had been wild caught some twenty-five years previously and had been kept in Colorado for more than twenty years. These facts strongly suggest that the macaw was one of the two shipped by Gordon Cooke from the U.K. in 1979 (see page 143). The Trust said that the bird, found in 2002, was the surviving member of a pair of birds originally shipped there; the other one had died in the early 1980s. Since then this special parrot had been kept as a household pet. Like the last wild Spix's Macaw, this Rip Van Winkle of the bird world had paired up with quite a different species, in his case another pet bird, a Yellow-naped Amazon (*Amazona auropalliata*). When the Amazon parrot had died in the summer of 2002, the woman who owned these two pet parrots decided to find a new home for the Spix's.

The previously unproven rumors of Spix's Macaws kept in the U.S.A. had always struck me as being a little bit like the periodic claimed sightings of Elvis after his death: tantalizing, almost believable, but never backed with hard evidence—until the 2002 that is. It was, perhaps, appropriate that this bird was called *Presley*. Certainly his example will encourage me to take future rumors seriously. I would encourage anyone with hard evidence as to the location of any more "unknown" birds to pass on details to those national and international agencies with responsibility for the enforcement of wildlife trade laws. In most countries, the local police or national conservation bodies will be able to tell you who this is. Had Presley come into a breeding program some years ago, it could be that his contribution to the salvation of his species would have been assured.

On his arrival in Brazil on December 23, 2002, Presley joined the breeding effort now under official government control. Although there are only nine birds in that Brazilian-led initiative (the rest being with the private owners who refuse to hand "their" birds back), the genetic diversity of this little group is believed to largely represent that of the wider captive flock and thus is seen as a viable group to start a separate breeding program. Certainly the addition of the surprise bird from the U.S. is a great boost, assuming that at twenty-five years old he is still in breeding condition.

Out in the Melância Creek there were developments too. In February 2002, the owner of the Concordia Farm decided to sell his land. A few months later, in June, the money available for the field-based activities finally ran out and the field project out in the hot dry caatinga was officially terminated. Happily, there are moves to buy this key bit of territory for future recovery efforts and Loro Parque Foundation offered $40,000 for this purpose.

Thus in 2003 there is a new glimmer of hope. Brazil has control of nine birds and in partnership with various other bodies, including Loro Parque, plans to begin breeding. At least some of the land where the birds last lived in the wild might be secured for a reintroduction attempt, and there is clear and constant pressure on those outside Brazil to return their Spix's Macaws to the country that owns them. There is a draft recovery program now under serious consideration and there are plans to develop a breeding center for both Spix's and Lear's Macaws at a location in the dry interior of Bahía, Brazil.

There is hope, but time is not on the side of this bird. Neither, apparently, are the various "owners" who refuse to collaborate in ensuring its salvation. There are more birds out there in some collection or other. If you know about them, pick up the phone to the relevant authorities and tell them all you know. You might just save an endangered species from oblivion.

Notes

1 All quotes attributed to Spix and Martius concerning their expedition to Brazil are taken from *An account of travels in Brazil at the command of his Majesty, Maximilian Joseph I, King of Bavaria, in the years 1817 to 1820.* The original work was published in German. An English translation of volumes one and two was completed by H. E. Lloyd and published in 1824.

2 Reiser, O. *Liste de Vogelarten welche auf der von der Kaiserl. Akademie der Wissenschaften 1903 nach Nordostbrasilien entsendeten Expedition unter Leitung des Herrn Hofrates Dr. F. Steindachner gesammelt wurden*, Denkschr. Akad. Wiss. Wien, Math-Naturwiss. Kl. 76, 1926.

3 See Pinto, O. M. O. *Catálogo de aves do Brasil.* São Paulo: Secretária da Agricultura, 1938.

4 Lei no. 5197 was passed in that year by the government's Forestry Institute and ended the legal export of native Brazilian wildlife.

5 CITES was signed in Washington, D.C., in 1973. The treaty operates through two main appendices. Appendix I includes species essentially banned from international trade that may only be shipped between countries under very restricted circumstances and with the relevant paperwork. Appendix II lists species that may be traded but only at a level that will not endanger them in the wild and with relevant CITES permits. In all cases, exports of wildlife listed in CITES may only be traded with other CITES sig-

natories in accordance with the laws of the exporting country. Spix's Macaw was included in Appendix I of the Convention from 1975.

6   Forshaw, J. M., and Cooper, W. T., *Parrots of the World*, Blandford 1989, and Tony Juniper and Michael Parr's *Parrots*, Pica and Yale University Press, 1998, provide comprehensive summaries of the parrot family, including details on the natural history, distribution, and conservation status of all known species.

7   For a review of key early parrot fossils, see Dyke, G. J., and Cooper, J. H. (2000). "A new Psittaciform bird from the London Clay (Lower Eocene) of England." *Palaeontology*, Vol. 43, Part 2, pp. 271–85 .

8   India and Africa broke away first from the great landmass of Gondwanaland, perhaps before the ancestors of modern parrots had appeared. These birds have since colonized Asia and Africa from their ancient stronghold but not reached the diversity seen in the places where they have a far longer evolutionary history.

9   These are the El Oro Conure (*Pyrrhura orcesi*) from Ecuador, the Amazonian Parrotlet (*Nannopsittaca dachilleae*) from the Andean foothills of southern Peru and northern Bolivia, and the White-faced Amazon (*Amazona kawalli*) of the central Amazon basin. A fourth 'new' new species of parrot belonging to the *Pionopsitta* genus was found in Central Brazil and was described in 2002.

10 There are exceptions to the vegetarian rule. The Australian rosellas and cockatoos, for example, eat a great many insects, including grubs from logs and trunks. This is an interesting fact given that woodpeckers are absent from Australia. It appears that the niche occupied by these birds elsewhere has left an ecological vacancy now taken by some parrots. Some South American species like insects, too—for example, the gorgeously marked *Pyrrhura* conures.

11 See, for example, Pepperberg, I. M., in *Animal Cognition in Nature: The Convergence of Psychology and Biology in Laboratory and Field*. Edited by Balda, R. P., Pepperberg, I. M., and Kamil, A. C., Academic Press, 1998.

12 See Cruikshank, A. J., *et al.*, "Vocal mimicry in wild African Grey Parrots *Psittacus erithacus*," *Ibis* 1993, 135: 293–9.

13 Brouwer, K., *et al.*, provide a useful summary of captive parrot longevity records. Their survey finds the oldest documented parrot in a zoological collection to be a Moluccan Cockatoo (*Cacatua*

moluccensis) that lived to be sixty-five years old at the San Diego Zoo in California. See *International Zoo Yearbook* 37, London Zoological Society, London, 2000.

14   The Fulmar (*Fulmarus glacialis*) is a common seabird found around North Atlantic coasts that is related to the albatrosses. This species has been recorded to live in excess of sixty years in the wild. Some larger species of albatross have lived longer than that.

15   Low, R. *Parrots: Their Care and Breeding*. Blandford Press, 1992.

16   For example, before Spain and Portugal entered the European Union in 1987 and later became bound by its CITES regulations, they were common ports of entry for rare wildlife into Europe. Once the borders tightened there, the wildlife traffickers went east, with Yugoslavia emerging as a popular first entry point. More recently, Yugoslavia became a problem for the importers because of its progressive isolation by the West, culminating in the NATO air raids and the trade blockade during the Kosovo war. At that time, the locus moved east again, to Russia, where corruption and organized crime were already seriously out of control and where wildlife was added to the growing range of freely traded commodities available at the right price. Despite the official import ban on wild birds to the U.S.A., rare parrots continue to enter the country at different points along the Rio Grande, via Caribbean islands, including Puerto Rico, or are simply smuggled in air freight.

17   ICBP was renamed BirdLife International in 1993.

18   *Birds to Watch*, International Council for Bird Preservation Technical Publication No. 8. ICBP, Cambridge, 1988.

19   These extracts are from d'Orbigny's *Voyages dans l'Amérique Méridionale*, published in parts between 1835 and 1847.

20   See Yamashita, C., and Valle, M. (1993), "On the linkage between *Anodorhynchus* macaws and palm nuts and the extinction of the Glaucous Macaw." *Bulletin of the British Ornithological Club*, 113 (1), 35–60.

21   See for example Sick, H., Teixeira, D. M., and Gonzaga, L. P., "Our discovery of the land of the Lear's Macaw (*Anodorhynchus leari*)," *Anais Acad. Bras. Ciênc.* 51 (1), 1979.

22   See Yamashita, C., "Field observations and comments on the Indigo Macaw (*Anodorhynchus leari*), a highly endangered species from northeastern Brazil," *Wilson Bulletin* 99 (2), 1987.

23   The survey was instigated by CITES to establish the parrot's status in relation to international wildlife trade rules.

24   See chapter 4, p. 77. There is no suggestion that his employer at Loro Parque or any of his colleagues there had any knowledge of Silva's illegal parrot-smuggling activities.

25   Queen of Bavaria's Conure is a name often used in avicultural circles. The species is more commonly known to ornithologists in English as the Golden Parakeet.

26   The charge sheet prepared for Silva's and his codefendants' hearing mentions Spix's Macaw as among the eighteen species of parrot illegally shipped into the U.S.A.

27   See for example Sick, H., *Ornitologia brasileira, uma introducão*, Brasilia: Editora Universidada de Brasília, 1989.

28   Police raids on outdoor city markets where wildlife is illegally traded have since become more routine. During one 1999 foray thirty members of the Rio forestry battalion donned flak jackets, packed rifles, and raided two Rio markets seizing illegally captured animals, including 174 live wild birds.

29   These smaller parrots were Blue-winged Macaws (*Propyrrhura maracana*). See chapter 1.

30   Data on the creekside vegetation and the apparent reasons for its scarcity was published by Juniper, A. T., and Yamashita, C., in "The Habitat and Status of Spix's Macaw, *Cyanopsitta spixii*." *Bird Conservation International* 1 (1), 1991.

31   International Council for Bird Preservation, *Putting Biodiversity on the Map: Priority Areas for Global Conservation*, Cambridge, U.K.: International Council for Bird Preservation, 1992.

32   Very few scientists have devoted serious effort to the study of the caatinga. There is however a body of material that describes the main characteristics. For a summary in English see Moody *et al.*, *Seasonally dry tropical forests*, Cambridge University Press, Cambridge, U.K., 1997. Andrade-Lima, D., "The caatingas dominium," *Revta. Brasil. Bot.* 4: 149–53, 1981. Both authors provide routes into the Portuguese language literature. Andrade-Lima also gives a useful account (in Portuguese) of some caatinga plants in *Plantas das caatingas*, 1989.

33   See chapter 5. See also Susan George's account of the debt crisis.

This provides a good summary of the origins and effects of huge external debts on countries like Brazil. See George, S., *A Fate Worse Than Debt*, Penguin Books, 1989.

34 BirdLife International, *Threatened Birds of the World*. Lynx Ediciós, Barcelona, Spain, and BirdLife International, Cambridge, U.K., 2000.

35 These details and other important material were published in "*Cyanopsitta spixii*: A non-recovery report," written by Thomsen and Munn in *Parrotletter*, 1, pp. 6–7.

36 Although "secret," some of the trade was quite blatant. Even in the early 1980s, over five years since the Spix's Macaw was added to Appendix I of CITES and in the face of a 15-year-old ban on the capture and export of native species, the trade in rare wildlife from Brazil was quite open. For example, a letter from the São Paulo-based Flora and Fauna Inc. to likely buyers in South Africa offered "the following animals for sale, trade and breeding loan," including "Harpy Eagles, Golden Conures, Hawkhead Parrot, Spix Macaw, Caninde and Scarlet Macaws, Bell Birds, Toucans." The list went on to offer rare mammals and reptiles too.

37 For example, the British aviculturist and veterinarian George Smith wrote about a meeting he and fellow bird keeper Tony Silva had in Paraguay in 1988, by which time—apart from the one remaining individual—Spix's Macaw was extinct in the wild. Smith said he interviewed a young trapper bringing birds in from Brazil. The trapper said he knew of three or four breeding pairs of Spix's Macaws and could supply the parents and chicks if they wanted. The price would be $7,500 for an entire family group delivered to Paraguay. Alternatively, if the foreigners traveled with him in Brazil and paid the expedition expenses, the price would drop to $2,500 per nest if they contained eggs, more if there were babies. The reason for the lower fee was because cross-border smuggling would not be the trapper's responsibility; neither would be the deaths of any birds in transit after capture. Smith said he didn't pursue the offer, so whether it was real was never proven, although it would appear implausible given the conclusions of the 1990 expedition. He said he was subsequently offered another adult bird taken from the wild in early 1990. Again, no concrete proof was produced to demonstrate its existence.

38 Antonio de Dios said that he received his wild-caught pair of Spix's Macaws in November 1979. Assuming these birds were the ones that appeared in *Singapore Aviculture*, the photos were taken at least four years before publication.

39 The Parrot Specialist Group was an expert body of scientists and conservation biologists established under the auspices of the International Union for the Conservation of Nature and Natural Resources (now known as the World Conservation Union). Its role was to set a strategic framework for parrot conservation and to assist with the conservation of the most threatened species. It did not, however, have any official or legal function that could require governments or individual owners of birds to act on its recommendations.

40 Brazil's official forestry institute, Instituto Brasileiro de Desenvolvimento Florestal (IBDF), was terminated, and its environmental protection responsibilities were adopted by the new environmental and natural resources agency called Instituto Brasileiro do Meio Ambiente e dos Recursos Naturais Renováveis (IBAMA).

41 The Permanent Committee for the Recovery of Spix's Macaw was formally established under Brazilian law (Portaria no. 330) in March 1990. Its statutes were set out in a separate decree (Portaria no. 331). This was nearly four years after the first attempt to get the interested parties to agree to a plan to save the species. The Committee adopted the acronym CPRAA (derived from the Portuguese title for the institution: Comitê Permanente para a Recuperação da Arahinha Azul), but for the sake of simplicity and brevity is referred to here as the Recovery Committee or the committee.

42 These details are according to the minutes of the first meeting of the Recovery Committee.

43 Euclides da Cunha's account of the Canudos war (in his famous book *Os Sertões*, Livraria Francisco Alves, Rio de Janeiro, 1902) gives a fascinating insight to life in the caatinga at the end of the nineteenth century. Samuel Putnam translated this volume into English under the title of *Rebellion in the Backlands*, University of Chicago Press, 1944 and 1985.

44 This is perhaps the locality mentioned by the planner with the Polaroid photo who met the ICBP team in 1990. He informed the search party about the patches of caraiba gallery woodlands that he knew about in the caatinga, one of which was in the catchment of the Rio Vasa Barris. Carlos Yamashita has traveled there frequently but could find no trace of Spix's Macaws. They might well have occurred there in the past, however. Yamashita found remnant patches of caraiba woodlands in this area (for example, southwest of Uauá), but these are degraded and much less dense than those remaining near Curaçá.

45 *The Status Survey and Conservation Action Plan 2000–2004* for the world's parrots published by leading conservation groups in 2000, for example, remarks that "New pairings [of captive Spix's Macaws] are expected to increase breeding success from the presently low rate of captive reproduction. However, recent negotiations for movement of individuals among breeding facilities have often been tortuous." Snyder, N., McGowan, P., Gilardi, J. and Grajal, A., *Parrots: Status Survey and Conservation Action Plan 2000–2004*, IUCN: Cambridge, U.K., and Gland, Switzerland, 2000.

46 The Great Auk (*Alca impennis*) was a flightless seabird allied to puffins and guillemots. It was hunted to extinction in its North Atlantic range during the nineteenth century. A significant contribution toward its final demise was the taking of birds for collections. The flightless moas were a family of birds once native to New Zealand. They were hunted out of existence by Maori colonists.

47 Standards laid out by the International Union of Directors of Zoological Gardens—the World Zoo Organisation (IUDZG-WZO) and the World Conservation Union Species Survival Commission (IUCN/SSC) require studbook keepers to update and distribute studbook data annually. No such document had ever been received by the International Zoo Yearbook editor, whose responsibility it is to oversee and coordinate approved international studbooks. Natasha Schischakin, the Spix's Macaw studbook coordinator, said that the studbook had not been published because of security concerns (even though the locations of all birds are quite well known). However, this position was not in line with that of other studbooks, where the sensitive locations of endangered animals have

been hidden via the use of codes. In any event, the policy of keeping the Spix's Macaw studbook secret was not one officially adopted by the Recovery Committee.

48   These details were included in a document (entitled *Visit of Mr Roland Messer to the Fauna General Coordination/IBAMA*) circulated in early 2002 to the former Recovery Committee members by the Brazilian authorities.

49   This request was issued in a notification to CITES member governments from the CITES headquarters in Geneva. It followed the transfer between Antonio de Dios and Sheikh Saud Al-Thani that led to the final collapse of the Recovery Committee. "The Government of Brazil earnestly requests all [CITES] Parties not to issue permits or certificates for import, export or re-export specimens of Spix's macaw" before obtaining permission from Brazil, it said. This request followed a September 2000 letter from Brazil to the Philippines CITES authorities in which Brazil states its displeasure thus: "it was established that the Spix's Macaws would not be commercialised, nor any transference would be done without the previous knowledge of the committee. Unfortunately this did not happen."

50   These were the two at São Paulo Zoo (males transferred there from the Philippines five years before), three in Recife with Mauricio dos Santos (one male and his two offspring hatched in early 2001), and the three in Loro Parque. The Loro Parque birds had been returned to Brazilian ownership by the unilateral decision of Wolfgang Kiessling.

51   A special working group for the conservation of Lear's Macaw was established by the Brazilian government in 1992. It was modeled in some respects on the effort to save the Spix's Macaw but was different in terms of the international ownership of birds being far more limited. Also, the circumstances of the Lear's Macaw in the wild were somewhat different.

52   The legal arguments that might have been used to recover Spix's Macaws known in captivity outside Brazil in the 1980s and early 1990s would have been different and less clear than those used in the Sissen case. This does not, however, alter the fact that Brazil has chosen to pursue a quite different policy in the case of the Lear's Macaw.

53 In order to protect their sovereign rights over their biological resources, some nations have recently adopted national legislation to
combat bioprospecting (the search for useful compounds or
species) and biopiracy. There is, however, no international legal
code aside from general commitments included in the 1992 U.N.
Convention on Biological Diversity.

54 The international political controversy that has raged over control
and ownership of wildlife species has mostly concerned the finan-
cially more important pharmaceuticals industry. In this case, tropical plant extracts used to manufacture drugs have generated
billions of dollars in profits for some multinational drugs firms.
But there has been no systematic recompense or recognition for
the developing countries from which the plants came. Very expensive rare parrots bred in captivity are arguably a parallel of the
same process of exploitation. Certainly the sale of birds aroused
bad feelings in Brazil, born of national pride.

Picture Credits

Figure 1: With kind permission of Zoologischen Staatsammlung, München, Germany

Figure 2: Tony Juniper

Figure 4: With kind permission of the Zoological Society of London

Figure 5: Illustration by David Johnston, from *Parrots* by Tony Juniper and Mike Parr, Pica and Yale University Press, 1998

Figure 6: Luiz Claudio Marigo

Figure 7: Luiz Claudio Marigo

Figure 8: Luiz Claudio Marigo

Figure 10: Jorgen Thomsen, Conservation International

Figure 11: Tony Juniper

Figure 12: With kind permission of Loro Parque Fundación

Figure 13: With kind permission of Loro Parque Fundación

Acknowledgments

I am very privileged to have had the opportunity to chart the saga of the world's rarest bird. In this endeavor, I have been assisted by many people.

Myles Archibald at HarperCollins first encouraged me to develop the idea and Marie Woolf from *The Independent* newspaper in London finally convinced me to write the proposal. I am indebted also to Mike McCarthy, the environment editor at *The Independent*, who inspired me to actually get on and do it.

Without Fourth Estate, who decided to publish it, there would be no book—so thanks to them, too, especially Clive Priddle and Mitzi Angel, who so expertly guided my writing into what I hope will appear to the reader as a reasonably coherent account. My wife, Sue Sparkes, was a determined research assistant, and my children, Maddie, Nye, and Sam, have, as ever, proved patient and understanding; so have my colleagues at Friends of the Earth. Ankin Ljungman and Otto Seiber from Friends of the Earth International kindly read a draft for me.

Dr. Nigel Collar at BirdLife International has been an invaluable source of information and advice and a spring of inspiration in digging up details. I have been greatly assisted in my endeavors by his colleagues, Sue Shutes, Jeremy Speck, and Christine Alder in the BirdLife International Secretariat in Cambridge, England. I have also been assisted by the National History Museum in Tring, the British Library, London; Cambridge University Library, Cambridge; the library in the Natural History Museum at South Kensington, London; and to the staff in the library at the Royal Botanic Gardens in Kew, London. Ray Simmonds in the Cambridge University Zoology Museum helped me too.

I would like to acknowledge the contribution of Wolfgang Kiessling and Yves de Soye at Loro Parque, who agreed to speak to me frankly about their experiences with Spix's Macaw and who assisted me with various details that otherwise would have eluded me. Roland Messer, Joseph Hämmerli, and His Excellency Sheikh Saud Al-Thani also provided me with interviews and information for which I am very grateful.

Juan Villalba-Macias in Uruguay gave me invaluable material and insights, as did Jorgen Thomsen of Conservation International in the United States. I would like to thank Tony Pittman, Roger Sweeney in Barbados, David Waugh at the Edinburgh Zoo, Miriam Behrens from Friends of the Earth Switzerland, Peter Olney of the London Zoological Society, and Mike Reynolds and Andrew Greenwood of the World Parrot Trust, all of whom gave me their time and much vital information. I would also like to thank Rosemary Low, Penny Walker, Paul Butler, Gordon Cooke, and Craig Bennett, who all furnished me valuable advice. I would like to thank my Brazilian friends Carlos Yamashita, Francisco Pontual, Luiz Claudio Marigo, and Roberto Otoch for all the help they provided—not only in the writing of this book, but for being such good companions during our search for wild Spix's Macaws back in 1990.

By contrast to the World Bank, who were not especially helpful with information about their funding for large dams in northeast Brazil, Nick Hildyard at the Cornerhouse in Dorset, England, was of great assistance to me. I would also like to thank Korinna Horta and Amy Boone at the Environmental Defense Fund in Washington, D.C., who aided me in this respect too.

Steve Broad, Teresa Mulliken, and Crawford Allan at TRAFFIC International and Stephanie Pendry of TRAFFIC UK all helped me in different ways. So did Jim Armstrong and John Barsdow at the CITES headquarters in Geneva. I am also grateful for the input of Swiss CITES officials in Bern.

I am also very thankful for the help of Sigrid Shreeve, Jim Sparkes, and Sheila Barnes de Shvetz, who aided me in translating German, Portuguese, French, and Spanish documents, and my very good friend, Tim Morris, in Munich, who not only helped with translation but picture research too.

—Tony Juniper
Cambridge
March 2002

Index